# THE

# UNITED

# MISCELLANY

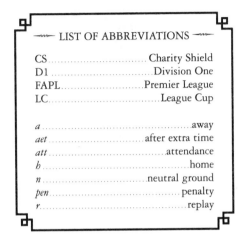

## LIST OF ABBREVIATIONS

| | |
|---|---|
| CS | Charity Shield |
| D1 | Division One |
| FAPL | Premier League |
| LC | League Cup |

| | |
|---|---|
| *a* | away |
| *aet* | after extra time |
| *att* | attendance |
| *h* | home |
| *n* | neutral ground |
| *pen* | penalty |
| *r* | replay |

This edition published in 2008
First published by Carlton Books in 2005

Text and design copyright © 2005, 2007, 2008 Carlton Books Limited

Manufactured and distributed by
Carlton Books Limited
20 Mortimer Street, London W1T 3JW

A CIP catalogue record for this book is available from the British Library

ISBN 978-1-84732-210-4

Commissioning editor: Martin Corteel
Assistant Editor: David Ballheimer
Project art editor: Paul Chattaway
Production: Lisa French

Printed in Great Britain

# THE
# UNITED
# MISCELLANY

### JOHN WHITE
WITH A FOREWORD BY THE LATE GREAT
### GEORGE BEST

UNOFFICIAL & UNAUTHORISED

THIRD EDITION

**CARLTON**
BOOKS

I was delighted when John, a fellow East Belfast man, approached me and asked me to write the foreword to his *United Miscellany*.

This truly is the book of all Manchester United books and one for United fans regardless of age. John has painstakingly researched the history of the club from its very early and humble beginnings in 1878 when Newton Heath was formed by Railway Workers from the Lancashire & Yorkshire Railways to the Theatre of Dreams and its vast array of Superstars today.

Manchester United and I have very much in common. We both started off in humble, but proud, beginnings and then we made our way to the top of our respective positions in the world of football. My own career has certainly been somewhat of a rollercoaster ride and I only wish I could get back on that thrill of a ride one more time and play alongside the likes of Roy Keane, Rio Ferdinand, Ruud van Nistelrooy, Wayne Rooney and Ryan Giggs today. That is not to say that I did not enjoy my time at Old Trafford. Nothing in fact could be further from the truth because my team-mates at United in the 1960s were all fantastic players. Players such as Paddy Crerand, who could chip and land a ball more precisely than Tiger Woods with a golf club in his hand; Alex Stepney, a wonderful goalkeeper; Bill Foulkes who was a tremendous servant to United; Shay Brennan and Tony Dunne, two fantastic full-backs; Brian Kidd and David Sadler, our tireless workers up front; Nobby Stiles who was a terrier in midfield; John Aston Jnr, who played the game of his life in our 1968 European Cup Final triumph over Benfica; Bobby Charlton, a true professional and of course, last but certainly not least, Denis Law, the King of the Stretford End.

I really enjoyed reading John's book and I love the way it has been set out with little cameos of players here, some quirky facts coupled with the odd statistic there and the occasional "Did You Know?" This book is so easy to read as it is not written as a wall of words and I can guarantee you that once you pick it up, like me you will find it difficult to put back down again. In fact you could read it over and over again and still want to read it time and time again. It is just that type of book whereby the more times you read it then the more you learn about the greatest football club in the world, Manchester United.

**George Best**
*Manchester United, 1963–1974*

## ⚊ ACKNOWLEDGEMENTS ⚊

Thanks to: Andy Mitten and Jim White, two true Reds, for their wonderful *Rough Guides to Man United*; Phil Hughes at *www.georgiebest.co.uk* for securing the foreword from George Best; Martin Corteel my editor at Carlton Books for having the faith in me to offer me the chance to write this book; Chris Marshall for analysing and organizing my original typescript; Darren Jordan for constructing the pages with meticulous care and great finesse; Nigel Matheson for all his help; Mark Baber at the Association of Football Statisticians; Frankie "Dodger" Dodds; Matthew Paton, Christie's, London; Bill Clarkson for his valued advice and guidance on my Busby Babe entries; David Roberts at Guinness Publishing Limited; Phil Matcham at the Official UK Charts Company; Jonathan McCleery at *wwwmanutdzone.com*; Paul Hinson at Red 11 – *http://red11.org*; the webmaster at *www.wikipedia.org* for providing such a comprehensive database on Manchester United which inspired several entries; Neil at *www.PrideOfManchester.com*; Iain McCartney, Keith Mellor, Joseph Muscat and Charles Zahra for their excellent book *Manchester United – Pictorial History and Club Record*, which provided the inspiration for several entries in my book; Michael Crick for *The Complete Manchester United Trivia Fact Book*, which helped clarify several entries; Garth Dykes for *The United Alphabet*, which helped me establish a number of facts about past players; Ian Morrison and Alan Shury for their informative *Manchester United – A Complete Record 1878–1992*, which helped settle a number statistical queries; Sir Bobby Charlton, Sir Alex Ferguson, Eamonn Holmes, Denis Law and Bryan Robson for their kind words in support of my book; George Best for his very generous foreword; and last, but certainly not least, I wish to thank my wife Janice and our two sons, Marc and Paul, for their continuous and unwavering help, love and support.

Welcome to this updated and expanded edition of *The United Miscellany*. So what exactly is a miscellany? Well, it is a mixture of facts, figures, statistics, trivia and quirky events that have helped fashion the story of Manchester United FC, from humble railway workers in 1878 to the highly paid world superstars of today, including Michael Carrick, Cristiano Ronaldo, Wayne Rooney et al. who we watch every other week at the Theatre of Dreams. There are quite a few entries on my own personal favourite United player, the Belfast Boy himself, George Best. Growing up in Belfast during the 1960s, I wanted to be just like Bestie. Alas I had to settle for the honour of The Genius agreeing to write the Foreword for my book.

As you pan through the book you will see that it is not actually structured in the chronological order of events that have shaped the club's illustrious history. Instead it is a little like stepping inside a time machine, not knowing what fascinating occurrences each page will turn up. However, I must admit to including some uniformity and structure in certain areas of the club's history. For instance, in respect of United's 18 championship-winning seasons, I have spread these throughout the book in the order they were won and included the final league table for each season. The same principle has been applied to United's record 11 FA Cup victories.

I have listed many quirky and unusual facts about Manchester United covering the odd, the bizarre, the unbelievable and the truly outrageous. Researching this book unveiled a plethora of interesting events that I did not know despite the fact that I have had three other books published about the club. However, I very carefully selected the best and juiciest items to include that would appeal most to United fans and here it is, *The United Miscellany*.

As you read through the book I hope it will teach you more about the club than you have ever read before. I have tried to encapsulate the most interesting events in the club's history coupled with the most important. And believe me, this was no easy task. Therefore, I trust like me, you will enjoy reading about United legends, cup triumphs, championship successes, the managers, Old Trafford, Newton Heath, and just about everything from the bankruptcy of the club in 1902 to the thrilling climax of the 2007–08 Premier League season.

**John White**
*Summer 2008*

## PORTENTOUS DEBUTS

The following players all made their debuts for Manchester United against a team they also played for or later managed:

| Player | Club |
| --- | --- |
| George Graham | Arsenal |
| Ian Greaves | Wolverhampton Wanderers |
| John Hall | Oldham Athletic |
| William Hunter | Liverpool |
| Joe Jordan | Bristol City |
| Brian Kidd | Everton |
| George Livingstone | Manchester City |
| Sammy McIlroy | Manchester City |
| Lou Macari | West Ham United |
| Albert Pape | Charlton Athletic |

## SCHMEICHEL'S SAFE HANDS

Unbelievably when Simon Charlton scored for Southampton at Old Trafford on 10 May 1995, it was the first time all season that Peter Schmeichel had conceded a Premier League goal at home. United conceded only four goals in their 19 home Premier League games, with Gary Walsh conceding the other three (two against Nottingham Forest and one against Leicester City).

## UNITED'S INTERNATIONAL CRICKETERS

Two Manchester United players have played international cricket. Noel Cantwell, a dual international, played cricket for Ireland as well as playing football for the Republic of Ireland. Arnold Sidebottom made 20 appearances for United from 1973 to 1975 but gave up football to concentrate on his cricket career. Arnold was a fast-medium bowler for Yorkshire and in 1985 was selected to play for England against Australia.

## ROUGH AND TUMBLE

United's 1–0 home defeat against Arsenal on 20 October 1990 was an ill-tempered affair that spilled over into an all-out brawl between players from both sides. After an FA enquiry, United were deducted one League point for misconduct while Arsenal were docked two points.

## ⚬⚬⚬ THE UNITED REVIEW ⚬⚬⚬

The *United Review*[†] is Manchester United's official match-day programme. It is unmistakable, with a distinctive masthead depicting a player shaking hands with a supporter. The most famous *United Review* is the programme produced for United's FA Cup Fifth Round tie with Sheffield Wednesday at Old Trafford on 19 February 1958. The title was "United Will Go On", and the programme was full of material relating to the Munich Air Disaster, which had taken place only 13 days earlier. The United line-up was left blank because Jimmy Murphy did not know which players would be available to play until close to kick-off.

## ⚬⚬⚬ CENTRE TUNNEL ⚬⚬⚬

The famous Centre Tunnel is located in Old Trafford's South Stand. It was part of the original stadium build in 1910 and is the only section that survived the German air raid of 1941. The tunnel slopes towards the pitch so steeply that it is difficult to walk down, and it is said that this is the reason why players got into the habit of jogging onto the pitch. The list of stars to have made the trip through this passageway over the years includes just about every famous player known to English football up until the tunnel ceased to be used in 1993, since when it has been retained for historical reasons. The benches for the managers, coaching staff, substitutes and physios are located over the Centre Tunnel. This position is much preferred to the old one as it provides a better view of the game.

## ⚬⚬⚬ MATCH-FIXING SCANDAL ⚬⚬⚬

On 2 April 1915 Manchester United beat Liverpool 2–0 at Old Trafford in a First Division game, but a lengthy investigation by the Football Association took place that discovered the match had been "fixed". Eight players, including United's Sandy Turnbull, Enoch West and Arthur Whalley, were banned for life. However, after the Great War, the Football Association lifted their suspensions in recognition of their services in fighting for their country. Sadly, Sandy was killed in action in France on 3 May 1917.

---

[†]*A United Review from United's postponed First Division game against Wolverhampton Wanderers scheduled for 8 February 1958 at Old Trafford was sold in 1997 for £1925. The price slightly bettered the £1887 paid for a programme from United's match against Red Star Belgrade on 5 February 1958, the last game the Busby Babes played together.*

Manchester United have spent longer in the UK hit parade than any other football team. These are the toe-tapping songs:

**Manchester United Football Club**
*UK, male football team vocalists (56 WEEKS)*     *pos/wks*

| | | | |
|---|---|---|---|
| 8 May 76 | **Manchester United** *Decca F 13633* | 50 | 1 |
| 21 May 83 | **Glory Glory Man United** *EMI 5390* | 13 | 5 |
| 18 May 85 • | **We All Follow Man United** | | |
| | *Columbia DB 9107* | 10 | 5 |
| 19 Jun 93 | **United (We Love You)** | | |
| | *Living Beat LBECD 026*   ① | 37 | 2 |
| 30 Apr 94 * | **Come On You Reds** *PolyGram TV MANU 2* | 1 | 15 |
| 13 May 95 • | **We're Gonna Do It Again** | | |
| | *PolyGram MANU 952*   ② | 6 | 6 |
| 4 May 96 • | **Move Move Move (The Red Tribe)** | | |
| | *Music Collection MANUCD 1*   ③ | 6 | 11 |
| 3 Aug 96 | **Move Move Move (The Red Tribe)** (re-entry) | | |
| | *Music Collection MANUCD 1*   ③ | 50 | 4 |
| 29 May 99 | **Lift It High (All About Belief)** | | |
| | *Music Collection MANUCD 4*   ④ | 11 | 6 |
| 21 Aug 99 | **Lift It High (All About Belief)** (re-entry) | | |
| | *Music Collection MANUCD 4*   ④ | 75 | 1 |

UK No. 1 *
UK Top 10 •

① Manchester United and the Champions
② Manchester United Football Squad featuring Stryker
③ 1996 Manchester United FA Cup Squad
④ 1999 Manchester United FA Cup Squad

© *Guinness World Records Book of Hit Singles/The Official UK Charts Company*

—w— THREE GAMES, THREE GOALKEEPERS —w—

On Christmas Day 1902 Herbert Birchenough played in goal for United in a 1–1 draw with Manchester City in Division Two. On Boxing Day Birchenough was replaced in goal by James Whitehouse for the 2–2 draw with Blackpool. The following day United used their third goalkeeper in three successive League games over three consecutive days when James Saunders was put in goal for the 2–1 win over Barnsley. All three matches were played at Clayton.

## — BOMBS FALL ON OLD TRAFFORD —

On the night of 11 March 1941 Old Trafford was virtually demolished as Hitler's bombers targeted the vast Trafford Park industrial complex in an attempt to halt engineering production for Britain's war effort. Only three days earlier, on the 8th, Manchester United had played what proved to be their last game at Old Trafford for quite some time, beating Bury 7–3 (Carey 3, Rowley 3, Smith). After the bombing, United filed a claim with the War Damage Commission for reconstruction of the ground and were awarded £22,278. Meanwhile, the club had to rent Maine Road from their City neighbours, for around £5000 a year plus a percentage of the gate receipts, until Old Trafford could be rebuilt – a process that took eight years.

## — DEFIANT EUROPEAN PIONEERS —

On 12 September 1956 United defied FA orders and participated in their first ever European competition fixture. United played Anderlecht in Belgium in the preliminary round (first leg) of the European Cup. The Reds won the game 2–0 in front of 35,000 people with goals from Viollet and Taylor.

## — MANAGERS SINCE 1903 —

| Dates | Name |
| --- | --- |
| 1903–12 | Ernest Mangnall |
| 1912–13 | JJ Bentley* |
| 1914–21 | John Robson |
| 1921–26 | John Chapman |
| 1926–27 | Clarence Hilditch |
| 1927–31 | Herbert Bamlett |
| 1931–32 | Walter Crickmer |
| 1932–37 | Scott Duncan |
| 1937–45 | Walter Crickmer |
| 1945–69 | Sir Matt Busby |
| 1969–70 | Wilf McGuinness |
| 1970–71 | Sir Matt Busby |
| 1971–72 | Frank O'Farrell |
| 1972–77 | Tommy Docherty |
| 1977–81 | Dave Sexton |
| 1981–86 | Ron Atkinson |
| 1986 to date | Sir Alex Ferguson |

*Club Secretary – responsible for team selection*

After only two seasons in the First Division, Newton Heath was relegated in season 1893–94 after losing their Test Match 2–0 against Liverpool, played at Blackburn on 28 April 1894. The Heathens avoided relegation at the end of their first season in the top flight by beating Small Heath 6–3 on aggregate over two Test Matches.

### *Football League Division 1*
### 1893–94

|    |                     | P  | W  | D | L | F  | A  | W | D | L  | F  | A  | Pts |
|----|---------------------|----|----|---|---|----|----|---|---|----|----|----|-----|
| 1. | Aston Villa         | 30 | 12 | 2 | 1 | 49 | 13 | 7 | 4 | 4  | 35 | 29 | 44  |
| 2. | Sunderland          | 30 | 11 | 3 | 1 | 46 | 14 | 6 | 1 | 8  | 26 | 30 | 38  |
| 3. | Derby County        | 30 | 9  | 2 | 4 | 47 | 32 | 7 | 2 | 6  | 26 | 30 | 36  |
| 4. | Blackburn Rovers    | 30 | 13 | 0 | 2 | 48 | 15 | 3 | 2 | 10 | 21 | 38 | 34  |
| 5. | Burnley             | 30 | 13 | 0 | 2 | 43 | 17 | 2 | 4 | 9  | 18 | 34 | 34  |
| 6. | Everton             | 30 | 11 | 1 | 3 | 63 | 23 | 4 | 2 | 9  | 27 | 34 | 33  |
| 7. | Nottingham Forest   | 30 | 10 | 2 | 3 | 38 | 16 | 4 | 2 | 9  | 19 | 32 | 32  |
| 8. | WBA                 | 30 | 8  | 4 | 3 | 35 | 23 | 6 | 0 | 9  | 31 | 36 | 32  |
| 9. | Wolverhampton W     | 30 | 11 | 1 | 3 | 34 | 24 | 3 | 2 | 10 | 18 | 39 | 31  |
| 10. | Sheffield United   | 30 | 8  | 3 | 4 | 26 | 22 | 5 | 2 | 8  | 21 | 39 | 31  |
| 11. | Stoke City         | 30 | 13 | 1 | 1 | 45 | 17 | 0 | 2 | 13 | 20 | 62 | 29  |
| 12. | Sheffield Wednesday | 30 | 7 | 3 | 5 | 32 | 21 | 2 | 5 | 8  | 16 | 36 | 26  |
| 13. | Bolton Wanderers   | 30 | 7  | 3 | 5 | 18 | 14 | 3 | 1 | 11 | 20 | 38 | 24  |
| 14. | Preston North End  | 30 | 7  | 1 | 7 | 25 | 24 | 3 | 2 | 10 | 19 | 32 | 23  |
| 15. | Darwen             | 30 | 6  | 4 | 5 | 25 | 28 | 1 | 1 | 13 | 12 | 55 | 19  |
| 16. | Newton Heath       | 30 | 5  | 2 | 8 | 29 | 33 | 1 | 0 | 14 | 7  | 39 | 14  |

*Test match: Liverpool 3, Newton Heath 0*

### ~~ NO PLACE LIKE HOME ~~

The club has called several grounds home since it was formed in 1878[†]:

| Date | Ground |
|------|--------|
| 1878–1893 | North Road, Newton Heath |
| 1893–1910 | Bank Street, Clayton |
| 1910–1941 | Old Trafford |
| 1941–1949 | Maine Road |
| 1949 to date | Old Trafford |

[†]1. *The club played at Harpurhey in 1902 when the Bank Street ground was closed by bailiffs.*

2. *United rented Maine Road after Old Trafford was damaged by bombing in World War II.*

## HOSPITAL BROADCAST

Commentary of the Manchester derby game at Old Trafford on 16 January 1954 was broadcast live to local hospitals for the first time. Patients were also given a complimentary copy of the *United Review*.

## BUFFET BATTLE

United ended Arsenal's record 49-game unbeaten run in the top flight with a 2–0 win at Old Trafford on 24 October 2004. After the game a scuffle broke out between players from both teams, which spread to the changing-room area. Somehow slices of pizza and even pea soup were thrown at Sir Alex Ferguson and several of the United players. This only resulted in an even more intense and bitter rivalry between the two sides. In the return game at Arsenal Stadium on 1 February 2005, Roy Keane and Patrick Vieira clashed in the tunnel before kick-off, while Mikael Silvestre was sent off during the game for headbutting Freddie Ljungberg. Despite only having 10 men, United won 4–2 to complete a unique treble over Arsenal, having already knocked them out of the League Cup earlier in the season. Sadly, United couldn't make it four out of four losing the 2005 FA Cup final to the Gunners.

## UNITED'S FIRST HARD MAN

Frank Barson[†] arrived at United in August 1922. Standing 6ft tall, weighing 12st 10lbs and sporting a broken, twisted nose, he was a blacksmith by trade and a no-nonsense, barrel-chested centre-half. Barson captained Manchester United from 1922 to 1928 and helped get the club back into the First Division for 1925–26. Reports suggest Barson was sent off 12 times in his career and once served a two-month ban following violent conduct during a game. Barson had many run-ins with the football authorities, but one famous story recalls a game in which he had been so badly fouled by an opposing player that he was limping when he got to his feet. The referee was about to send the offender off when Barson intervened and asked the official to allow the player to remain on the pitch so that he could kick him off personally in the second half.

[†]*Prior to arriving at Old Trafford, Barson was promised a public house if he could captain United back into the top flight. After securing First Division football for the 1925–26 season, Barson was given the keys to a hotel in Ardwick Green. Fifteen minutes into his tenancy, he handed the keys to the head waiter and walked out. Hundreds of well-wishers had turned up for the opening of the hotel, and Barson got so fed up with the praise and flattery he decided that being a licensee was not the job for him.*

① Peter **SCHMEICHEL**

② John **SIVEBAEK**   ⑥ Jaap **STAM**   ⑤ Nemanja **VIDIC**   ③ Patrice **EVRA**

⑦ Cristiano **RONALDO**   ⑧ Arnold **MUHREN**   ④ Juan Sebastian **VERON**   ⑪ Andrei **KANCHELSKIS**

⑨ Ruud *van* **NISTELROOY**   ⑩ Eric **CANTONA**

*Substitutes*
Fabien **BARTHEZ**, Nikola **JOVANOVIC**, Eric **DJEMBA-DJEMBA**, **NANI**,
**ANDERSON**, Jesper **OLSEN**, Carlos **TEVEZ**
*Manager*
Sir Alex **FERGUSON CBE**

*Did You Know That?*
Peter Schmeichel was asked by the BBC to select the Top 5 goals scored during the month of March 2005 for their *Match of the Day* monthly competition. It was the first time in the show's history, covering more than 40 years, that at least one viewer's selection did not match the expert's choice of 1st, 2nd and 3rd.

━ MUNICH CLOCK ━

On 25 February 1960, Dan Marsden, chairman of the Ground Committee, unveiled the Munich Clock, a poignant reminder commemorating the players, club officials, members of the press and others who died in the Munich Air Disaster on 6 February 1958. The clock is situated under the Manchester United Football Club sign at the front of Old Trafford's South Stand. On the United Road corner of K Stand is the Munich Plaque, once again in memory of those who died in the tragedy; it was unveiled, also on 25 February 1960, by Matt Busby, who almost lost his life in the crash.

## CAPTAIN STAFFORD

Harry Stafford was the only player to captain Newton Heath and Manchester United. He was the Heathens' captain from 1896 to 1902 and the first ever captain of Manchester United.

## FIVE OUT OF FIVE FOR HERD

David Herd[†] scored on his debut in all five major cup competitions in which he played for United:

FA Cup ................................... v Bolton Wanderers *(h)* ..... 06/01/62
European Cup Winners' Cup ... v Willem II Tilburg *(a)* .... 25/09/63
Inter-Cities Fairs Cup ............. v Djurgardens IF *(a)* ........ 23/09/64
European Cup ...................... v HJK Helsinki *(a)* ......... 22/09/65
Football League Cup ............. v Blackpool *(a)* ............... 14/09/66

## PRAWN SANDWICH ANYONE?

Following a crucial UEFA Champions League game against Dynamo Kiev at Old Trafford in November 2000*, Keano made his infamous "prawn sandwich" swipe at some of the less vociferously appreciative sections of the Old Trafford crowd: "Sometimes you wonder, do they understand the game of football? We're 1–0 up, then there are one or two stray passes and they're getting on players' backs. It's just not on. At the end of the day they need to get behind the team. Away from home our fans are fantastic, I'd call them the hardcore fans. But at home they have a few drinks and probably the prawn sandwiches, and they don't realize what's going on out on the pitch. I don't think some of the people who come to Old Trafford can spell football, never mind understand it."

\* *Incidentally, United won the game 1–0.*

## TEENAGE KICKS

Three United 17-year-olds have been capped by Northern Ireland.

| Player | Age first capped |
| --- | --- |
| Jimmy Nicholson | 17 years, 256 days |
| George Best | 17 years, 328 days |
| Sammy McIlroy | 17 years, 356 days |

[†]*David failed to score on his League debut for United but did score in his second League game in a 3–2 win over Chelsea at Old Trafford on 23 August 1961.*

In their third season as Manchester United, the club won promotion to Division One as runners-up. United missed promotion the previous season when they finished third in the 1904–05 season.

### *Football League Division 2*
### 1905–06

|  |  | P | W | D | L | F | A | W | D | L | F | A | Pts |
|---|---|---|---|---|---|---|---|---|---|---|---|---|---|
| 1. | Bristol City | 38 | 17 | 1 | 1 | 43 | 8 | 13 | 5 | 1 | 40 | 20 | 66 |
| 2. | MANCHESTER UNITED | 38 | 15 | 3 | 1 | 55 | 13 | 13 | 3 | 3 | 35 | 15 | 62 |
| 3. | Chelsea | 38 | 13 | 4 | 2 | 58 | 16 | 9 | 5 | 5 | 32 | 21 | 53 |
| 4. | WBA | 38 | 13 | 4 | 2 | 53 | 16 | 9 | 4 | 6 | 26 | 20 | 52 |
| 5. | Hull City | 38 | 10 | 5 | 4 | 38 | 21 | 9 | 1 | 9 | 29 | 33 | 44 |
| 6. | Leeds City | 38 | 11 | 5 | 3 | 38 | 19 | 6 | 4 | 9 | 21 | 28 | 43 |
| 7. | Leicester City | 38 | 10 | 3 | 6 | 30 | 21 | 5 | 9 | 5 | 23 | 27 | 42 |
| 8. | Grimsby Town | 38 | 11 | 7 | 1 | 33 | 13 | 4 | 3 | 12 | 13 | 33 | 40 |
| 9. | Burnley | 38 | 9 | 4 | 6 | 26 | 23 | 6 | 4 | 9 | 16 | 30 | 38 |
| 10. | Stockport County | 38 | 11 | 6 | 2 | 36 | 16 | 2 | 3 | 14 | 8 | 40 | 35 |
| 11. | Bradford City | 38 | 7 | 4 | 8 | 21 | 22 | 6 | 4 | 9 | 25 | 38 | 34 |
| 12. | Barnsley | 38 | 11 | 4 | 4 | 45 | 17 | 1 | 5 | 13 | 15 | 45 | 33 |
| 13. | Lincoln City | 38 | 10 | 1 | 8 | 46 | 29 | 2 | 5 | 12 | 23 | 43 | 30 |
| 14. | Blackpool | 38 | 8 | 3 | 8 | 22 | 21 | 2 | 6 | 11 | 15 | 41 | 29 |
| 15. | Gainsborough Trinity | 38 | 10 | 2 | 7 | 35 | 22 | 2 | 2 | 15 | 9 | 35 | 28 |
| 16. | Glossop North End | 38 | 9 | 4 | 6 | 36 | 28 | 1 | 4 | 14 | 13 | 43 | 28 |
| 17. | Port Vale | 38 | 10 | 4 | 5 | 34 | 25 | 2 | 0 | 17 | 15 | 57 | 28 |
| 18. | Chesterfield | 38 | 8 | 4 | 7 | 26 | 24 | 2 | 4 | 13 | 14 | 48 | 28 |
| 19. | Burton United | 38 | 9 | 4 | 6 | 26 | 20 | 1 | 2 | 16 | 8 | 47 | 26 |
| 20. | Leyton Orient | 38 | 6 | 4 | 9 | 19 | 22 | 1 | 3 | 15 | 16 | 56 | 21 |

—— HEALY MATCHED BEST ——

On 6 September 2006, ex Manchester United Player, David Healy (now at Leeds United) became the first Northern Ireland player to score a hat-trick on home soil since the legendary George Best scored a hat-trick against Cyprus in 1971. Healy's hat-trick earned Northern Ireland a historic 3–2 win over Spain, who were at number seven in the official FIFA world rankings, after twice falling behind in a Euro 2008 qualifying game at Windsor Park, Belfast.

### *Did You Know That?*
David Healy made only three appeareances at United.

## UNITED IN COURT OVER SALE OF ALCOHOL

In September 1904 Manchester United found themselves involved in a court case concerning the sale of alcohol at their Bank Street ground. Prior to that date the licensee at the ground had been the club captain, Harry Stafford. However, when the club secretary, James West, submitted an application to have his name registered as the licensee it was refused. In court the club was represented by Mr Fred Brocklehurst, who argued that if the club was prevented from selling alcohol during a game then the fans would bring their own, probably drink more and might even throw the bottles at the referee if a decision went against United. The licence was eventually granted.

## THE RED FLAG

United's flag is deepest red
It shrouded all our Munich dead
Before their limbs grew stiff and cold
Their heart's blood dyed it's ev'ry fold
Then raise United's banner high
Beneath it's shade we'll live and die
So keep the faith and never fear
We'll keep the Red Flag flying here
We'll never die, we'll never die
We'll never die, we'll never die
We'll keep the Red flag flying high
'Cos Man United will never die

## PLAYING SURFACE

Old Trafford boasts a superb grass playing surface, measuring 116 yards by 76 yards; it is cut three times a week from April to November and once a week from November to March. The pitch has an excellent drainage system – the centre is nine inches higher than the wings – and this coupled with the heating delivered by some 23 miles of plastic pipe 10 inches below the surface means that it is virtually unheard of now for a game to be postponed because of bad weather. To protect the pitch, Old Trafford is rarely used for training or reserve games, although visiting European sides are allowed to practise at the ground for one hour the night before a game. The quality of the Old Trafford pitch was recognised in 1995, when the head groundsman, Keith Kent, and his team were presented with the Premier League Groundsman of the Year Award.

## IMMORTAL LAWMAN

On 23 February 2002 Manchester United legend Denis Law celebrated his immortality at Old Trafford when he unveiled a 10-foot-tall statue of himself at the Stretford End. The statue was commissioned by Manchester United from sculptor Ben Panting. Said Denis during the ceremony, "I'm very glad to be here doing this. And I hope my family are happy I'm here too, because usually when you unveil a statue it's when the person is no longer around. This would truly be a great honour for any footballer but it is especially so for me to be back in the Stretford End where the fans will always hold a special place in my heart." Later that day Manchester United beat Aston Villa 1–0 at Old Trafford in the Premier League thanks to a Ruud van Nistelrooy goal.

## CANTONA IN THE MOVIES

2007 *Le Deuxième Soufflé (Second Wind* – French)
Eric is bartender Alban in a film about a recently freed gangster.

1999 *La Vie Est a Nous (It's Our Life* – French)
Eric plays a hunky striking trucker named Pierre.

1999 *L'Outremangeur (The Overeater* – French)
Eric put on two stone to play a lonely 160 kg (25 st) Marseille police investigator in a twist on Disney's *Beauty and the Beast.*

1999 *Les Enfants du Marais (Children of the Marshland* – Subtitles)
Eric plays Jo Sardi, an evil boxer, a film set in 1930s France.

1998 *Mookie* (French)
Eric plrays a boxer who meets a monk and his talking chimp. Eric joins them in their attempt to escape from scientists.

1998 *Elizabeth* (English)
Eric plays French ambassador Monsieur de Foix alongside British actor and United fan, Christopher Ecclestone in the Oscar-winning movie about the early years of Queen Elizabeth I's reign.

1997 *Question d'Honneur (A Question of Honour)* – Subtitles)
Eric plays a boxing promoter in this, his first major film role.

1995 *Le Bonheur est dans le Pre (Happiness in the Field* – Subtitles)
In this, Eric's first screen role, he plays Lionel, a rugby player.

## ⚊ UNITED'S HISTORICAL LEAGUE STATUS ⚊

| Seasons | League/Division |
|---|---|
| 1888–89 | Football Combination |
| 1889–92 | Football Alliance |
| 1892–94 | Division One |
| 1894–1906 | Division Two |
| 1906–15 | Division One |
| 1915–19 | Wartime League (Lancashire Section) |
| 1919–22 | Division One |
| 1922–25 | Division Two |
| 1925–31 | Division One |
| 1931–36 | Division Two |
| 1936–37 | Division One |
| 1937–38 | Division Two |
| 1938–39 | Division One |
| 1939–40 | Wartime Regional League (Western Division) |
| 1940–46 | Wartime Football League (Northern Section) |
| 1946–74 | Division One |
| 1974–75 | Division Two |
| 1975–92 | Division One |
| 1992 to date | FA Premier League |

## ⚊ PRE-LEAGUE FOOTBALL ⚊

Before the start of the 1888–89 season Newton Heath applied to join the Football League. Their application received a solitary vote and was subsequently rejected. The Heathens then joined forces with other disappointed applicants and formed the Football Combination. Newton Heath were the first "unofficial" winners of this newly created league, which lasted only one season before being wound up on 5 April 1889 and the balance of the funds donated to an orphanage in Derby. Newton Heath together with many other teams from the Football Combination then became founder members of the Football Alliance. The Heathens played three seasons of Alliance football, their best finish being as runners-up in 1891–92.

## ⚊ KEEPING IT TIGHT AT THE BACK ⚊

When Nottingham Forest's Stan Collymore scored in the 65th minute against United at Old Trafford on 17 December 1994, his strike was the first Premier League goal that United had conceded at home in 1133 minutes of play. United lost the game 2–1.

## ⸺ UNITED FORCE FA TO SCRAP THE CUP ⸺

When Manchester United won the FA Cup for the first time in 1909 they celebrated by having a duplicate made of the famous trophy. The Football Association were furious with the club, claiming their trophy was unique, and had a new FA Cup made in time for the 1911 final. United later handed over the duplicate to the Football Association, while the FA presented the original to Lord Kinnaird, who played in nine of the first eleven finals, when he completed 21 years' service with the association.

## ⸺ NO CUP TIES ⸺

Stan Crowther became the only FA Cup finalist in the competition's history to appear for two clubs in the Cup in the same season. On 19 February 1958, as an Aston Villa player, Crowther was brought to Old Trafford by Eric Houghton, Villa's manager, to watch the FA Cup fifth round game between Manchester United and Sheffield Wednesday. A few days earlier, United caretaker manager Jimmy Murphy (Matt Busby lay injured in a Munich hospital) had spoken to Houghton about the possibility of signing Crowther, but the Villa player did not want to leave the Midlands. However, an hour before the game against Wednesday kicked off, Crowther signed for United. As a mark of sympathy for United in the aftermath of the Munich Air Disaster, the FA waived their rule that a player cannot appear for two different teams in the Cup in the same season. Crowther played and United won 3–0.

## ⸺ BAND OF BROTHERS ⸺

United players with brothers who also played League football:

| United player(s) | Brother(s) | Team played for |
|---|---|---|
| Roger & Jack Doughty | – | both Newton Heath |
| Fred & Harry Erentz | – | both Newton Heath |
| James & John Hodge | – | both United |
| Jackie Blanchflower | Danny | Tottenham Hotspur |
| Bobby Charlton | Jack | Leeds United |
| Martin & George Buchan | – | both United |
| Jimmy & Brian Greenhoff | – | both United |
| Bryan Robson | Gary | WBA |
| Danny Wallace | Rod & Ray | Southampton |
| Gary & Philip Neville | – | both United |

## WE ARE THE CHAMPIONS (1)

On the last day of the 1907–08 season United beat Preston North End 2–1 (Halse, Rodway o.g.) to win the First Division Championship for the first time in the club's history. In winning the Championship, United set a then season record for the most League points – 52.

### *Football League Division 1*
### 1907–08

|     |                     | P  | W  | D | L | F  | A  | W | D | L  | F  | A  | Pts |
|-----|---------------------|----|----|---|---|----|----|---|---|----|----|----|-----|
| 1.  | MANCHESTER UNITED   | 38 | 15 | 1 | 3 | 43 | 19 | 8 | 5 | 6  | 38 | 29 | 52  |
| 2.  | Aston Villa         | 38 | 9  | 6 | 4 | 47 | 24 | 8 | 3 | 8  | 30 | 35 | 43  |
| 3.  | Manchester City     | 38 | 12 | 5 | 2 | 36 | 19 | 4 | 6 | 9  | 26 | 35 | 43  |
| 4.  | Newcastle United    | 38 | 11 | 4 | 4 | 41 | 24 | 4 | 8 | 7  | 24 | 30 | 42  |
| 5.  | Sheffield Wednesday | 38 | 14 | 0 | 5 | 50 | 25 | 5 | 4 | 10 | 23 | 39 | 42  |
| 6.  | Middlesbrough       | 38 | 12 | 2 | 5 | 32 | 16 | 5 | 5 | 9  | 22 | 29 | 41  |
| 7.  | Bury                | 38 | 8  | 7 | 4 | 29 | 22 | 6 | 4 | 9  | 29 | 39 | 39  |
| 8.  | Liverpool           | 38 | 11 | 2 | 6 | 43 | 24 | 5 | 4 | 10 | 25 | 37 | 38  |
| 9.  | Nottingham Forest   | 38 | 11 | 6 | 2 | 42 | 21 | 2 | 5 | 12 | 17 | 41 | 37  |
| 10. | Bristol City        | 38 | 8  | 7 | 4 | 29 | 21 | 4 | 5 | 10 | 29 | 40 | 36  |
| 11. | Everton             | 38 | 11 | 4 | 4 | 34 | 24 | 4 | 2 | 13 | 24 | 40 | 36  |
| 12. | Preston North End   | 38 | 9  | 7 | 3 | 33 | 18 | 3 | 5 | 11 | 14 | 35 | 36  |
| 13. | Chelsea             | 38 | 8  | 3 | 8 | 30 | 35 | 6 | 5 | 8  | 23 | 27 | 36  |
| 14= | Arsenal             | 38 | 9  | 8 | 2 | 32 | 18 | 3 | 4 | 12 | 19 | 45 | 36  |
| 14= | Blackburn Rovers    | 38 | 10 | 7 | 2 | 35 | 23 | 2 | 5 | 12 | 16 | 40 | 36  |
| 16. | Sunderland          | 38 | 11 | 2 | 6 | 53 | 31 | 5 | 1 | 13 | 25 | 44 | 35  |
| 17. | Sheffield United    | 38 | 8  | 6 | 5 | 27 | 22 | 4 | 5 | 10 | 25 | 36 | 35  |
| 18. | Notts County        | 38 | 9  | 3 | 7 | 24 | 19 | 4 | 5 | 10 | 15 | 32 | 34  |
| 19. | Bolton Wanderers    | 38 | 10 | 3 | 6 | 35 | 26 | 4 | 2 | 13 | 17 | 32 | 33  |
| 20. | Birmingham City     | 38 | 6  | 6 | 7 | 22 | 28 | 3 | 6 | 10 | 18 | 32 | 30  |

## 88 POINTS NOT GOOD ENOUGH

United's total of 88 League points in 1994–95 was the highest ever accumulated by a team that did not win England's top division. However, if the old scoring system of two points for a win and one for a draw had been in place, then United, and not Blackburn Rovers, that season's champions, would have finished top. Blackburn ended up with 27 wins, 8 draws and 7 defeats – 62 points under the old system. United finished with 26 wins, 10 draws and 6 defeats – also 62 points under the old system. However, United boasted the superior goal difference of +49 to Blackburn's +41.

## ──── UNITED WORLD CUP WINNERS ────

Six Manchester United players have featured in World Cup winning squads:

| Player | Country | Year |
| --- | --- | --- |
| Bobby Charlton | England | 1966 |
| John Connelly | England | 1966 |
| Nobby Stiles | England | 1966 |
| Fabien Barthez | France | 1998 |
| Laurent Blanc | France | 1998 |
| Jose Kleberson Pereira | Brazil | 2002 |

## ──── ALL OVER IN 12 SECONDS ────

Nick Culkin made his debut in goal for Manchester United away against Arsenal on 22 August 1999. When the referee blew his whistle for full-time, he'd been on the pitch for a mere 12 seconds, and he never got another game.

## ──── ROUGH JUSTICE FOR HEATHENS ────

On 14 January 1893 the Heathens comfortably beat West Bromwich Albion 4–1 with goals from Peden (2), Donaldson and Erentz. However, shortly after the game an article appeared in the *Birmingham Daily Gazette* which criticized some of the Newton Heath players, claiming they had used dirty tactics in the game. The Heathens sued the newspaper for £200 damages and won their case at Manchester Assizes. Unfortunately for the club the jury decided that the damage sustained should be compensated to the tune of the lowest value coin of the realm, which amounted to a farthing. The judge ordered both parties to pay their own legal costs, in Newton Heath's case £145. The court's ruling put a severe financial strain on the club.

## ──── PROUD HOME RECORD FALLS ────

When Fenerbahce beat Manchester United at Old Trafford on 30 October 1996 in the UEFA Champions League, they took United's proud 40-year home unbeaten record in European competition back to Turkey with them. The record had stood for 57 games; the 1–0 reverse also meant that United had failed to score for the first time in 27 home games in the European Cup.

—— GLITTERING PRIZES ——

***Premier League champions*** *(record 10 occasions)*
1993, 1994, 1996, 1997, 1999, 2000, 2001, 2003, 2007, 2008
Runners-up: 1995, 1998

***FA Cup winners*** *(record 11 occasions)*
1909, 1948, 1963, 1977, 1983, 1985, 1990,
1994, 1996, 1999, 2004
Runners-up: 1957, 1958, 1976, 1979, 1995, 2005, 2007

***European Cup/UEFA Champions League winners*** *(3 occasions)*
1968, 1999, 2008

***European Cup Winners' Cup winners*** *(1 occasion)*
1991

***Super Cup winners*** *(1 occasion)*
1991
Runners-up: 1999

***Intercontinental Cup winners*** *(1 occasion)*
1999
Runners-up: 1968

***League Division One champions*** *(7 occasions)*
1908, 1911, 1952, 1956, 1957, 1965, 1967
Runners-up: 1947, 1948, 1951, 1959, 1964,
1968, 1980, 1988, 1992

***League Division Two champions*** *(2 occasions)*
1936, 1975

***League Cup winners*** *(2 occasions)*
1992, 2006
Runners-up: 1983, 1991, 1994, 2003

***FA Charity / Community Shield winners*** *(12 occasions)*
1908, 1911, 1952, 1956, 1957, 1983,
1993, 1994, 1996, 1997, 2003, 2007
Joint-winners: 1965, 1967, 1977, 1990
Runners-up: 1948, 1963, 1985, 1998,
1999, 2000, 2001, 2004

## ⚬— THE CAPTAINS' LOG —⚬

The following players have all captained Manchester United:

| | | |
|---|---|---|
| Harry Stafford | Albert Quixall | Mike Duxbury |
| Jack Peddie | Ernie Taylor | Bryan Robson |
| Charlie Roberts | Maurice Setters | Frank Stapleton |
| George Stacey | Noel Cantwell | Norman Whiteside |
| George Hunter | David Herd | Steve Bruce |
| Frank Barson | Pat Crerand | Brian McClair |
| Hugh McLenahan | Denis Law | Paul Ince |
| Louis Page | John Connelly | Gary Pallister |
| Jimmy Brown | Willie Morgan | Mike Phelan |
| Johnny Carey | Ian Ure | Neil Webb |
| Stan Pearson | Martin Buchan | Eric Cantona |
| Jack Warner | Sammy McIlroy | Peter Schmeichel |
| Allenby Chilton | George Graham | Roy Keane |
| Charlie Mitten | Lou Macari | Ryan Giggs |
| Ray Wood | Brian Greenhoff | Gary Neville |
| Johnny Berry | Stewart Houston | Nicky Butt |
| Roger Byrne | Arthur Albiston | Ruud van Nistelrooy |
| Bill Foulkes | Steve Coppell | Phil Neville |
| Dennis Viollet | Kevin Moran | Rio Ferdinand |
| Bobby Charlton | Ray Wilkins | Cristiano Ronaldo |

## ⚬— BEATEN BY UNDERDOGS —⚬

Manchester United have lost two Wembley finals to teams from a lower division. In the 1976 FA Cup final they were beaten by Southampton from Division Two; in 1991 they lost in the League Cup final to Sheffield Wednesday, also from Division Two.

## ⚬— SPARKY'S 100TH WINS TITLE FOR UNITED —⚬

Mark Hughes scored his 100th League goal for United in the 2–0 Premiership win over Crystal Palace at Selhurst Park on 21 April 1993 that effectively won the Reds their first FA Premier League Championship title.

## ⚬— MASTER FERGUSON —⚬

On 8 October 1997 Alex Ferguson was awarded an Honorary Master of Arts Degree by Manchester University.

## LAL HILDITCH BOWS OUT

On 30 January 1932 Clarence "Lal" Hilditch played his last game for United in a 3–2 win over Nottingham Forest at Old Trafford. Hilditch spent 16 seasons at Old Trafford and was the only player-manager in the history of the club. He was appointed to the post in 1924 and held it for a year until Herbert Bamlett took over as manager.

## JUST CALL ME "SIR"

Warren Bradley played 66 times for United from 1958 to 1962, scoring 21 goals. He was selected to play for England against Italy at Wembley on 6 May 1959 and scored on his international debut in a 2–2 draw (Bobby Charlton scored the other England goal). After Warren retired from football, he took up teaching and was the headmaster of Stretford Secondary School during the early 1970s.

## THE UNITED CALYPSO

Manchester, Manchester United;
A bunch of bouncing Busby Babes;
They deserve to be knighted!
If ever they are playing in your town;
You must get to that football ground;
Take a lesson come and see;
Football taught by Matt Busby.

## UP FOR THE CUP (1)

Both teams were making their FA Cup final debuts and because the two sides wore red shirts, the FA instructed them to wear a change of strip. United wore white shirts with a red "V". A record crowd of 70,000 turned up at the Crystal Palace to see United win the Cup thanks to a goal from Sandy Turnbull. Charlie Roberts had the honour of becoming the first Manchester United player to lift the FA Cup.

**FA CUP FINAL**
*24 April 1909, The Crystal Palace*
MANCHESTER UNITED (1) *1*     *vs*     BRISTOL CITY (0) *0*
A. Turnbull
*Att. 71,401*
*Manchester United:* Moger, Stacey, Hayes, Duckworth, Roberts, Bell, Meredith, Halse, J. Turnbull, A. Turnbull, Wall

## ⚬ ROCK OF GIBRALTAR ⚬

It should have been no surprise to anyone when Rock of Gibraltar, co-owned by Sir Alex Ferguson, won his first seven Group One races in succession to set a new record. The Rock's father, Danehill, was the champion Australian sire seven times, champion juvenile sire six times and the champion European juvenile sire three times. The trainer Aidan O'Brien bred The Rock in partnership with his wife, Anne-Marie, and his father-in-law, John Crowley, mating Danehill with the stable's mare Offshore Boom. In 2002 Rock of Gibraltar completed his three-year-old season in Europe with the highest ever Timeform season rating of 133; not surprisingly he was voted World Horse of the Year. In 2003 The Rock entered stud in Australia and Ireland, but not before the settlement of a long and drawn-out dispute of ownership of stud fees between Sir Alex Ferguson and the Coolmore Stud.

**The Rock's race record**

| Age | Starts | Wins | Seconds | Thirds |
|---|---|---|---|---|
| 2 | 7 | 5 | 1 | – |
| 3 | 6 | 5 | 1 | _ |
| | 13 | 10 | 2 | _ |

Stakes won: £1,164,804          *World Horse of the Year, 2002*

## ⚬ RECORD ATTENDANCE FOR MIDWEEK ⚬

On 4 September 1957 United travelled to Goodison Park for a First Division encounter with Everton. The game ended 3–3, but the crowd of 72,077 set an all-time high attendance for a midweek Football League game.

## ⚬ THE OUTCASTS ⚬

At the end of the 1907–08 season, when Manchester United were crowned League champions for the first time in their history, many of the club's players found themselves the target of the football authorities for having played a significant role in the formation of the Players' Union. In 1908 a strike was threatened by the players, who ended up having to train at nearby Fallowfield; they named themselves "The Outcasts". However, a strike was avoided when the Football Association and the Football League decided to recognize the Players' Union prior to the start of the 1908–09 season.

## MANGNALL MEETS THE MAGYARS

As a reward for winning the club its first Championship in 1907–08, the United board sent the team on a trip to the Austro-Hungarian Empire. As part of the tour, United played two games in Budapest against Ferencvaros. United won the first 6–2, but the second match sparked a minor diplomatic incident. To the admiring applause of the Hungarian fans, the visitors seemed to be cruising to a second win, when the referee sent three United players off, bringing about a mini-riot. United finished the game with eight players, and a 7–0 win, but when the referee blew the final whistle, trouble flared again, leading the police to charge with swords drawn to disperse the crowd. Unbelievably United were then transported to their hotel by open-top bus. *En route* they encountered another missile-hurling mob, and a few of the team sustained head wounds. The Hungarian authorities apologized profusely to United, who diplomatically shrugged off the incidents and promised to return to Hungary the following year. However, when he arrived back in Manchester, United manager Ernest Mangnall vowed he would never go back.

## PUSKAS ALMOST JOINED UNITED

Shortly after the Munich Air Disaster the great Hungarian striker Ferenc Puskas offered to join United to help their rebuilding programme following the deaths of eight first-team players. However, Puskas could not speak English and the proposed move never materialized.

## CENTURION GOALSCORERS

This table covers all competitive games including the Charity Shield.

| Player | Number of goals | Player | Number of goals |
|---|---|---|---|
| Joe Cassidy | 100 | Stan Pearson | 148 |
| George Wall | 100 | Ruud van Nistelrooy | 150 |
| Sandy Turnbull | 101 | Mark Hughes | 163 |
| Andy Cole | 121 | Joe Spence | 168 |
| Ole Gunnar Solskjaer | 126 | Dennis Viollet | 179 |
| Brian McClair | 127 | George Best | 179 |
| Tommy Taylor | 131 | Jack Rowley | 211 |
| Paul Scholes | 139* | Denis Law | 237 |
| Ryan Giggs | 144* | Bobby Charlton | 249 |
| David Herd | 145 | *up to the end of the 2007–08 season | |

## —— DOUBLE RED ——

Eric Cantona was the first United player to be sent off in consecutive games. He was shown the red card for stamping on Swindon Town's John Moncur in a Premier League game on 19 March 1994, and three days later received his marching orders at Arsenal, also in the League.

## —— BOXING DAY TREBLE ——

Brian McClair's goal for United against Sheffield Wednesday on 26 December 1992 gave him the distinction of having scored in three consecutive Boxing Day games.

## —— NUMERO UNO ——

Steve Bruce was the inaugural winner of the FA Carling Premiership No. 1 Award in the 1992–93 season, for his "commitment and leadership".

## —— NINE TESTIMONIALS ——

| Date | Player | Opposition |
| --- | --- | --- |
| 18 October 1972 | Bobby Charlton | Glasgow Celtic |
| 3 October 1973 | Denis Law | Ajax Amsterdam |
| 17 August 1983 | Martin Buchan | Aberdeen |
| 13 May 1984 | Lou Macari | Glasgow Celtic |
| 8 May 1988 | Arthur Albiston | Manchester City |
| 16 May 1994 | Mark Hughes | Glasgow Celtic |
| 15 April 1996 | Brian McClair | Glasgow Celtic |
| 12 October 1999 | Sir Alex Ferguson | Rest of the World XI |
| 1 August 2001 | Ryan Giggs | Glasgow Celtic |

## —— MEN OF LEARNING ——

The following university graduates all played for United:

| Player | Subject |
| --- | --- |
| Gary Bailey | Physics |
| Warren Bradley | General Studies |
| Steve Coppell | Economics |
| Alan Gowling | Economics |
| Kevin Moran | Commerce |
| Mike Pinner | Law |

United defeated Sunderland 5–1 (Halse 2, Turnbull, West, Milton o.g.) at Old Trafford on the last day of the 1910–11 season to clinch their second First Division Championship in three years. However, two world wars would be fought before United were crowned champions again.

### *Football League Division 1*
### 1910–11

| | | P | W | D | L | F | A | W | D | L | F | A | Pts |
|---|---|---|---|---|---|---|---|---|---|---|---|---|---|
| 1. | MANCHESTER UNITED | 38 | 14 | 4 | 1 | 47 | 18 | 8 | 4 | 7 | 25 | 22 | 52 |
| 2. | Aston Villa | 38 | 15 | 3 | 1 | 50 | 18 | 7 | 4 | 8 | 19 | 23 | 51 |
| 3. | Sunderland | 38 | 10 | 6 | 3 | 44 | 22 | 5 | 9 | 5 | 23 | 26 | 45 |
| 4. | Everton | 38 | 12 | 3 | 4 | 34 | 17 | 7 | 4 | 8 | 16 | 19 | 45 |
| 5. | Bradford City | 38 | 13 | 1 | 5 | 33 | 16 | 7 | 4 | 8 | 18 | 26 | 45 |
| 6. | Sheffield Wednesday | 38 | 10 | 5 | 4 | 24 | 15 | 7 | 3 | 9 | 23 | 33 | 42 |
| 7. | Oldham Athletic | 38 | 13 | 4 | 2 | 30 | 12 | 3 | 5 | 11 | 14 | 29 | 41 |
| 8. | Newcastle United | 38 | 8 | 7 | 4 | 37 | 18 | 7 | 3 | 9 | 24 | 25 | 40 |
| 9. | Sheffield United | 38 | 8 | 3 | 8 | 27 | 21 | 7 | 5 | 7 | 22 | 22 | 38 |
| 10. | Arsenal | 38 | 9 | 6 | 4 | 24 | 14 | 4 | 6 | 9 | 17 | 35 | 38 |
| 11. | Notts County | 38 | 9 | 6 | 4 | 21 | 16 | 5 | 4 | 10 | 16 | 29 | 38 |
| 12. | Blackburn Rovers | 38 | 12 | 2 | 5 | 40 | 14 | 1 | 9 | 9 | 22 | 40 | 37 |
| 13. | Liverpool | 38 | 11 | 3 | 5 | 38 | 19 | 4 | 4 | 11 | 15 | 34 | 37 |
| 14. | Preston North End | 38 | 8 | 5 | 6 | 25 | 19 | 4 | 6 | 9 | 15 | 30 | 35 |
| 15. | Tottenham Hotspur | 38 | 10 | 5 | 4 | 40 | 23 | 3 | 1 | 15 | 12 | 40 | 32 |
| 16. | Middlesbrough | 38 | 9 | 5 | 5 | 31 | 21 | 2 | 5 | 12 | 18 | 42 | 32 |
| 17. | Manchester City | 38 | 7 | 5 | 7 | 26 | 26 | 2 | 8 | 9 | 17 | 32 | 31 |
| 18. | Bury | 38 | 8 | 9 | 2 | 27 | 18 | 1 | 2 | 16 | 16 | 53 | 29 |
| 19. | Bristol City | 38 | 8 | 4 | 7 | 23 | 21 | 3 | 1 | 15 | 20 | 45 | 27 |
| 20. | Nottingham Forest | 38 | 5 | 4 | 10 | 28 | 31 | 4 | 3 | 12 | 27 | 44 | 25 |

~~ AGAINST THE ODDS ~~

United, in the wake of the Munich Air Disaster, made it to Wembley for the 1958 FA Cup final against all the odds. Jimmy Murphy led the United team out as Matt Busby sat in the stadium watching. However, their makeshift side were not good enough on the day to beat Nat Lofthouse and his Bolton team-mates, who won 2–0. United became the first team in the twentieth century to lose consecutive FA Cup finals and also had their goalkeeper injured for the second year running. None of the Bolton side that beat United had previously played for another club; the first time that had ever been the case in a final.

### ICE CREAM SIGNING

It is reported that when Manchester United signed Hugh McLenahan from Stockport County in 1928, the United assistant manager, Louis Rocca, donated a freezer of ice cream in return for the 18-year-old's services. Rocca, a well-known ice-cream dealer in Manchester, had learned that Stockport County were holding a bazaar in an attempt to raise money for the club.

### WAR HERO

John Scott (Manchester United 1921–22) was awarded the Military Medal during World War I.

### HEATHEN WITNESS

On 19 October 1892 James Brown played for Newton Heath Reserves against Darwen Reserves. During the game Brown was involved in an accidental collision with Joseph Apsden, the Darwen centre forward, when he missed the ball and caught Apsden in the stomach with his knee. Apsden was taken to the tent where injured players were treated and then sent home after the game, but a short time later he died. Brown was called to give evidence to the Coroner's Court; a ruling of "Accidental Death" was recorded.

### UNDER THE HAMMER

In October 1992 Bill Foulkes' collection of more than 20 items of football memorabilia raised £35,000 at auction at Christie's, Glasgow. Bill's 1968 European Cup medal was sold for £11,000 while his shirt from the final was sold for £1800.

In March 2000 Christie's sold a pair of David Beckham's red, black and white Adidas Predator football boots worn in the 1997–98 season for £13,800[†].

In October 1997 a 1915 FA Cup final programme from the game played at Old Trafford was sold at Christie's for £11,270.

In September 2002 Jimmy Delaney's 1948 FA Cup winner's medal was sold at Christie's for £10,575.

[†]*A Beckham shirt can fetch anything from £700 to £2500 at auction.*

## —•— GOING, GOING, GOING, GONE —•—

The following businessmen[†] have all at some point attempted to purchase Manchester United:

*Robert Maxwell*   entered into negotiations with Martin Edwards in February 1984 to purchase Manchester United for £10 million. The deal never materialized.

*Michael Knighton* famously took to the Old Trafford pitch showing off his ball-juggling skills after agreeing a £20-million takeover deal with Martin Edwards. Two months later the deal collapsed when Knighton could not produce the agreed amount.

*Rupert Murdoch*   in September 1998 his BSkyB Group bid £575 million for control of Manchester United; the bid was rejected and later increased to £625 million, which was subsequently accepted. In accordance with the Fair Trading Act 1973, BSkyB's proposed acquisition of the club was referred to the Monopolies and Mergers Commission (MMC) to determine whether the merger would act against the public interest. The MMC blocked the deal.

*Malcolm Glazer*   is the owner of the 2003 Super Bowl winners, the Tampa Bay Buccaneers, and on 23 May 2005 he acquired 76.2% of the club's shares at a cost of £790 million, effectively making him the new owner of Manchester United.

## —•— BUSBY BABES' LAST GAME AT OLD TRAFFORD —•—

On 25 January 1958 the Old Trafford faithful saw the Busby Babes play at home for the last time. Matt Busby's all-conquering team beat Ipswich Town 2–0 in this FA Cup fourth round encounter. One of the greatest Busby Babes of all, Bobby Charlton, scored both goals for the Reds. Before the next round of the Cup was played, seven of Charlton's team-mates were dead; an eighth, Duncan Edwards, died two days after United's fifth round win over Sheffield Wednesday.

---

[†]*In September 1998 Roger Taylor of Queen was the man behind attempts by Manchester United fans to mobilize opposition to Sky TV's proposed takeover plan. The Queen drummer donated £10,000 to the Independent Manchester United Supporters Association (IMUSA). The money was needed to secure a headquarters for the campaign and organize a rally at Bridgewater Hall.*

At the end of the 1921–22 season United were relegated to Division Two after finishing the season with just 28 points from their 42 League games. During the season John Robson resigned as manager and was replaced by John Chapman.

### *Football League Division 1*
### 1921–22

|  |  | P | W | D | L | F | A | W | D | L | F | A | Pts |
|---|---|---|---|---|---|---|---|---|---|---|---|---|---|
| 1. | Liverpool | 42 | 15 | 4 | 2 | 43 | 15 | 7 | 9 | 5 | 20 | 21 | 57 |
| 2. | Tottenham Hotspur | 42 | 15 | 3 | 3 | 43 | 17 | 6 | 6 | 9 | 22 | 22 | 51 |
| 3. | Burnley | 42 | 16 | 3 | 2 | 49 | 18 | 6 | 2 | 13 | 23 | 36 | 49 |
| 4. | Cardiff City | 42 | 13 | 2 | 6 | 40 | 26 | 6 | 8 | 7 | 21 | 27 | 48 |
| 5. | Aston Villa | 42 | 16 | 3 | 2 | 50 | 19 | 6 | 0 | 15 | 24 | 36 | 47 |
| 6. | Bolton Wanderers | 42 | 12 | 4 | 5 | 40 | 24 | 8 | 3 | 10 | 28 | 35 | 47 |
| 7. | Newcastle United | 42 | 11 | 5 | 5 | 36 | 19 | 7 | 5 | 9 | 23 | 26 | 46 |
| 8. | Middlesbrough | 42 | 12 | 6 | 3 | 46 | 19 | 4 | 8 | 9 | 33 | 50 | 46 |
| 9. | Chelsea | 42 | 9 | 6 | 6 | 17 | 16 | 8 | 6 | 7 | 23 | 27 | 46 |
| 10. | Manchester City | 42 | 13 | 7 | 1 | 44 | 21 | 5 | 2 | 14 | 21 | 49 | 45 |
| 11. | Sheffield United | 42 | 11 | 3 | 7 | 32 | 17 | 4 | 7 | 10 | 27 | 37 | 40 |
| 12. | Sunderland | 42 | 13 | 4 | 4 | 46 | 23 | 3 | 4 | 14 | 14 | 39 | 40 |
| 13. | WBA | 42 | 8 | 6 | 7 | 26 | 23 | 7 | 4 | 10 | 25 | 40 | 40 |
| 14. | Huddersfield Town | 42 | 12 | 3 | 6 | 33 | 14 | 3 | 6 | 12 | 20 | 40 | 39 |
| 15. | Blackburn Rovers | 42 | 7 | 6 | 8 | 35 | 31 | 6 | 6 | 9 | 19 | 26 | 38 |
| 16. | Preston North End | 42 | 12 | 7 | 2 | 33 | 20 | 1 | 5 | 15 | 9 | 45 | 38 |
| 17. | Arsenal | 42 | 10 | 6 | 5 | 27 | 19 | 5 | 1 | 15 | 20 | 37 | 37 |
| 18. | Birmingham City | 42 | 9 | 2 | 10 | 25 | 29 | 6 | 5 | 10 | 23 | 31 | 37 |
| 19. | Oldham Athletic | 42 | 8 | 7 | 6 | 21 | 15 | 5 | 4 | 12 | 17 | 35 | 37 |
| 20. | Everton | 42 | 10 | 7 | 4 | 42 | 22 | 2 | 5 | 14 | 15 | 33 | 36 |
| 21. | Bradford City | 42 | 8 | 5 | 8 | 28 | 30 | 3 | 5 | 13 | 20 | 42 | 32 |
| 22. | MANCHESTER UNITED | 42 | 7 | 7 | 7 | 25 | 26 | 1 | 5 | 15 | 16 | 47 | 28 |

### —~~— SIX MERSEYSIDE CUP FINALS —~~—

| Year | Competition | Result | Venue |
|---|---|---|---|
| 1977 | FA Cup | United 2, Liverpool 1 | Wembley |
| 1983 | League Cup | United 1, Liverpool 2 *aet* | Wembley |
| 1985 | FA Cup | United 1, Everton 0 | Wembley |
| 1995 | FA Cup | United 0, Everton 1 | Wembley |
| 1996 | FA Cup | United 1, Liverpool 0 | Wembley |
| 2003 | League Cup | United 0, Liverpool 2 | Cardiff |

## —— THE GOAL THAT INSPIRED THE DOUBLE ——

On 10 April 1994 United met Oldham Athletic at Wembley in the FA Cup semi-finals and after 90 minutes the game was scoreless. Then in the first minute of the second period of injury time Neil Pointon scored for Oldham, and United's dreams of winning the Double were fast disappearing. United's season was on the line, but cometh the hour, cometh the man. With a minute of the game remaining, Brian McClair headed the ball into the Oldham box where Mark Hughes met it on the volley and sent it scorching past a dumbstruck Jon Hallworth and into the Oldham goal. United were off the hook, and after easily disposing of Oldham in the replay, went on to win the coveted Double for the first time in the club's history.

## —— THREE HAT-TRICKS IN 22 DAYS ——

At the beginning of the 1951–52 League season Jack Rowley scored three hat-tricks in 22 days for United. His first came on the opening day of the season (18 August), in a 3–3 draw away at West Bromwich Albion. His second came four days later as United beat Middlesbrough 4–2 at Old Trafford, and his third was against Stoke City in a 4–0 Old Trafford win on 8 September. In between he found the net a further five times for a total of 14 League goals in only seven games.

## —— KEEPER SAVES TWO PENALTIES ON DEBUT ——

Manchester United's Tim Howard saved two penalties on his debut in the 2003 FA Community Shield,[†] denying Arsenal's Giovanni van Bronckhorst and Robert Pires. United won the Shield on penalties. As it happened, Arsenal's Jens Lehmann also made his debut in the same game – and saved a penalty from Ruud van Nistelrooy.

## —— WORTHY WINNERS ——

On their way to winning the FA Cup in 1948, Manchester United became the competition's first winners to play First Division opposition in every round. United beat Aston Villa, Liverpool, Charlton Athletic, Preston North End, Derby County, and then Blackpool in the final.

[†]*In 2002 the FA Charity Shield was renamed the FA Community Shield after a government report in March 2002 stated that the Football Association had breached fund-raising regulations in the way it handled cash raised from the game.*

## UNITED'S FIRST TEN ENGLAND CAPS

| Player | Year capped |
|---|---|
| Charles Roberts | 1905 |
| George Wall | 1907 |
| Harold Halse | 1909 |
| John Mew | 1920 |
| John Silcock | 1921 |
| Joseph Spence | 1926 |
| Henry Cockburn | 1946 |
| John Aston Sr | 1948 |
| Stan Pearson | 1948 |
| Jack Rowley | 1948 |

## DURING THE WAR

During World War II, United played in the Football League North and notched up some impressive victories:

| Date | Result |
|---|---|
| 28 December 1940 | United 9, Blackburn Rovers 0 |
| 30 August 1941 | United 13, New Brighton Tower 1 |
| 11 October 1941 | United 7, Chester 0 |
| 18 October 1941 | United 8, Chester 1 |
| 6 December 1941 | United 10, Wrexham 3 |
| 20 February 1943 | United 7, Crewe Alexandra 0 |
| 15 April 1944 | United 9, Burnley 0 |

## WORST EVER FA CUP DEFEAT

On 13 February 1901 United (then Newton Heath) suffered their worst ever FA Cup defeat, in a first round replay away to Burnley, losing 7–1. Only four days earlier the two sides had drawn 0–0 in their first meeting.

## CAPTAIN BLOOD

United defender Kevin Moran[†] was tagged "Captain Blood" by the press as a result of claims that he had over 100 stitches inserted into his face and head as a result of injuries sustained during games.

[†]*Prior to becoming a professional soccer player, Kevin was an accomplished Gaelic footballer, winning an All-Ireland winner's medal with Dublin in 1976 and again in 1977.*

## WORST EVER HOME DEFEATS

United have suffered 6–0 home defeats on two occasions. The first took place at the hands of Aston Villa at Old Trafford in a First Division game on 14 March 1914. Sixteen years later Huddersfield Town beat United by the same score, also at Old Trafford in a League game.

## LAST-MINUTE SIGNING

On 7 February 1925 Albert Pape arrived at Old Trafford with his Clapton Orient team-mates for a Second Division game. An hour or so prior to kick-off United signed Pape and he made his debut in the match against the players he had travelled to Manchester with. To really rub it in, Pape scored in United's 4–2 win.

## MANCHESTER UNITED SCOTLAND XI

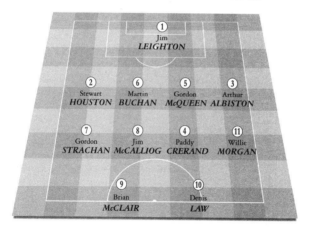

*Substitutes*
Andy *GORAM*, Alex *FORSYTH*, Jim *HOLTON*, Darren *FLETCHER*,
Lou *MACARI*, Joe *JORDAN*
*Manager*
Sir Matt *BUSBY*

### *Did You Know That?*
Three Manchester United managers also managed Scotland: Sir Matt Busby, Tommy Docherty and Sir Alex Ferguson.

After three seasons in Division Two United were finally promoted back into Division One. On their way to securing promotion United finished runners-up in the League conceding just 23 goals from their 42 League games. This was a record for Division Two.

### *Football League Division 2*
### 1924–25

|  |  | P | W | D | L | F | A | W | D | L | F | A | Pts |
|---|---|---|---|---|---|---|---|---|---|---|---|---|---|
| 1. | Leicester City | 42 | 15 | 4 | 2 | 58 | 9 | 9 | 7 | 5 | 32 | 23 | 59 |
| 2. | MANCHESTER UNITED | 42 | 17 | 3 | 1 | 40 | 6 | 6 | 8 | 7 | 17 | 17 | 57 |
| 3. | Derby County | 42 | 15 | 3 | 3 | 49 | 15 | 7 | 8 | 6 | 22 | 21 | 55 |
| 4. | Portsmouth | 42 | 7 | 13 | 1 | 28 | 14 | 8 | 5 | 8 | 30 | 36 | 48 |
| 5. | Chelsea | 42 | 11 | 8 | 2 | 31 | 12 | 5 | 7 | 9 | 20 | 25 | 47 |
| 6. | Wolverhampton W | 42 | 14 | 1 | 6 | 29 | 19 | 6 | 5 | 10 | 26 | 32 | 46 |
| 7. | Southampton | 42 | 12 | 8 | 1 | 29 | 10 | 1 | 10 | 10 | 11 | 26 | 44 |
| 8. | Port Vale | 42 | 12 | 4 | 5 | 34 | 19 | 5 | 4 | 12 | 14 | 37 | 42 |
| 9. | Gateshead | 42 | 9 | 6 | 6 | 33 | 21 | 3 | 11 | 7 | 9 | 17 | 41 |
| 10. | Hull City | 42 | 12 | 6 | 3 | 40 | 14 | 3 | 5 | 13 | 10 | 35 | 41 |
| 11. | Leyton Orient | 42 | 8 | 7 | 6 | 22 | 13 | 6 | 5 | 10 | 20 | 29 | 40 |
| 12. | Fulham | 42 | 11 | 6 | 4 | 26 | 15 | 4 | 4 | 13 | 15 | 41 | 40 |
| 13. | Middlesbrough | 42 | 6 | 10 | 5 | 22 | 21 | 4 | 9 | 8 | 14 | 23 | 39 |
| 14. | Sheffield Wednesday | 42 | 12 | 3 | 6 | 36 | 23 | 3 | 5 | 13 | 14 | 33 | 38 |
| 15. | Barnsley | 42 | 8 | 8 | 5 | 30 | 23 | 5 | 4 | 12 | 16 | 36 | 38 |
| 16. | Bradford City | 42 | 11 | 6 | 4 | 26 | 13 | 2 | 6 | 13 | 11 | 37 | 38 |
| 17. | Blackpool | 42 | 8 | 5 | 8 | 37 | 26 | 6 | 4 | 11 | 28 | 35 | 37 |
| 18. | Oldham Athletic | 42 | 9 | 5 | 7 | 24 | 21 | 4 | 6 | 11 | 11 | 30 | 37 |
| 19. | Stockport County | 42 | 10 | 6 | 5 | 26 | 15 | 3 | 5 | 13 | 11 | 42 | 37 |
| 20. | Stoke City | 42 | 7 | 8 | 6 | 22 | 17 | 5 | 3 | 13 | 12 | 29 | 35 |
| 21. | Crystal Palace | 42 | 8 | 4 | 9 | 23 | 19 | 4 | 6 | 11 | 15 | 35 | 34 |
| 22. | Coventry City | 42 | 10 | 6 | 5 | 32 | 26 | 1 | 3 | 17 | 13 | 58 | 31 |

—— ONE GAME, THREE CAPTAINS ——

When Manchester United rested Roy Keane for the home game against Portsmouth on 26 February 2005, Gary Neville was made captain for the match. During the game Neville was injured and handed the captain's armband over to Ruud van Nistelrooy. When van Nistelrooy was substituted near the end of the match, he passed the armband over to Ryan Giggs. The crowd for the game, which United won 2–1 (Rooney 2), was a record for the Premiership of 67,989.

## GOOSE AND GOAT

During the late 1890s Newton Heath were so desperate to get crowds to attend their home games at Bank Street that they tried a number of novel ideas. Two particular attractions to lure the crowds in were a goose and a goat. Posters would encourage spectators to come to Bank Street and hear the "Bank Street Canary" sing. In fact, the canary referred to was a goose housed in a pen in a far corner of the ground. It was being fattened for the club's Christmas dinner. The goat belonged to one of the players and was employed as a club mascot. After home games the players and the goat would visit the nearby pub, where the animal was given pints of ale to slake its thirst.

## FIRST TEN CAPPED SCOTLAND PLAYERS

| Player | Year capped |
|---|---|
| Alex Bell | 1912 |
| Thomas Miller | 1921 |
| Neil McBain | 1922 |
| Jimmy Delaney | 1947 |
| Denis Law | 1962 |
| Paddy Crerand | 1963 |
| Francis Burns | 1969 |
| Martin Buchan | 1972 |
| Willie Morgan | 1972 |
| Alex Forsyth | 1973 |

## BEST MAGIC

On 7 February 1970 George Best returned from suspension and was in the United line-up that faced Northampton Town away in the fifth round of the FA Cup. Best was unstoppable as he carved through the home defence time after time, scoring two hat-tricks in the process. United won 8–2, with Brian Kidd helping himself to United's other two goals.

## CHARLTON 75 NOT OUT

Bobby Charlton played his 75th consecutive FA Cup tie for the club in United's 1–0 defeat away to Wolverhampton Wanderers in the third round on 13 January 1973. Although the game was Charlton's last FA Cup game for Manchester United, he went on to play a further four FA Cup ties for Preston North End.

During his playing career, Eric Cantona had more than the odd run in with team-mates and officialdom. Here are some of his misdemeanours:

1987  Punched his team-mate, goalkeeper Bruno Martini, at Auxerre. Received a heavy fine.

1988  Called the former French national team coach Henri Michel a "shitbag". Banned for one year.

1989  Kicked the ball into the crowd and threw his shirt into the crowd while playing for Marseilles. Banned indefinitely by the French club, who subsequently loaned him out to Bordeaux and Montpellier.

1990  Clattered team-mate Jean Claude Lemoult with his boots at Montpellier. Returned to Marseilles.

1991  Banned for three games playing for his new club, Rimes, after throwing the ball at the referee. At the disciplinary hearing before the French FA, he approached each member of the panel, looked him in the face and called him an "idiot". His ban was increased to two months. Eric decided it was time to retire at the age of 24.

1991  Stormed out of Sheffield Wednesday, where he was on a six-week trial, after Trevor Francis delayed a decision to sign him. The trial had been limited to indoor games because of poor weather conditions at the time. Eric said he was insulted, and joined Howard Wilkinson at Leeds United.

1993  Sent off after the final whistle had been blown after accusing the referee, Kurt Rothlisberger, of cheating in United's drawn European game with Galatasaray. On the way back to the changing rooms he got involved in a fight with Turkish police. UEFA gave him a four-match ban.

1994  Sent off in successive games against Swindon Town and Arsenal in March – on the former occasion for stamping on Swindon's John Moncur; on the latter for two yellow card offences. The FA handed down a five-match ban.

1994  Commentating on the World Cup finals for French television, Eric was arrested and placed in handcuffs prior to the semi-final between Brazil and Sweden at the Pasadena Rose Bowl after allegedly throwing a punch at a fellow reporter in the press box. Following the swift intervention of FIFA press officer Guido Tognoni, Eric was released without charge.

1994  In a pre-season friendly against Glasgow Rangers, Eric was sent off for the fourth time in nine months. The sending-off prompted Alex Ferguson to say that he would never play another friendly at Rangers. The FA gave Eric a three-match ban for his offence.

1995    Sent off at Crystal Palace on 25 January. On his way back to the changing rooms Eric was verbally abused by a Crystal Palace supporter. The red mist descended and Eric jumped into the crowd "kung-fu style", attacking the supporter. The FA fined Eric £20,000 and banned him from playing in all games until the end of the season; they subsequently increased the fine to £30,000 and extended his ban to 30 September 1995.

1995    At his court hearing Eric was given a two-week jail sentence for his part in the incident at Selhurst Park; the sentence was later reduced on appeal to 120 hours of community service. Eric returned to France, where he contemplated retirement for a second time but was persuaded by Alex Ferguson to return to Old Trafford and serve out the full term of his ban.

## ⚊⚊ EIGHT FROM EIGHT FOR WHELAN ⚊⚊

Between 5 September 1956 and 20 October 1956, Liam Whelan scored in eight consecutive first division matches for Manchester United.

## ⚊⚊ FIRST GAME AFTER MUNICH ⚊⚊

On 19 February 1958, amid an emotional atmosphere at Old Trafford, United played their first game since the Munich Air Disaster. The crowd of almost 60,000 wept openly in memory of those who had lost their lives at Munich, and their red-and-white scarves were draped in black as a mark of respect[†]. Sheffield Wednesday were the visitors for an FA Cup fifth round tie. United were forced to put a makeshift team together but won the game 3–0, with Shay Brennan (two goals on debut) and Alex Dawson the scorers. What made the victory even more remarkable, though, was that United had lost their previous three FA Cup ties against Wednesday and hadn't managed to score in any of them (0–6, 0–1, 0–2). The Sheffield Wednesday captain on the night, Albert Quixall, later became a Manchester United player.

---

[†]1. *The space for the Manchester United line-up inside the programme produced for the game was left blank as no one knew what the team would be following the air crash 13 days earlier.*

2. *From United's first game after the Cup tie with Sheffield Wednesday, red, white and black were adopted as the club's official colours.*

A 4–4 draw with Middlesbrough (Reid 2, Bennison, Gallimore) was United's final League game of the 1930–31 season. United finished bottom of Division One, with 27 defeats from their 42 matches; it was their worst ever season for League defeats. Nine of the losses were at Old Trafford, which is also a club record figure. The team also suffered their worst ever season for away defeats, losing 18 of their 21 games on the road. After the game, Herbert Bamlett resigned as manager and the post was filled by Walter Crickmer.

### *Football League Division 1*
### 1930–31

|  |  | P | W | D | L | F | A | W | D | L | F | A | Pts |
|---|---|---|---|---|---|---|---|---|---|---|---|---|---|
| 1. | Arsenal | 42 | 14 | 5 | 2 | 67 | 27 | 14 | 5 | 2 | 60 | 32 | 66 |
| 2. | Aston Villa | 42 | 17 | 3 | 1 | 86 | 34 | 8 | 6 | 7 | 42 | 44 | 59 |
| 3. | Sheffield Wednesday | 42 | 14 | 3 | 4 | 65 | 32 | 8 | 5 | 8 | 37 | 43 | 52 |
| 4. | Portsmouth | 42 | 11 | 7 | 3 | 46 | 26 | 7 | 6 | 8 | 38 | 41 | 49 |
| 5. | Huddersfield Town | 42 | 10 | 8 | 3 | 45 | 27 | 8 | 4 | 9 | 36 | 38 | 48 |
| 6. | Derby County | 42 | 12 | 6 | 3 | 56 | 31 | 6 | 4 | 11 | 38 | 48 | 46 |
| 7. | Middlesbrough | 42 | 13 | 5 | 3 | 57 | 28 | 6 | 3 | 12 | 41 | 62 | 46 |
| 8. | Manchester City | 42 | 13 | 2 | 6 | 41 | 29 | 5 | 8 | 8 | 34 | 41 | 46 |
| 9. | Liverpool | 42 | 11 | 6 | 4 | 48 | 28 | 4 | 6 | 11 | 38 | 57 | 42 |
| 10. | Blackburn Rovers | 42 | 14 | 3 | 4 | 54 | 28 | 3 | 5 | 13 | 29 | 56 | 42 |
| 11. | Sunderland | 42 | 12 | 4 | 5 | 61 | 38 | 4 | 5 | 12 | 28 | 47 | 41 |
| 12. | Chelsea | 42 | 13 | 4 | 4 | 42 | 19 | 2 | 6 | 13 | 22 | 48 | 40 |
| 13. | Grimsby Town | 42 | 13 | 2 | 6 | 55 | 31 | 4 | 3 | 14 | 27 | 56 | 39 |
| 14. | Bolton Wanderers | 42 | 12 | 6 | 3 | 45 | 26 | 3 | 3 | 15 | 23 | 55 | 39 |
| 15. | Sheffield United | 42 | 10 | 7 | 4 | 49 | 31 | 4 | 3 | 14 | 29 | 53 | 38 |
| 16. | Leicester City | 42 | 12 | 4 | 5 | 50 | 38 | 4 | 2 | 15 | 30 | 57 | 38 |
| 17. | Newcastle United | 42 | 9 | 2 | 10 | 41 | 45 | 6 | 4 | 11 | 37 | 42 | 36 |
| 18. | West Ham United | 42 | 11 | 3 | 7 | 56 | 44 | 3 | 5 | 13 | 23 | 50 | 36 |
| 19. | Birmingham City | 42 | 11 | 3 | 7 | 37 | 28 | 2 | 7 | 12 | 18 | 42 | 36 |
| 20. | Blackpool | 42 | 8 | 7 | 6 | 41 | 44 | 3 | 3 | 15 | 30 | 81 | 32 |
| 21. | Leeds United | 42 | 10 | 3 | 8 | 49 | 31 | 2 | 4 | 15 | 19 | 50 | 31 |
| 22. | MANCHESTER UNITED | 42 | 6 | 6 | 9 | 30 | 37 | 1 | 2 | 18 | 23 | 78 | 22 |

~~~ UNITED THE FIRST BIG SPENDERS ~~~

Manchester United became the first British club to pay a six-figure sum for a player when they bought Denis Law from Torino in July 1962 for £115,000.

## ⚬⚬⚬ FIRST NIGHT-TIME GAME ⚬⚬⚬

The first "floodlit" match in United's history took place at Clayton in 1899–1900, when the club was still known as Newton Heath. A benefit match was organized for Harry Stafford and Walter Cartwright in recognition of their service to the club. Stafford insisted the game be played at night, in the hope that more people would turn up, with a gilded ball to be used in association with the Wells lighting system. A strong gale on the night meant the stewards had great difficulty in keeping the lights lit. No sooner had they relit one when another one blew out. When only a single lamp remained alight, the referee blew the whistle and abandoned the game early. When the officials reached the changing rooms they discovered that many of the 22 players who started the game had already showered and dressed. The lighting was so poor none of the officials noticed them walk off the pitch.

## ⚬⚬⚬ MEDALLION MAN ⚬⚬⚬

Ryan Giggs is the most successful player in the history of Manchester United. To the end of the 2007–08 season, Giggs had won a staggering 20 medals during his time at Old Trafford:

| | |
|---|---|
| Premier League | 10 |
| FA Cup | 4 |
| League Cup | 2 |
| UEFA Champions League | 2 |
| European Super Cup | 1 |
| World Club Championship | 1 |

## ⚬⚬⚬ ON THE BRINK OF DIVISION THREE ⚬⚬⚬

On the final day of the 1933–34 season Manchester United travelled to London to play Millwall in a game that would ultimately decide which club remained in Division Two and which club played in the Third Division in 1934–35. United had 32 points from 41 games, Millwall 33 from 41 and Swansea 33 from 41. Goals from John Cape and Tom Manley secured United's survival with a 2–0 win that sent Millwall down. Two years later United won Division Two to return to top-flight football.[†]

[†]*Prior to the game United changed the colour of their shirts for luck. They played in white shirts with cherry hoops.*

## ⚬⚬⚬ HEATHENS TAKEN TO COURT ⚬⚬⚬

In January 1900 Newton Heath signed Gilbert Godsmark from the Kent League side Ashford FC. The fee agreed between the two clubs was £40, with half to be paid upon the player's signing and the remainder to be handed over after a satisfactory trial period had been served. After only nine appearances for the Heathens, in which he scored four times, in April 1900 Godsmark, a reservist, was called up to fight in the Boer War. The Heathens retained his playing registration for the following season, but sadly Godsmark was killed in action in February 1901. Following his death, Ashford FC served a writ on Newton Heath for the outstanding £20.

## ⚬⚬⚬ A KNIGHT OF 1000 GAMES ⚬⚬⚬

On 23 November 2004 Sir Alex Ferguson took charge of Manchester United for the 1000th time in his illustrious career. Lyon were the visitors to Old Trafford for a UEFA Champions League game that United won 2–1 thanks to goals from Gary Neville and Ruud van Nistelrooy. Speaking about his 1000th game in charge, Sir Alex said: "I can still remember my very first game in charge away at Oxford. I had done my team-talk and was going into the dugout when I saw the bus driver sitting there. He was even giving the tea out at half-time. Let's say that quickly stopped."

The following is a breakdown of Manchester United's first 1000 games under Sir Alex Ferguson:

| P | W | D | L | F | A |
|------|-----|-----|-----|------|-----|
| 1000 | 568 | 242 | 190 | 1784 | 945 |

## ⚬⚬⚬ SPOOKY GOAL ⚬⚬⚬

Liam O'Brien scored for United against Coventry City at Old Trafford on 6 February 1988. It was the 30th anniversary of the Munich Air Disaster, and O'Brien's goal, the winner as it proved to be, was scored just three minutes after the exact time the plane crashed in Munich in 1958.

## ⚬⚬⚬ BASKETBALL DEVILS ⚬⚬⚬

In 1984 Manchester United formed their own basketball team to compete in the British Basketball League. Appropriately the team were named the Red Devils.

## THE TROPHY COLLECTOR

Sir Alex Ferguson has amassed a trophy collection that is the envy of other managers. He has won 39 trophies in his managerial career with three different clubs, including 28 with Manchester United:

*St Mirren*
First Division winners ............................................. 1977
*Aberdeen*
Premier League winners ........................... 1980, 1984, 1985
Scottish Cup winners ...................... 1982, 1983, 1984, 1986
League Cup winners ................................................ 1986
European Cup Winners' Cup winners ........................... 1983
European Super Cup winners ..................................... 1983
*Manchester United*
FA Cup winners ..................... 1990, 1994, 1996, 1999, 2004
European Cup Winners' Cup winners ........................... 1991
European Super Cup winners ..................................... 1991
League Cup winners ....................................... 1992, 2006
Premier League winners .......... 1993, 1994, 1996, 1997, 1999,
2000, 2001, 2003, 2007, 2008
FA Charity Shield winners 1993, 1994, 1996, 1997, 2003, 2007
European Cup winners ..................................... 1999, 2008
World Club champions ............................................ 1999

## OLD TRAFFORD OFFICIALLY OPENED

United's move from Bank Street[†] to Old Trafford took place midway through the 1909–10 season, and the very first game at the ground took place against Liverpool on 19 February 1910 in front of a crowd of 45,000. Although United had several injury problems, they raced to a 3–1 lead with goals from Homer, Sandy Turnbull and Wall. The Merseysiders fought back to level the game at 3–3 before grabbing a winner to spoil United's big day. That day's *Sporting Chronicle* had this to say about United's new stadium: "The most handsomest, the most spacious and the most remarkable arena I have ever seen. As a football ground it is unrivalled in the world, it is an honour to Manchester and the home of a team who can do wonders when they are so disposed."

[†]*On 17 February 1910, two days before the official opening of United's new home – Old Trafford – fierce gales struck the Manchester area. The old wooden stand at Bank Street, Clayton, was ripped apart by the winds, and wreckage from it blew across the roadway, damaging a number of houses in the area. Mercifully it wasn't a match day and no one was injured.*

With a 3–2 away win at Bury (Manley 2, Mutch) on 29 April 1936, United clinched the Second Division title.

### *Football League Division 2*
### 1935–36

|  |  | P | W | D | L | F | A | W | D | L | F | A | Pts |
|---|---|---|---|---|---|---|---|---|---|---|---|---|---|
| 1. | MANCHESTER UNITED | 42 | 16 | 3 | 2 | 55 | 16 | 6 | 9 | 6 | 30 | 27 | 56 |
| 2. | Charlton Athletic | 42 | 15 | 6 | 0 | 53 | 17 | 7 | 5 | 9 | 32 | 41 | 55 |
| 3. | Sheffield United | 42 | 15 | 4 | 2 | 51 | 15 | 5 | 8 | 8 | 28 | 35 | 52 |
| 4. | West Ham United | 42 | 13 | 5 | 3 | 51 | 23 | 9 | 3 | 9 | 39 | 45 | 52 |
| 5. | Tottenham Hotspur | 42 | 12 | 6 | 3 | 60 | 25 | 6 | 7 | 8 | 31 | 30 | 49 |
| 6. | Leicester City | 42 | 14 | 5 | 2 | 53 | 19 | 5 | 5 | 11 | 26 | 38 | 48 |
| 7. | Plymouth Argyle | 42 | 15 | 2 | 4 | 50 | 20 | 5 | 6 | 10 | 21 | 37 | 48 |
| 8. | Newcastle United | 42 | 13 | 5 | 3 | 56 | 27 | 7 | 1 | 13 | 32 | 52 | 46 |
| 9. | Fulham | 42 | 11 | 6 | 4 | 58 | 24 | 4 | 8 | 9 | 18 | 28 | 44 |
| 10. | Blackpool | 42 | 14 | 3 | 4 | 64 | 34 | 4 | 4 | 13 | 29 | 38 | 43 |
| 11. | Norwich City | 42 | 14 | 2 | 5 | 47 | 24 | 3 | 7 | 11 | 25 | 41 | 43 |
| 12. | Bradford City | 42 | 12 | 7 | 2 | 32 | 18 | 3 | 6 | 12 | 23 | 47 | 43 |
| 13. | Swansea City | 42 | 11 | 3 | 7 | 42 | 26 | 4 | 6 | 11 | 25 | 50 | 39 |
| 14. | Bury | 42 | 10 | 6 | 5 | 41 | 27 | 3 | 6 | 12 | 25 | 57 | 38 |
| 15. | Burnley | 42 | 9 | 8 | 4 | 35 | 21 | 3 | 5 | 13 | 15 | 38 | 37 |
| 16. | Bradford Park Av | 42 | 13 | 6 | 2 | 43 | 26 | 1 | 3 | 17 | 19 | 58 | 37 |
| 17. | Southampton | 42 | 11 | 3 | 7 | 32 | 24 | 3 | 6 | 12 | 15 | 41 | 37 |
| 18. | Doncaster Rovers | 42 | 10 | 7 | 4 | 28 | 17 | 4 | 2 | 15 | 23 | 54 | 37 |
| 19. | Nottingham Forest | 42 | 8 | 8 | 5 | 43 | 22 | 4 | 3 | 14 | 26 | 54 | 35 |
| 20. | Barnsley | 42 | 9 | 4 | 8 | 40 | 32 | 3 | 5 | 13 | 14 | 48 | 33 |
| 21. | Port Vale | 42 | 10 | 5 | 6 | 34 | 30 | 2 | 3 | 16 | 22 | 76 | 32 |
| 22. | Hull City | 42 | 4 | 7 | 10 | 33 | 45 | 1 | 3 | 17 | 14 | 66 | 20 |

⎯⎯ TOMMY DOCHERTY SACKED ⎯⎯

Under Tommy Docherty, the good days returned to Old Trafford. However, shortly after United's 1977 FA Cup final victory over Liverpool, the news broke that Docherty was having an affair with Mary Brown, the wife of the club's physio. United, with their strong Catholic traditions, felt compelled to ask Docherty to step down. On 4 July 1977 Tommy Docherty was called before the United board at the home of Louis Edwards in Alderley Edge. The directors asked Docherty for his resignation and when he refused he was sacked. And so ended the reign of the man fondly remembered as "The Doc".

## ONLY 18 PLAYERS USED

Throughout the 1964–65 League Championship winning campaign, Manchester United used only 18 players (19 players in all competitions).

## CENTRE-HALF OR CENTRE-FORWARD?

Steve Bruce holds the record for the most goals from penalties in a season for United. In 1990–91 he converted 11 spot kicks.

## THE TRIUMPH OF YOUTH

In 1968 George Best, aged 22, became the youngest ever winner of the European Footballer of the Year Award. In the same year he was also voted the Player of the Year both in England and in Northern Ireland.

## OLD TRAFFORD SENTINEL

Matt Busby personified Manchester United, and shortly after his death on 20 January 1994 the idea of memorializing him was discussed. Numerous suggestions were made about how to mark his contribution to the club, but in the end it was decided that a statue would be an appropriate monument. Manchester United entrusted Philip Jackson with the commission. He depicted Sir Matt in relaxed mood, wearing the club blazer of 1968; his right hand rests on his hip while in his other hand is a football. The Busby family were consulted at the various stages of the project, and the statue was unveiled by Sandy and Sheena Busby, Sir Matt's son and daughter, on 27 April 1996. It is situated outside Old Trafford's new North Stand above the Executive Entrances and Souvenir Shop, looking across Sir Matt Busby Way.

## SPLASHING OUT ON KEEPERS

Manchester United have paid a British record transfer fee for a goalkeeper on four occasions:

| Goalkeeper | Fee | From | Date |
|---|---|---|---|
| Reg Allen | £11,000 | Queens Park Rangers | June 1950 |
| Harry Gregg | £23,000 | Doncaster Rovers | Dec 1957 |
| Alex Stepney | £60,000 | Chelsea | Sept 1966 |
| Fabien Barthez | £7.8m | AS Monaco | July 2000 |

## RYAN'S DOUBLE

Ryan Giggs was the first ever player to be voted PFA Young Player of the Year twice. He won the award in 1992 and again in 1993.

## WHICH OLD TRAFFORD?

When George Best and Eric McMordie, both aged 15, arrived in Manchester in 1961 for their trial at Old Trafford, they jumped into a taxi and asked the driver to take them to Old Trafford. When the driver asked them "Which Old Trafford?" the two lads were slightly embarrassed, since neither of them knew there was also an Old Trafford cricket ground.

## MANCHESTER UNITED ENGLAND XI

*Substitutes*

Gary *BAILEY*, Eddie *COLMAN*, Mark *JONES*, Ray *WILKINS*, Steve *COPPELL*, Gordon *HILL*, Jack *ROWLEY*, Dennis *VIOLLET*, David *BECKHAM*, Wayne *ROONEY*

*Manager*

Ron *ATKINSON*

### Did You Know That?

Walter Winterbottom, a Manchester United half back from 1936 to 1938, managed England from 1946 to 1962, guiding them to four successive World Cup finals tournaments.

## ⚬⚬⚬ FIRST EUROPEAN TIE AT OLD TRAFFORD ⚬⚬⚬

Having played their home quarter-final leg at Maine Road in February, on 25 April 1957 United brought competitive European football to Old Trafford for the first time when they played Real Madrid in the second leg of their European Cup semi-final[†]. The match ended in a 2–2 draw (Taylor, Charlton), but it was the Spanish champions who went through to the final, having already beaten United 3–1 in the first leg at the Santiago Bernabeu Stadium.

## ⚬⚬⚬ SHAGGY DOG STORY ⚬⚬⚬

With Newton Heath plunged into bankruptcy, in early 1902 club captain Harry Stafford organized a Grand Bazaar in St James's Hall, Manchester, to help raise cash, employing his St Bernard, Major, as an overnight guard dog. Major, however, escaped from the hall and failed to come back. Stafford, heartbroken, placed an advertisement in the local press for the return of his pet. According to legend, the dog turned up at the house of John H. Davies, a local brewery owner, who contacted Stafford. When the two men met, conversation naturally turned to Newton Heath's predicament. The upshot was that on 28 April 1902, at a club meeting at Islington Public Hall, Ancoats, Harry Stafford was able to announce that he and John H. Davies had a plan to save the Heathens. Davies and three other local businessmen had pledged to invest £500 each, thus guaranteeing the club's existence. It was at this meeting that Newton Heath changed its name to Manchester United and John H. Davies was appointed the club's new president. Had a much-loved St Bernard not escaped from St James's Hall, it is doubtful that we would even have a Manchester United today.

## ⚬⚬⚬ FOULKES THE INDESTRUCTIBLE ⚬⚬⚬

Despite being involved in the Munich Air Disaster, Bill Foulkes ended the 1957–58 season having played in all 42 of United's League games. Dennis Viollet was the only other player to have played in both the opening and last League games of the season.

---

[†]1. *European football first arrived at Old Trafford on 12 May 1951 when United hosted Red Star Belgrade in a Festival of Britain game. The score was 1–1.*

2. *On 11 April 1957, 135,000 had turned up at the Santiago Bernabeu Stadium to watch the first leg of the Real Madrid–Manchester United European Cup semi-final. The crowd remains the largest that United have ever played in front of.*

United, the Division Two Champions in season 1935–36 slipped back into the Second Division after finishing in 21st place in Division One at the end of the 1936–37 season. However, United did manage to win the Manchester Senior Cup in 1936–37.

### *Football League Division 1*
### 1936–37

| | | P | W | D | L | F | A | W | D | L | F | A | Pts |
|---|---|---|---|---|---|---|---|---|---|---|---|---|---|
| 1. | Manchester City | 42 | 15 | 5 | 1 | 56 | 22 | 7 | 8 | 6 | 51 | 39 | 57 |
| 2. | Charlton Athletic | 42 | 15 | 5 | 1 | 37 | 13 | 6 | 7 | 8 | 21 | 36 | 54 |
| 3. | Arsenal | 42 | 10 | 10 | 1 | 43 | 20 | 8 | 6 | 7 | 37 | 29 | 52 |
| 4. | Derby County | 42 | 13 | 3 | 5 | 58 | 39 | 8 | 4 | 9 | 38 | 51 | 49 |
| 5. | Wolverhampton W | 42 | 16 | 2 | 3 | 63 | 24 | 5 | 3 | 13 | 21 | 43 | 47 |
| 6. | Brentford | 42 | 14 | 5 | 2 | 58 | 32 | 4 | 5 | 12 | 24 | 46 | 46 |
| 7. | Middlesbrough | 42 | 14 | 6 | 1 | 49 | 22 | 5 | 2 | 14 | 25 | 49 | 46 |
| 8. | Sunderland | 42 | 17 | 2 | 2 | 59 | 24 | 2 | 4 | 15 | 30 | 63 | 44 |
| 9. | Portsmouth | 42 | 13 | 3 | 5 | 41 | 29 | 4 | 7 | 10 | 21 | 37 | 44 |
| 10. | Stoke City | 42 | 12 | 6 | 3 | 52 | 27 | 3 | 6 | 12 | 20 | 30 | 42 |
| 11. | Birmingham City | 42 | 9 | 7 | 5 | 36 | 24 | 4 | 8 | 9 | 28 | 36 | 41 |
| 12. | Grimsby Town | 42 | 13 | 3 | 5 | 60 | 32 | 4 | 4 | 13 | 26 | 49 | 41 |
| 13. | Chelsea | 42 | 11 | 6 | 4 | 36 | 21 | 3 | 7 | 11 | 16 | 34 | 41 |
| 14. | Preston North End | 42 | 10 | 6 | 5 | 35 | 28 | 4 | 7 | 10 | 21 | 39 | 41 |
| 15. | Huddersfield Town | 42 | 12 | 5 | 4 | 39 | 21 | 0 | 10 | 11 | 23 | 43 | 39 |
| 16. | WBA | 42 | 13 | 3 | 5 | 45 | 32 | 3 | 3 | 15 | 32 | 66 | 38 |
| 17. | Everton | 42 | 12 | 7 | 2 | 56 | 23 | 2 | 2 | 17 | 25 | 55 | 37 |
| 18. | Liverpool | 42 | 9 | 8 | 4 | 38 | 26 | 3 | 3 | 15 | 24 | 58 | 35 |
| 19. | Leeds United | 42 | 14 | 3 | 4 | 44 | 20 | 1 | 1 | 19 | 16 | 60 | 34 |
| 20. | Bolton Wanderers | 42 | 6 | 6 | 9 | 22 | 33 | 4 | 8 | 9 | 21 | 33 | 34 |
| 21. | MANCHESTER UNITED | 42 | 8 | 9 | 4 | 29 | 26 | 2 | 3 | 16 | 26 | 52 | 32 |
| 22. | Sheffield Wednesday | 42 | 8 | 5 | 8 | 32 | 29 | 1 | 7 | 13 | 21 | 40 | 30 |

~~~ SEVENTH HEAVEN ~~~

On 15 October 1892 Newton Heath registered their first ever win in League football with a 10–1 demolition of Wolverhampton Wanderers in a Division One game at North Road. It was the Heathens' seventh game of the season. The scoreline was not only the first 10–1 result in League football but also a club record. Donaldson (3), Stewart (3), Carson, Farman, Hendry and Hood were on the scoresheet for the Heathens.

### ⚬ THE STRETFORD END ⚬

Old Trafford's West Stand, or Stretford End, situated next to the players' tunnel, has a special place in the heart of every Manchester United fan. The new stand was completed in 1993 at a cost of £10.3 million, a huge sum when compared with the £350,000 cost of building the first cantilever stand in 1964. Besides the banqueting suite – the International – the West Stand contains the Family Stand, which is open only to parents and children who are either Manchester United members or on an organized tour from a visiting club. Above the Family Stand sits the TV studio, from which television presenters provide match coverage.

### ⚬ PRESTON CONNECTION ⚬

Four Manchester United players have also managed Preston North End:

Bobby Charlton ............................. May 1973 – August 1975
Nobby Stiles ................................. July 1977 – June 1981
Brian Kidd .................................. January 1986 – March 1986
Sammy McIlroy .............................. February 1990 – July 1991

### ⚬ ONE WEDDING AND A RESIGNATION ⚬

Neil Dewar left Manchester United in December 1933 and joined Sheffield Wednesday. Shortly after leaving Old Trafford he eloped with the daughter of United director Councillor A.E. Thomson. The couple ran into "residential" problems when they attempted to marry at a register office and there were some difficulties before the wedding could proceed. There was so much publicity surrounding the episode that Councillor Thomson felt obliged to resign his United directorship.

### ⚬ GIBSON'S GUARANTEE ⚬

During the 1931–32 season Manchester United were struggling in Division Two and finding it difficult to make ends meet. When the secretary, Walter Crickmer, announced that the bank had refused to advance United any more money, the club could not even afford to purchase the players their traditional Christmas turkey let alone meet their wages. Enter James W. Gibson, who guaranteed the players' wages until the end of the season, at which point he became the club's new chairman.

## ⟿ HOLY TRINITY ⟿

When United beat West Brom 4–1 at the Hawthorns on 18 January 1964 it was the first game in which Matt Busby played the trio of Law, Best and Charlton in the same match. United, with the predatory instincts of Law, the class and drive of Charlton and the maverick genius of the young Irishman, were simply too good for the home side, who suffered a 4–1 defeat. The goals, appropriately to mark the occasion, were scored by Law (2), Best and Charlton – a sign of things to come.

## ⟿ FINALLY OFF THE MARK ⟿

In his 30th game for Manchester United following his move from Nottingham Forest in October 1980, Garry Birtles, United's first £1 million player (he cost £1.25 million), finally scored his first League goal. He netted the only goal of the game in a 1–0 home win over Swansea City on 19 September 1981. Birtles was never able to reproduce his previous goalscoring form at United and within two years of his arrival the club had sold him back to Forest for £250,000.

## ⟿ PITCH SIGNING ⟿

On 3 October 1981 Bryan Robson signed for Manchester United on the Old Trafford pitch in front of a crowd of 46,837. Robson did not play in the game that followed, but the man he was bought to replace, Sammy McIlroy, scored a hat-trick in United's 5–0 win over Wolverhampton Wanderers.

## ⟿ FERGIE'S FLEDGLINGS ⟿

Fergie's Fledglings – David Beckham, Nicky Butt, Chris Casper, Gary Neville, John O'Kane, Paul Scholes and Ben Thornley – all signed professional forms for Manchester United on 23 January 1993.

## ⟿ FORTRESS CARRINGTON ⟿

Six miles west of Old Trafford lies Carrington, Manchester United's state-of-the-art training complex. The site covers 70 acres and boasts 14 pitches (all visible from Sir Alex Ferguson's office), plus training and rehabilitation areas, physiotherapy rooms, massage rooms and remedial and hydrotherapy pools. The complex, as you would expect, is extremely well guarded and often nicknamed "Fortress Carrington".

## RECORD UNBEATEN RUN

United set their all-time record of 34 games without defeat in the League and in cup competitions when they beat Sheffield Wednesday 4–2 at Hillsborough in the second leg of their Coca-Cola Cup semi-final on 2 March 1994. The record stretched back to 25 September 1993, when United beat Swindon Town by the same score in the Premiership.

## UNITED WIN 9–0

On 4 March 1995 United recorded the biggest win in FA Premier League history, beating Ipswich Town 9–0 at Old Trafford. Andy Cole scored five (the highest number of goals in a League game by a United player) and Roy Keane, Mark Hughes (2) and Paul Ince were the other goalscorers. Meanwhile, a little farther up the motorway, David Beckham scored directly from a corner in a 2–2 draw against Doncaster Rovers while on loan at Preston North End.

## RECORD LEAGUE ATTENDANCE

On 17 January 1948 a crowd of 82,950 attended United's 1–1 (Rowley) home draw with Arsenal. The game was played at Manchester City's Maine Road ground as Old Trafford was still under reconstruction after the war. The crowd is a record for an English Football League game.

## TOP MARKSMAN WITH SIX

Bobby Charlton scored his sixth and last League goal of the 1972–73 season in United's 2–0 away win at Southampton on 31 March 1973. Remarkably Charlton finished the season as United's top marksman in the League with those six goals.

## INAUGURAL FA CHARITY SHIELD

Manchester United, the Northern League champions, won the first ever FA Charity Shield when they beat Southern League champions Queens Park Rangers 4–0 at Stamford Bridge on 29 August 1908 in a replay. Sandy Turnbull scored a hat-trick, with George Wall also making the scoresheet. The original game had been played four months earlier, on 27 April, also at Stamford Bridge, and had ended in a 1–1 draw. Meredith scored for United.

After winning the Division Two Championship in 1935–36, then suffering relegation back to Division Two in 1936–37, United were promoted to Division One for the second time in three seasons after finishing in runners-up spot in Division Two at the end of the 1937–38 season. United also won the Lancashire Senior Cup in 1937–38.

### *Football League Division 2*
### 1937–38

| | | P | W | D | L | F | A | W | D | L | F | A | Pts |
|---|---|---|---|---|---|---|---|---|---|---|---|---|---|
| 1. | Aston Villa | 42 | 17 | 2 | 2 | 50 | 12 | 8 | 5 | 8 | 23 | 23 | 57 |
| 2. | MANCHESTER UNITED | 42 | 15 | 3 | 3 | 50 | 18 | 7 | 6 | 8 | 32 | 32 | 53 |
| 3. | Sheffield United | 42 | 15 | 4 | 2 | 46 | 19 | 7 | 5 | 9 | 27 | 37 | 53 |
| 4. | Coventry City | 42 | 12 | 5 | 4 | 31 | 15 | 8 | 7 | 6 | 35 | 30 | 52 |
| 5. | Tottenham Hotspur | 42 | 14 | 3 | 4 | 46 | 16 | 5 | 3 | 13 | 30 | 38 | 44 |
| 6. | Burnley | 42 | 15 | 4 | 2 | 35 | 11 | 2 | 6 | 13 | 19 | 43 | 44 |
| 7. | Bradford Park Ave | 42 | 13 | 4 | 4 | 51 | 22 | 4 | 5 | 12 | 18 | 34 | 43 |
| 8. | Fulham | 42 | 10 | 7 | 4 | 44 | 23 | 6 | 4 | 11 | 17 | 34 | 43 |
| 9. | West Ham United | 42 | 13 | 5 | 3 | 34 | 16 | 1 | 9 | 11 | 19 | 36 | 42 |
| 10. | Bury | 42 | 12 | 3 | 6 | 43 | 26 | 6 | 2 | 13 | 20 | 34 | 41 |
| 11. | Chesterfield | 42 | 12 | 2 | 7 | 39 | 24 | 4 | 7 | 10 | 24 | 39 | 41 |
| 12. | Luton Town | 42 | 10 | 6 | 5 | 53 | 36 | 5 | 4 | 12 | 36 | 50 | 40 |
| 13. | Plymouth Argyle | 42 | 10 | 7 | 4 | 40 | 30 | 4 | 5 | 12 | 17 | 35 | 40 |
| 14. | Norwich City | 42 | 11 | 5 | 5 | 35 | 28 | 3 | 6 | 12 | 21 | 47 | 39 |
| 15. | Southampton | 42 | 12 | 6 | 3 | 42 | 26 | 3 | 3 | 15 | 13 | 51 | 39 |
| 16. | Blackburn Rovers | 42 | 13 | 6 | 2 | 51 | 30 | 1 | 4 | 16 | 20 | 50 | 38 |
| 17. | Sheffield Wednesday | 42 | 10 | 5 | 6 | 27 | 21 | 4 | 5 | 12 | 22 | 35 | 38 |
| 18. | Swansea City | 42 | 12 | 6 | 3 | 31 | 21 | 1 | 6 | 14 | 14 | 52 | 38 |
| 19. | Newcastle United | 42 | 12 | 4 | 5 | 38 | 18 | 2 | 4 | 15 | 13 | 40 | 36 |
| 20. | Nottingham Forest | 42 | 12 | 3 | 6 | 29 | 21 | 2 | 5 | 14 | 18 | 39 | 36 |
| 21. | Barnsley | 42 | 7 | 11 | 3 | 30 | 20 | 4 | 3 | 14 | 20 | 44 | 36 |
| 22. | Stockport County | 42 | 8 | 6 | 7 | 24 | 24 | 3 | 3 | 15 | 19 | 46 | 31 |

⚊ RECORD WORST START EVER ⚊

United had made the worst start to a First Division League campaign by any club when they were beaten 4–1 at Portsmouth on 25 October 1930. It was their twelfth successive defeat since the opening day of the season, and in those 12 games United had scored 14 goals and conceded 49. Their first points of the season came in their thirteenth game, when they beat Birmingham City 2–0 at Old Trafford.

## OLDEST POST-WAR PLAYER

On 22 April 1950 Jack Warner, aged 38, became United's oldest post-war player when he played for the Reds in a League game at Newcastle United. Ironically Warner took the place in the team of Jeff Whitefoot, who only one week earlier had become United's youngest post-war League player. United were beaten 2–1 (Downie).

## JESUS AND JUDAS SUPPORT UNITED

On Saturday 19 February 2005 actors Ian McShane[†] and Robert Powell were guests on Eamonn Holmes' BBC Radio Five Live show to discuss the Malcolm Glazer bid to purchase Manchester United. Both Ian and Robert are patrons of Shareholders' United. During the broadcast Eamonn pointed out that Robert played Jesus Christ and Ian played Judas Iscariot in the BBC mini-series *Jesus of Nazareth*, which was screened in 1977.

## TREBLE WINNERS' PLAQUE

Towards the end of 2000 a bronze plaque celebrating United's 1999 Treble winning year was unveiled by Sir Alex Ferguson and placed at the front of the Red Café. The plaque depicts the Premier League trophy, FA Cup and UEFA Champions League trophy in front of the Old Trafford stadium. The artist, Michael Browne, who once famously depicted Eric Cantona as Jesus Christ in a painting, got his inspiration for the plaque from a fourteenth-century Greek image. Michael said: "It is a permanent celebration of the club's triumph and reflects the achievements of Sir Alex so I was especially proud that he could unveil the work."

## DERBY CHARITY SHIELD

United (the League champions) met City (FA Cup winners) in the FA Charity Shield for the first and only time on 24 October 1956. Although United as League champions had the right to host the game at Old Trafford, the match was played at Maine Road because Old Trafford did not have any floodlights. The Busby Babes lifted the Shield thanks to a goal from Dennis Viollet in the 75th minute.

[†]*Ian McShane's father, Harry, was a forward with United from 1950 to 1954. He played 57 games for the Reds, scoring eight times. Harry went on to become the PA announcer at Old Trafford in the late 1960s and early 1970s.*

## STRAWBERRY YOGHURT

In January 2005 Manchester United star Rio Ferdinand was reported to have been absolutely furious when some of his team-mates covered his new £200,000 6.8-litre Bentley Arnage convertible with strawberry yoghurt at United's Carrington training complex. According to reports, the United defender had to have it professionally cleaned. An official at United said: "Rio's face was a picture when he saw it, he went absolutely mad. It was the first time he had taken the car out and it looked absolutely pristine. The lads at United are always taking the mickey out of Rio for being so flash and they couldn't resist the wind-up."

## THE CLIFF

The Cliff, situated in Salford on the banks of the River Irwell, was United's main training and practice facility until replaced by Carrington in 1999. Nevertheless, the Cliff is still used for Academy, Junior and Manchester United Ladies' side games. Manchester United's "Football in the Community" project headquarters is located here, and the England team have trained at the Cliff ahead of an international staged at Old Trafford.

## TWO GAMES, TWO CUP FINALS

When Les Sealey replaced the suspended Peter Schmeichel in goal for United's 1994 Coca-Cola Cup final clash with Aston Villa at Wembley, it was only his second start for the team in three years. His previous start had been in the 1991 European Cup Winners' Cup final.

## 100 POINTS

When they defeated Oldham Athletic 5–2 at Boundary Park on 29 December 1993, Manchester United notched up a total of 100 League points for the calendar year.

## SEQUENTIALLY ORDERED

When Manchester United beat Sheffield Wednesday 3–0 at Hillsborough in the Premier League on 7 December 1993, it was the first time since the introduction of squad numbers that United had taken to the field with players numbered 1 to 11. Roy Keane (No 16) came on as a substitute.

Usually with ghostly assistance, many United notables have penned their memoirs. With no intended comment on their respective literary merits, *Cantona On Cantona*, *Keane* and other self-explanatory book titles have been omitted from this list.

*After The Ball* – Nobby Stiles (2003)
*Back At The Top* – Bill Foulkes (1965)
*Behind The Dream* – Joe Jordan (2005)
*Black Pearl of Inchicore* – Paul McGrath (1994)
*Blessed* – George Best (2001)
*Call The Doc* – Tommy Docherty (1981)
*Father of Football* – Sir Matt Busby (1994)
*For Club and Country* – Gary & Phil Neville (1998)
*Forward For England* – Bobby Charlton (1967)
*Frankly Speaking* – Frank Stapleton (1991)
*Harry's Game* – Harry Gregg (2002)
*Head To Head* – Jaap Stam (2002)
*Heading For Victory* – Steve Bruce (1994)
*In Safe Keeping* – Alex Stepney (1969)
*Living For Kicks* – Denis Law (1963)
*Managing My Life* – Alex Ferguson (2001)
*Moments* – Cristiano Ronaldo (2007)
*My Manchester United Years* – Sir Bobby Charlton (2007)
*My Memories of Manchester United* – Norman Whiteside (2003)
*My Side* – David Beckham (2003)
*My Story So Far* – Wayne Rooney (2006)
*Never Turn The Other Cheek* – Pat Crerand (2007)
*Odd Man Out* – Brian McClair (1997)
*Rio: My Story* – Rio Ferdinand (2006)
*Soccer – My Battlefield* – Nobby Stiles (1968)
*Soccer At The Top* – Sir Matt Busby (1974)
*The King* – Denis Law (2003)
*The Lawman* – Denis Law (2001)
*The Red Dragon* – Mark Hughes (1994)
*Touch And Go* – Steve Coppell (1998)
*Un Reve Modeste et Fou* – Eric Cantona (1993)
*United I Stand* – Bryan Robson (1984)
*United To Win* – Ron Atkinson (1994)
*United We Stand* – Noel Cantwell (1965)
*We Shall Not Be Moved* – Lou Macari (1976)
*A Will To Win* – Alex Ferguson (1997)

## ⟶ UP FOR THE CUP (2) ⟶

Thirty-nine years after their first FA Cup final appearance, United were at Wembley for the 1948 final. The Blackpool side, which included great players such as Stanley Matthews and Stan Mortensen, took the lead in the 12th minute when Shimwell scored from a penalty. In the 28th minute Jack Rowley levelled the scores, only for Mortensen to put Blackpool 2–1 up at half-time. In the second half United managed to shackle Matthews and thereby control the Blackpool attack. In the 69th minute Rowley made the score 2–2, and shortly afterwards Stan Pearson put United ahead for the first time in the game. With only seven minutes remaining, Anderson's cross ended up in the back of the Blackpool net via a deflection off Blackpool's Kelly. United captain Johnny Carey collected the Cup from King George VI.

### FA CUP FINAL
*24 April 1948, Wembley Stadium*

MANCHESTER UNITED (1) *4*    *vs*    BLACKPOOL (2) *2*
Rowley (2), Pearson,    Shimwell (pen), Mortensen
Anderson

*Att. 99,000*

*Manchester United:* Crompton, Carey, Aston, Anderson, Chilton, Cockburn, Delaney, Morris, Rowley, Pearson, Mitten

### ⟶ FIRST TEN NORTHERN IRELAND CAPS ⟶

| Player | Year capped |
|---|---|
| Michael Hamill | 1912 |
| W. Crooks | 1922 |
| David Lyner | 1922 |
| Walter McMillen | 1933 |
| Tommy Breen | 1937 |
| Johnny Carey | 1946 |
| Jackie Blanchflower | 1954 |
| Harry Gregg | 1958 |
| James Nicholson | 1960 |
| William Briggs | 1962 |

### ⟶ INAUSPICIOUS START ⟶

Newton Heath played their first game in the Football League on 3 September 1892 against Blackburn Rovers and lost 4–3.

## HEATHENS' GOALKEEPER GOES AWOL

The Heathens' first ever season in the Football League started badly, and on 7 January 1893 matters got worse when their goalkeeper, Jimmy Warner, failed to turn up for a League game away to Stoke City. Playing with only ten men the Heathens were thrashed 7–1. Warner had missed his train to Stoke, but the directors were far from impressed and suspended him. Warner played only twice more after that for Newton Heath and moved on to Walsall Town Swifts.

## USA 1 ENGLAND 0

Eddie McIlvenny, captain of the USA when they beat England 1–0 in Belo Horizonte in 1950, played the first two games of the following season for United. To add insult to injury, McIlvenny was one of three non-Americans to have played in the win over England. He was born in Greenock, Scotland.

## SAME AGAIN, PLEASE

Between 6 December 1975 and 28 February 1976, United played 18 games (13 League and 5 FA Cup) with an unchanged starting line-up.

## FOR CLUB AND COUNTRIES

During his time at Old Trafford, United's flying winger Andrei Kanchelskis won international caps with three different countries: Russia, Ukraine and the USSR/CIS.

## DUDLEY'S FAVOURITE SON

Duncan Edwards' home town of Dudley contains several memorials and tributes to the United legend, who died on 21 February 1958 as a result of injuries sustained in the Munich Air Disaster. Duncan was buried in Dudley Cemetery, Stourbridge Road, and his grave is still a place of pilgrimage for football fans. In the town centre stands the Duncan Edwards Statue, created by James Butler, while in St Francis' Church, Dudley, Duncan is commemorated in two stained-glass windows. Dudley Leisure Centre houses an exhibition containing many of Duncan's medals, shirts and trophies, and the town also has a pub named after the late Busby Babe. On 14 September 2001 "The Wren's Nest", situated 100 yards from where Duncan was born, was officially reopened as the "Duncan Edwards".

## ⚽ MATT BUSBY'S FIRST SIGNING ⚽

In February 1946 Jimmy Delaney became the first player to be signed by Matt Busby when he left Glasgow Celtic for Manchester United on a £4000 transfer.

## BACK HOME

After Old Trafford was badly damaged during a wartime German bombing raid, Manchester United took to playing "home" matches at Maine Road until their ground could be rebuilt. On 24 August 1949 United played their first Football League game at Old Trafford for ten years. A crowd of 41,748 watched them beat Bolton Wanderers 3–0, with goals from John Downie, Charlie Mitten and Jack Rowley.

## LIVERPOOL GIFT UNITED THE TITLE

When Manchester United lost 4–2 at Aston Villa on 22 April 1911, the First Division Championship was delicately poised. Villa's victory put them level on points (50) with United. However, the Birmingham side had a game in hand, which they drew at Blackburn Rovers two days later to put them one point clear at the top of the table with only one game remaining. On the final Saturday of the season, Villa travelled to Liverpool while United were at home to Sunderland. Villa lost 3–1; United beat Sunderland 5–1. The Reds finished one point ahead of Villa and were crowned champions for the second time in three years.

## THE FIRST EVER GOALSCORER

Chas Richards holds the unique distinction of being the first player to score a goal for United. He scored in the newly formed Manchester United's opening Division Two game of the 1902–03 season – a 1–0 away win over Gainsborough Trinity.

## BILLY MEREDITH BIDS FAREWELL

On the same day that Old Trafford recorded its lowest ever attendance (13 people are believed to have watched Stockport County against Leicester City in a Division Two game), Billy Meredith played his last game for United. A crowd of 10,000 watched United beat Derby County 3–0 (Spence 2, Sapsford).

## LAW THE CENTURY MAKER

Denis Law scored his 100th goal for Manchester United in their 2–1 win over Everton at Goodison Park on 23 August 1966. Denis registered his first 100 goals in only 139 games.

## OLD TRAFFORD ALL LIT UP

Old Trafford's first floodlight system cost Manchester United £40,000. Four 160ft-high steel towers were erected, with each tower containing 54 floodlights. The first ever floodlit match at the ground was a first division game against Bolton Wanderers on 25 March 1957. The occasion attracted a crowd of 60,862, United's largest of the season. However, the home fans went away disappointed after their side went down 2–0.

## TIGHT PURSE STRINGS

Matt Busby did not buy any players between 1953 and 1957, although when you consider the talent he had available among his Busby Babes at the time, why would he have needed to enter the transfer market! Indeed, in the 13 years preceding the 1958 Munich Air Disaster Busby purchased only 16 players, and four of those were goalkeepers. During the period 1964–72 Manchester United bought just three players: Willie Morgan, Alex Stepney and Ian Ure. By way of comparison, Tommy Docherty bought seven players during his first four months in charge at Old Trafford (December 1972 to April 1973).

## TAKING IT TO THE WIRE

On the final day of the 1967–68 season Manchester United and Manchester City were level on 56 points. City had to travel to Newcastle United while United entertained Sunderland at Old Trafford. United lost 2–1 while City won 4–3 to take the title.

|  | P | W | D | L | F | A | Pts |
|---|---|---|---|---|---|---|---|
| City | 42 | 26 | 6 | 6 | 86 | 43 | 58 |
| UNITED | 42 | 24 | 8 | 10 | 89 | 55 | 56 |

## A UNITED OLYMPIAN

Alan Gowling was in Great Britain's 1968 Olympic football squad.

## "GIVE IT TO JOE!"

"Give it to Joe!" was a regular chant from the terraces at Old Trafford and away grounds from 1919 to 1933. Joe Spence was the first player to make more than 500 appearances for Manchester United. In all he played 510 games for the club (481 League and 29 FA Cup), scoring 168 times; his last game was on 1 April 1933 in a 1–0 away defeat at Fulham. It was Spence's magical wing play that led the crowd to chant "Give it to Joe!" when a game appeared a little dull.

## FIRST TEN WALES CAPS

| Player | Year capped |
|---|---|
| John Doughty | 1887 |
| John Powell | 1887 |
| Thomas Burke | 1887 |
| Joseph Davies | 1888 |
| Roger Doughty | 1888 |
| W. Owen | 1888 |
| George Owen | 1889 |
| John Owen | 1892 |
| Caesar Jenkyns | 1897 |
| Billy Meredith | 1907 |

## KEEP THE CHANGE

When Tommy Taylor joined Manchester United in March 1953 from Barnsley the agreed fee was £30,000, but because Matt Busby did not want to burden the young striker with a £30,000 price tag, he paid £29,999 for him and gave a tea lady the other £1.

## SCORING A QUICK CENTURY

Ruud van Nistelrooy scored his first goal for Manchester United on his debut, against Arsenal in the Charity Shield on 12 August 2001. Less than three years later Ruud netted his 100th goal for United in their pulsating 4–3 away win at Everton on 7 February 2004. Amazingly it took Ruud only 131 games to reach his first 100 goals for United.

## HIGH FREQUENCY

In his 33 European games for United, Denis Law managed to find the back of the net an amazing 28 times.

United hammered Arsenal, the only team that could catch them, 6–1 in the final game of the 1951–52 season to capture the First Division Championship for the first time since 1911; it was United's third Championship overall. Jack Rowley scored a hat-trick while Pearson (2) and Byrne were the other goalscorers. Prior to the game, Arsenal could still have won the title, but they would have needed to beat United 7–0!

### *Football League Division 1*
### 1951–52

| | | P | W | D | L | F | A | W | D | L | F | A | Pts |
|---|---|---|---|---|---|---|---|---|---|---|---|---|---|
| 1. | MANCHESTER UNITED | 42 | 15 | 3 | 3 | 55 | 21 | 8 | 8 | 5 | 40 | 31 | 57 |
| 2. | Tottenham Hotspur | 42 | 16 | 1 | 4 | 45 | 20 | 6 | 8 | 7 | 31 | 31 | 53 |
| 3. | Arsenal | 42 | 13 | 7 | 1 | 54 | 30 | 8 | 4 | 9 | 26 | 31 | 53 |
| 4. | Portsmouth | 42 | 13 | 3 | 5 | 42 | 25 | 7 | 5 | 9 | 26 | 33 | 48 |
| 5. | Bolton Wanderers | 42 | 11 | 7 | 3 | 35 | 26 | 8 | 3 | 10 | 30 | 35 | 48 |
| 6. | Aston Villa | 42 | 13 | 3 | 5 | 49 | 28 | 6 | 6 | 9 | 30 | 42 | 47 |
| 7. | Preston North End | 42 | 10 | 5 | 6 | 39 | 22 | 7 | 7 | 7 | 35 | 32 | 46 |
| 8. | Newcastle United | 42 | 12 | 4 | 5 | 62 | 28 | 6 | 5 | 10 | 36 | 45 | 45 |
| 9. | Blackpool | 42 | 12 | 5 | 4 | 40 | 27 | 6 | 4 | 11 | 24 | 37 | 45 |
| 10. | Charlton Athletic | 42 | 12 | 5 | 4 | 41 | 24 | 5 | 5 | 11 | 27 | 39 | 44 |
| 11. | Liverpool | 42 | 6 | 11 | 4 | 31 | 25 | 6 | 8 | 7 | 26 | 36 | 43 |
| 12. | Sunderland | 42 | 8 | 6 | 7 | 41 | 28 | 7 | 6 | 8 | 29 | 33 | 42 |
| 13. | WBA | 42 | 8 | 9 | 4 | 38 | 29 | 6 | 4 | 11 | 36 | 48 | 41 |
| 14. | Burnley | 42 | 9 | 6 | 6 | 32 | 19 | 6 | 4 | 11 | 24 | 44 | 40 |
| 15. | Manchester City | 42 | 7 | 5 | 9 | 29 | 28 | 6 | 8 | 7 | 29 | 33 | 39 |
| 16. | Wolverhampton W | 42 | 8 | 6 | 7 | 40 | 33 | 4 | 8 | 9 | 33 | 40 | 38 |
| 17. | Derby County | 42 | 10 | 4 | 7 | 43 | 37 | 5 | 3 | 13 | 20 | 43 | 37 |
| 18. | Middlesbrough | 42 | 12 | 4 | 5 | 37 | 25 | 3 | 2 | 16 | 27 | 63 | 36 |
| 19. | Chelsea | 42 | 10 | 3 | 8 | 31 | 29 | 4 | 5 | 12 | 21 | 43 | 36 |
| 20. | Stoke City | 42 | 8 | 6 | 7 | 34 | 32 | 4 | 1 | 16 | 15 | 56 | 31 |
| 21. | Huddersfield Town | 42 | 9 | 3 | 9 | 32 | 35 | 1 | 5 | 15 | 17 | 47 | 28 |
| 22. | Fulham | 42 | 5 | 7 | 9 | 38 | 31 | 3 | 4 | 14 | 20 | 46 | 27 |

—⁓⁓— FISH AND CHIPS FOR THE WINNERS —⁓⁓—

As a result of Newton Heath's financial problems of the late 1800s and early 1900s, the players received an unusual win bonus of a trip to the local fish and chip shop, where they were treated to supper paid for by the directors.

## THE GREY KIT

Only three Manchester United players scored for the club wearing the infamous 1995–96 grey Umbro kit. They were David Beckham (v Aston Villa), Eric Cantona (penalty v Nottingham Forest) and Ryan Giggs (v Southampton). United scrapped the strip after wearing it only five times in the FA Premier League. They lost four and drew one of those games.

## UNITED JOTTINGS

David Meek was the Manchester United correspondent of the *Manchester Evening News* from 5 March 1958 until his retirement in January 1995. David reported on the highs and lows of the club, home and abroad, for 37 years. His first article for the *United Review* was penned under the heading "United Jottings" and appeared in the match programme for the FA Cup sixth round replay against West Bromwich Albion. United won the game 1–0.

## GEORGE BEST OPENS HIS ACCOUNT

On 28 December 1963 George Best scored his first goal for United in the 5–1 home win over Burnley.

## THE FIRST SUBSTITUTE

John Fitzpatrick holds the unique distinction of being the first ever substitute used by Manchester United. On 16 October 1965 he came on for Denis Law, United's scorer in the 5–1 defeat by Tottenham Hotspur at White Hart Lane.

## CHURCH EVICTS HEATHENS

Newton Heath's first ground at North Road, Newton Heath, was owned by the Cathedral Authorities in Manchester. During the 1892–93 season the authorities decided that the Heathens could no longer charge spectators an admission fee to a game. The club objected, so the authorities served them with notice to quit. Newton Heath then acquired a piece of muddy land at Bank Street, Clayton, and a large enclosure was erected in time for the beginning of the 1893–94 season. Arthur Farman scored Newton Heath's first goal at Bank Street on 2 September 1893, going on to net a hat-trick in a 3–2 win over Burnley.

*Substitutes*

Billy **BEHAN**, Shay **BRENNAN**, Tony **DUNNE**, Noel **CANTWELL**, Mick **MARTIN**,
Liam **O'BRIEN**, Don **GIVENS**

*Manager*

Frank **O'FARRELL**

### *Did You Know That?*

Johnny Carey, who captained Manchester United to FA Cup success in 1948 and the League Championship in 1952, won seven caps for Northern Ireland and 29 for the Republic of Ireland.

### —— TREBLE DOUBLE WINNERS ——

Ryan Giggs, Roy Keane and Peter Schmeichel are the only players in the history of English football to have won three sets of Double winner's medals, with Manchester United in 1994, 1996 and 1999.

### —— BIGGEST DERBY CROWDS ——

The largest attendance for a Derby at Old Trafford is 75,970 which was set when United lost 2–1 to City in a Premier League game played on 10 February 2008. The biggest Derby crowd for a game on City's home ground stands at 71,364, at Maine Road in the old First Division on 20 September 1947. The game ended 0–0.

### COLE BRIDGES LAW GAP

Andy Cole's hat-trick for United in their 3–1 UEFA Champions League win over Feyenoord on 4 November 1997 was the first scored in the European Cup by a Manchester United player since Denis Law did so in 1968.

### HARDMAN'S DOUBLE

Harold Hardman, United chairman from 1951 to 1965, won an FA Cup winner's medal as an amateur with Everton in 1906 and an Olympic gold medal as a member of the England football team at the London Olympics in 1908.

### YOUNG NORMAN WHITESIDE

When Norman Whiteside scored for United in their 2–0 home win over Stoke City on 15 May 1982, he became the youngest player to score for the club, aged 17 years and 8 days. When he scored in United's 1983 League Cup final defeat to Liverpool, Norman became the youngest player to score in a League Cup final, aged 17 years and 323 days. When he scored for United in the 1983 FA Cup final replay win over Brighton & Hove Albion, Whiteside became the youngest player to score in an FA Cup final, aged 18 years and 18 days.

### MANCHESTER FA SENIOR CUP

The Manchester FA Senior Cup was introduced in the 1884–85 season. Newton Heath reached the inaugural final, losing 3–0 to rivals Hurst at Whatley Range on 25 April 1885. Newton Heath dominated the early years of the competition, reaching eight of the first nine finals. The club recorded five wins, were runners-up three times and suffered a rare semi-final defeat to Bolton Wanderers in 1892.

### UNBEATEN, BUT OUT OF THE FA CUP

Newton Heath first participated in the FA Cup during the 1886–87 season. The Heathens played Fleetwood Rangers away on 30 October 1886 and the game ended 2–2. When the referee asked the Heathens to play extra time they refused and so the game was awarded to the home side. Newton Heath did not enter the Cup again until 1889–90, when they lost 6–1 at Preston North End in the first round on 18 January 1890.

On the final day of the 1955–56 season United, having already clinched the First Division Championship 14 days earlier, beat Portsmouth 1–0 with Dennis Viollet's 20th League goal of the campaign. United won the title by 11 points from Blackpool, thus equalling the record winning margin set in the late 1800s by Preston North End, Sunderland and Aston Villa.

### *Football League Division 1*
### 1955–56

|    |                      | P  | W  | D | L  | F  | A  | W | D | L  | F  | A  | Pts |
|----|----------------------|----|----|---|----|----|----|---|---|----|----|----|-----|
| 1. | MANCHESTER UNITED    | 42 | 18 | 3 | 0  | 51 | 20 | 7 | 7 | 7  | 32 | 31 | 60  |
| 2. | Blackpool            | 42 | 13 | 4 | 4  | 56 | 27 | 7 | 5 | 9  | 30 | 35 | 49  |
| 3. | Wolverhampton W      | 42 | 15 | 2 | 4  | 51 | 27 | 5 | 7 | 9  | 38 | 38 | 49  |
| 4. | Manchester City      | 42 | 11 | 5 | 5  | 40 | 27 | 7 | 5 | 9  | 42 | 42 | 46  |
| 5. | Arsenal              | 42 | 13 | 4 | 4  | 38 | 22 | 5 | 6 | 10 | 22 | 39 | 46  |
| 6. | Birmingham City      | 42 | 12 | 4 | 5  | 51 | 26 | 6 | 5 | 10 | 24 | 31 | 45  |
| 7. | Burnley              | 42 | 11 | 3 | 7  | 37 | 20 | 7 | 5 | 9  | 27 | 34 | 44  |
| 8. | Bolton Wanderers     | 42 | 13 | 3 | 5  | 50 | 24 | 5 | 4 | 12 | 21 | 34 | 43  |
| 9. | Sunderland           | 42 | 10 | 8 | 3  | 44 | 36 | 7 | 1 | 13 | 36 | 59 | 43  |
| 10. | Luton Town          | 42 | 12 | 4 | 5  | 44 | 27 | 5 | 4 | 12 | 22 | 37 | 42  |
| 11. | Newcastle United    | 42 | 12 | 4 | 5  | 49 | 24 | 5 | 3 | 13 | 36 | 46 | 41  |
| 12. | Portsmouth          | 42 | 9  | 8 | 4  | 46 | 38 | 7 | 1 | 13 | 32 | 47 | 41  |
| 13. | WBA                 | 42 | 13 | 3 | 5  | 37 | 25 | 5 | 2 | 14 | 21 | 45 | 41  |
| 14. | Charlton Athletic   | 42 | 13 | 2 | 6  | 47 | 26 | 4 | 4 | 13 | 28 | 55 | 40  |
| 15. | Everton             | 42 | 11 | 5 | 5  | 37 | 29 | 4 | 5 | 12 | 18 | 40 | 40  |
| 16. | Chelsea             | 42 | 10 | 4 | 7  | 32 | 26 | 4 | 7 | 10 | 32 | 51 | 39  |
| 17. | Cardiff City        | 42 | 11 | 4 | 6  | 36 | 32 | 4 | 5 | 12 | 19 | 37 | 39  |
| 18. | Tottenham Hotspur   | 42 | 9  | 4 | 8  | 37 | 33 | 6 | 3 | 12 | 24 | 38 | 37  |
| 19. | Preston North End   | 42 | 6  | 5 | 10 | 32 | 36 | 8 | 3 | 10 | 41 | 36 | 36  |
| 20. | Aston Villa         | 42 | 9  | 6 | 6  | 32 | 29 | 2 | 7 | 12 | 20 | 40 | 35  |
| 21. | Huddersfield Town   | 42 | 9  | 4 | 8  | 32 | 30 | 5 | 3 | 13 | 22 | 53 | 35  |
| 22. | Sheffield United    | 42 | 8  | 6 | 7  | 31 | 35 | 4 | 3 | 14 | 32 | 42 | 33  |

—— BABES BEATEN AT LAST ——

On 8 April 1957 United's highly successful youth team were beaten 3–2 at Old Trafford by Southampton in the semi-finals of the FA Youth Cup. It was the side's first ever defeat in the competition since it began in 1952, but they still managed to progress to the final, having won the first leg at The Dell 5–1.

### ⚬⚬⚬ BUSBY ALMOST PLAYED FOR UNITED ⚬⚬⚬

In the early days of his career at Maine Road, Matt Busby almost became a Manchester United player. Louis Rocca telephoned Manchester City manager Peter Hodge and said he wanted to sign Busby to ease United's mounting injury problems. City asked for £150, but United did not have the money.

### ⚬⚬⚬ WARTIME CHAMPIONS OF THE NORTH ⚬⚬⚬

A 3–1 win (Worrall 2, Whatley) at Maine Road over local rivals Manchester City on the final day of the 1941–42 season saw United crowned champions of the wartime Football League Northern Section. The season had been divided into two championships with a winner declared at the end of the first half of the season (when United finished fourth) and a winner at the end of May.

### ⚬⚬⚬ YOUNGEST POST-WAR PLAYER ⚬⚬⚬

David Gaskell became United's youngest post-war player when he started in place of Ray Wood in the United goal in the 1956 Charity Shield match. Gaskell was 16 years and 19 days old. Dennis Viollet scored to give the Reds a 1–0 victory.

### ⚬⚬⚬ FIRST GAME, FIRST GOAL; LAST GAME, LAST GOAL ⚬⚬⚬

Albert J. Kinsey played his one and only game for Manchester United against Chester in a 1964–65 FA Cup third-round tie at Old Trafford. Kinsey scored in United's 2–1 win. William Bainbridge also played only one game for Manchester United, against Accrington Stanley in the second leg of an FA Cup third-round tie in 1946. He scored too.

### ⚬⚬⚬ LOCKERBIE AIR DISASTER APPEAL GAME ⚬⚬⚬

On 1 March 1989 Manchester United played Queen of the South in a friendly at Palmerston Park to help raise money for the families of the Lockerbie Air Disaster. United won an entertaining game 6–3.

### ⚬⚬⚬ UNITED FIRST SIX-FIGURE CLUB ⚬⚬⚬

In 1958 Manchester United became the first football club to record a profit of £100,000.

## ⚬ GOALSCORING GOALKEEPERS ⚬

Alex Stepney was handed the responsibility of taking United's penalties by Tommy Docherty during the 1973–74 season, when the club's regular penalty taker, Willie Morgan, was injured. By Christmas, Alex was United's joint top goalscorer with two goals, having converted penalties against Leicester City (away) and Birmingham City (home). Alex's penalty-taking ability was first spotted in a pre-season friendly in Spain.

Peter Schmeichel scored 13 goals in his long and distinguished career, including heading Manchester United's equalizer from a corner in a 1995–96 UEFA Cup tie against SC Rotor Volgograd that preserved United's proud unbeaten European home record.

In the 1967 Charity Shield at Old Trafford, Tottenham Hotspur goalkeeper Pat Jennings kicked the ball from his own area. The ball bounced in front of Alex Stepney as he approached it, then sailed over his head and into the empty net. The game ended 3–3, and unluckily for Stepney not only did 54,106 spectators turn up to watch it but the BBC's *Match of the Day* cameras were also there and filmed it.

## ⚬ FIRST TEN CAPPED EIRE PLAYERS ⚬

| Player | Year capped |
|---|---|
| Johnny Carey | 1937 |
| Tommy Breen | 1937 |
| Liam Whelan | 1956 |
| Joseph Carolan | 1959 |
| Johnny Giles | 1959 |
| Noel Cantwell | 1961 |
| Shay Brennan | 1965 |
| Tony Dunne | 1965 |
| Pat Dunne | 1965 |
| Don Givens | 1969 |

## ⚬ THE PORTRAIT OF ERIC CANTONA ⚬

On 15 April 1997 a painting by local artist Michael Browne was unveiled at the Manchester City Art Gallery. The painting, based on two Renaissance works, *Resurrection* by Piero della Francesca and *Julius Caesar* by Mantegna, caused uproar because of its portrayal of Eric Cantona as Jesus Christ. Cantona himself liked Browne's work so much, he bought it. He subsequently lent the painting to the National Portrait Gallery, where it remains on display.

### ⚬⚬⚬ WORLD'S RICHEST CLUB ⚬⚬⚬

In February 2005 aacountatnts Deloitte named Manchester United the world's richest football club for the eighth successive year, with an income of £171.5 million for the 2003–04 season. In February 2006, Real Madrid dethroned United when they took over the mantle of the world's richest club after posting profits of £186.2 million. United moved down to second place on £166.4 million.

### ⚬⚬⚬ LOWEST POST-WAR LEAGUE ATTENDANCE ⚬⚬⚬

United's 1–1 draw "at home" to Stoke City on the afternoon of Wednesday 5 February 1947 at Maine Road drew a crowd of 8456, United's lowest post-war attendance for a home League match.

### ⚬⚬⚬ UNITED'S FIRST FLOTATION ⚬⚬⚬

Manchester United were first floated as a public limited company in the 1907–08 season.

### ⚬⚬⚬ RECORD-BUSTERS ⚬⚬⚬

Manchester United brought an end to Arsenal's record unbeaten run of 49 League games when they defeated them 2–0 at Old Trafford on 24 October 2004; the result ended Arsenal's 27-game unbeaten away run in the League as well. United also hold the distinction of bringing to a close Arsenal's 33-game unbeaten run in the League at home (record of 63 held by Liverpool) when they beat them 4–2 on 1 February 2005.

### ⚬⚬⚬ SPURS HUMBLE CHAMPIONS ⚬⚬⚬

Manchester United, First Division champions in 1952, went on a tour of the United States and Canada during the summer of that year. United met Spurs in Toronto on 13 June and lost 5–0. Two days later United played Spurs in New York, hoping to get revenge for that earlier defeat. The Reds lost 7–1.

### ⚬⚬⚬ LAST OF THE HEATHENS ⚬⚬⚬

On 1 March 1902 James Higson made his Newton Heath debut versus Lincoln City at home. Higson was the last League player signed by Newton Heath prior to them becoming bankrupt.

Alex Dawson scored for United in their 1–1 home draw with West Bromwich Albion on the last day of the 1956–57 season. The result gave United their second successive First Division Championship and their third title in the past five seasons. United's total of 103 League goals was a season record (later equalled by the club in 1958–59), and in all competitions they hit the back of the net 143 times.

### *Football League Division 1*
### 1956–57

|     |                       | P  | W  | D | L  | F  | A  | W | D | L  | F  | A  | Pts |
|-----|-----------------------|----|----|---|----|----|----|---|---|----|----|----|-----|
| 1.  | MANCHESTER UNITED     | 42 | 14 | 4 | 3  | 55 | 25 | 14 | 4 | 3  | 48 | 29 | 64 |
| 2.  | Tottenham Hotspur      | 42 | 15 | 4 | 2  | 70 | 24 | 7 | 8 | 6  | 34 | 32 | 56 |
| 3.  | Preston North End      | 42 | 15 | 4 | 2  | 50 | 19 | 8 | 6 | 7  | 34 | 37 | 56 |
| 4.  | Blackpool              | 42 | 14 | 3 | 4  | 55 | 26 | 8 | 6 | 7  | 38 | 39 | 53 |
| 5.  | Arsenal                | 42 | 12 | 5 | 4  | 45 | 21 | 9 | 3 | 9  | 40 | 48 | 50 |
| 6.  | Wolverhampton W        | 42 | 17 | 2 | 2  | 70 | 29 | 3 | 6 | 12 | 24 | 41 | 48 |
| 7.  | Burnley                | 42 | 14 | 5 | 2  | 41 | 21 | 4 | 5 | 12 | 15 | 29 | 46 |
| 8.  | Leeds United           | 42 | 10 | 8 | 3  | 42 | 18 | 5 | 6 | 10 | 30 | 45 | 44 |
| 9.  | Bolton Wanderers       | 42 | 13 | 6 | 2  | 42 | 23 | 3 | 6 | 12 | 23 | 42 | 44 |
| 10. | Aston Villa            | 42 | 10 | 8 | 3  | 45 | 25 | 4 | 7 | 10 | 20 | 30 | 43 |
| 11. | WBA                    | 42 | 8  | 8 | 5  | 31 | 25 | 6 | 6 | 9  | 28 | 36 | 42 |
| 12. | Birmingham City        | 42 | 12 | 5 | 4  | 52 | 25 | 3 | 4 | 14 | 17 | 44 | 39 |
| 13. | Chelsea                | 42 | 7  | 8 | 6  | 43 | 36 | 6 | 5 | 10 | 30 | 37 | 39 |
| 14. | Sheffield Wednesday    | 42 | 14 | 3 | 4  | 55 | 29 | 2 | 3 | 16 | 27 | 59 | 38 |
| 15. | Everton                | 42 | 10 | 5 | 6  | 34 | 28 | 4 | 5 | 12 | 27 | 51 | 38 |
| 16. | Luton Town             | 42 | 10 | 4 | 7  | 32 | 26 | 4 | 5 | 12 | 26 | 50 | 37 |
| 17. | Newcastle United       | 42 | 10 | 5 | 6  | 43 | 31 | 4 | 3 | 14 | 24 | 56 | 36 |
| 18. | Manchester City        | 42 | 10 | 2 | 9  | 48 | 42 | 3 | 7 | 11 | 30 | 46 | 35 |
| 19. | Portsmouth             | 42 | 8  | 6 | 7  | 37 | 35 | 2 | 7 | 12 | 25 | 57 | 33 |
| 20. | Sunderland             | 42 | 9  | 5 | 7  | 40 | 30 | 3 | 3 | 15 | 27 | 58 | 32 |
| 21. | Cardiff City           | 42 | 7  | 6 | 8  | 35 | 34 | 3 | 3 | 15 | 18 | 54 | 29 |
| 22. | Charlton Athletic      | 42 | 7  | 3 | 11 | 31 | 44 | 2 | 1 | 18 | 31 | 76 | 22 |

### ――― THE LONGEST GOAL ―――

David Beckham's 57-yard strike against Wimbledon at Selhurst Park on 17 August 1996 was the longest-range goal in the Premier League. Xabi Alonso beat it for Liverpool against Newcastle on 20 September 2006, but on 17 March 2007, Tottenham and England goalkeeper Paul Robinson scored from 95 yards against Watford.

### ⚬ NOBBY STILES ⚬

On 1 October 1960 Nobby Stiles made his debut for United in a 1–1 away draw with Bolton Wanderers. Stiles was a Busby Babe, a product of United's highly successful Youth Team set-up during the 1950s. He was an aggressive half-back for club and country and one of the first names entered on Matt Busby's team-sheet during the late 1960s. On the pitch he was a fearless competitor. Some have described Nobby as a dirty player but he was never that, he just couldn't see properly without his glasses! Nobby won two Championships with the Reds in 1965 and 1967 and helped England to victory in the 1966 World Cup Final, where everyone still remembers his victory jig on the Wembley pitch to this day. In 1968 Nobby was a member of United's European Cup winning side and in May 1971 he joined Middlesbrough for £20,000.

### ⚬ LONGEST-SERVING CAPTAIN ⚬

Bryan Robson (1982–94) is the longest-serving captain in the history of Manchester United.

### ⚬ KEEP IT IN THE FAMILY ⚬

Brian and Jimmy Greenhoff became the first pair of Manchester United brothers to play in the same FA Cup winning side. The Reds beat Liverpool 2–1 in the 1977 Final and Jimmy scored the winner. Gary and Phil Neville were in United's Cup-winning teams of 1996 and 1999.

### ⚬ FERGUSON FACING THE SACK? ⚬

On 7 January 1990 Alex Ferguson was reportedly under pressure at Old Trafford, and the luck of the FA Cup draw was not on his side as United were drawn away to Nottingham Forest in the third round. Nevertheless, United won the game 1–0 thanks to a Mark Robins strike, and the match was considered by many to be Fergie's watershed. United went on to win the Cup and dominate the domestic game over the following decade and beyond.

### ⚬ FIRST UNITED PLAYER CAPPED BY ENGLAND ⚬

Club captain Charlie Roberts was the first Manchester United player to be capped by England when he appeared for his country against Scotland in a Home International game at the Crystal Palace on 1 April 1905. England won 1–0.

### THE EYES HAVE IT

In the song, the late United legend Jim Holton is described as being "Six foot two with eyes of blue". Jim actually had brown eyes.

### MAKE IT A DOUBLE

At the end of the 1995–96 season, Alex Ferguson was voted the Carling Manager of the Season and Eric Cantona won the Carling Player of the Season Award.

### LAW'S HAT-TRICK OF HAT-TRICKS

Denis Law is the only Manchester United player to have scored a hat-trick in each of the three major European competitions. Overall, "The King" scored 18 hat-tricks during his time at Old Trafford, including a record seven during the 1963–64 season.

### BRUCE IS SPOT ON

In United's 1990–91 European Cup Winners' Cup winning season, Steve Bruce scored 19 goals, 11 of them from the penalty spot – an unbelievable total for a centre-half.

### UNITED'S ALL-GREEN KIT

On 31 August 1968 United turned out in an unusual strip when they played Drumcondra Select at Dalymount Park, Dublin, in a testimonial match for John Whelan (brother of United's Liam, who died in the Munich Air Disaster). United's colours for the game were green shirts, green shorts and green socks.

### MISERLY AWAY FROM HOME

During the 1947–48 season United conceded more League goals at home (27) than they conceded away (21).

### BOBBY CHARLTON'S LAST GAME

In his last ever game for the club, Bobby Charlton scored twice in United's 4–1 away win over Verona in a Group One Anglo-Italian Cup match played on 2 May 1973. The other United scorers were Olney and Fletcher.

## GOODISON CUP HOODOO ENDED

United's 2–0 win over Everton in the 1993–94 League Cup was the club's first victory in any cup competition over Everton at Goodison Park.

## TEN OUT OF TEN FOR UNITED

At the beginning of the 1985–86 season Manchester United won their opening ten First Division matches. Luton Town brought United's winning run to an end on 3 October in a 1–1 draw at Kenilworth Road. Manchester United just failed to equal the record of 11 wins set by Tottenham Hotspur in season 1960–61.

## THE ULTIMATE LONG THROW

United's Irish goalkeeper, Tommy Breen, is credited with conceding the first goal scored directly from a throw-in. Breen touched the ball during an FA Cup fourth round tie away at Barnsley on 2 January 1938.

## FIRST DERBY GAME AT MAINE ROAD

United visited Maine Road for a League Derby game for the first time on 12 September 1925. The First Division game ended 1–1 with Clatworthy Renoox becoming the first United player to score at Maine Road. In the return game at Old Trafford, City thrashed United 6–1.

## THE PENALTY KING

Charlie Mitten, who played for Manchester United between 1946 and 1950, took 17 penalties for Manchester United and scored all 17, including three in one game. When Mitten left United he joined Sante Fe in Bogota, Colombia where a lot of First Division players decided to play their football given the restrictive maximum wage available in English football at the time.

## VICTORY V

For their first appearance in an FA Cup final United were forced to change from their red shirts as their opponents, Bristol City, also wore red. United adopted an all-white kit with a large red V on the front of the shirt for the 1909 final which they won 1–0.

United reached the 1963 FA Cup final despite fighting a rearguard action all season against relegation. Their opponents, Leicester City, were clear favourites to lift the trophy, having finished fourth in Division One. In the 29th minute, "The King", Denis Law[†], opened the scoring with a fine turn and shot inside the box, which Gordon Banks, in the City goal, could do nothing about. Twelve minutes into the second half David Herd, whose father played alongside Matt Busby for Manchester City in the 1933 and 1934 FA Cup finals, made it 2–0 to the Reds. With five minutes of the game remaining, Keyworth pulled a goal back for Leicester, but moments later Herd grabbed his second, and United's third, goal of the game to ensure the Cup was going back to Old Trafford for the first time since 1948.

### FA CUP FINAL

*25 May 1963, Wembley Stadium*

MANCHESTER UNITED (1) *3*    *vs*    LEICESTER CITY (0) *1*

Herd (2), Law             Keyworth

*Att. 100,000*

*Manchester United:* Gaskell, Dunne, Cantwell, Crerand, Foulkes, Setters, Giles, Quixall, Herd, Law, Charlton

—∼∼— ONE-CAP WONDERS —∼∼—

The following Manchester United players won only one full international cap for their country:

| Player | Country |
| --- | --- |
| Francis Burns | Scotland |
| Peter Davenport | England |
| Bill Foulkes | England |
| Stewart Houston | Scotland |
| Caesar Jenkyns | Wales |
| David Pegg | England |
| Mike Phelan | England |
| Jimmy Rimmer | England |
| Alex Stepney | England |
| Ian Storey-Moore | England |
| Danny Wallace | England |

[†]*In the third round Denis Law scored a hat-trick in a 5–0 win over the club where he began his professional career – Huddersfield Town. In total Denis scored six goals in United's six Cup ties.*

## ⎯ SIR MATT BUSBY ⎯

On 15 February 1945 Matt Busby was appointed manager of Manchester United and the legend began. Matt Busby was born in Bellshill, Lanarkshire in 1909. His father was a miner, who died on the Somme in World War I, and the young Busby followed in his father's footsteps down the pit. In his youth Busby always had a dream that one day he would earn his living as a footballer and in 1928 that dream became a reality when he joined Manchester City. An outstanding right-half for United's neighbours, he won an FA Cup winner's medal with them in 1934 and then moved on to Liverpool in 1936.

Matt Busby built three great teams at United. His first great side were First Division runners-up in 1947, 1948 and 1949 and winners of the FA Cup in 1948. Busby's style of management was a breath of fresh air and unlike his predecessors he joined his players on the training field, a concept unheard of at the time. Matt Busby built a dynasty at Old Trafford and put all his faith and trust in youth. The Busby Babes side of the 1950s dominated the domestic game. During the 1950s United won the First Division Championship three times (1952, 1956 and 1957), were runners-up twice (1951 and 1959), FA Cup finalists in 1957 and 1958, FA Charity Shield Winners three times (1952, 1956 and 1957) and United's Youth Team won the first five FA Youth Cups (1953–1957). The football world was at their feet with players including Duncan Edwards, Eddie Colman and Bobby Charlton, all products of Matt's youth policy. However, on the 6 February 1958 the heart was ripped out of Manchester United when the Elizabethan jet, carrying the players home from their European Cup quarter-final tie with Red Star Belgrade, crashed on take-off at Munich Airport.

His rebuilt team of the 1960s thrilled fans up and down the country with their swashbuckling style. Matt's philosophy to his players was simply for them to go on to the field and enjoy themselves. In the 1960s United won the FA Cup in 1963, were First Division Champions in 1965 and 1967, First Division runners-up in 1964 and 1968, joint-holders of the FA Charity Shield in 1965 and 1967 and winners of the FA Youth Cup for the sixth time under his leadership in 1964. But the greatest night in Matt Busby's football life came at Wembley in May 1968 when his third great side beat Benfica of Portugal 4–1 after extra time to claim the European Cup. Later that year he was knighted. Matt Busby was a man of the people, honest and hard working, respected by everyone and loved by the fans of his beloved Manchester United. He was, and always will be remembered as "The Father of Manchester United".

## ⚬ VICTIMS OF THE MUNICH AIR DISASTER ⚬

The Busby Babes who lost their lives in the Munich crash were: Geoff Bent, Roger Byrne, Eddie Colman, Mark Jones, David Pegg, Tommy Taylor and Liam Whelan. Walter Crickmer, the club secretary, first-team trainer Tom Curry and coach, Bert Whalley and eight of the nine journalists on the flight (Alf Clarke, Don Davies, George Follows, Tom Jackson, Archie Ledbrooke, Henry Rose, Frank Swift and Eric Thompson) also died in the crash, as did one of the aircrew, the travel agent who arranged the trip, a supporter and two other passengers. In all, 23 people died in the crash (Duncan Edwards and Captain Rayment died in hospital from their injuries) with 16 survivors. Two of the United players who survived the crash, Jackie Blanchflower and Johnny Berry, never played competitive football again. The Munich Air Disaster is undoubtedly one of football's blackest days.

## ⚬ MAINE ROAD DEBUTANTS ⚬

The following players all made their debut for Manchester United against Manchester City at Maine Road:

| | | |
|---|---|---|
| Tommy O'Neill | 5 May 1971 | 4–3 *win* |
| Sammy McIlroy | 6 November 1971 | 3–3 *(McIlroy scored)* |
| Paul Bielby | 13 March 1974 | 0–0 |

## ⚬ THE CORONATION CUP ⚬

In 1953 Manchester United participated in the Coronation Cup that was held to commemorate the crowning of Queen Elizabeth II. The top teams in England and Scotland were invited, and United beat Glasgow Rangers 2–1 in the first round before losing 2–1 in the semi-final at Hampden Park to the eventual winners, Celtic.

## ⚬ FORTRESS OLD TRAFFORD ⚬

United won their final League home game of the 1982–83 season, beating Luton Town 3–0, and finished third in Division One. The win meant that United were unbeaten at Old Trafford, in all competitions, throughout the season and thereby equalled their previous achievements during seasons 1896–97 and 1955–56. In all, United played 29 games at home: 21 League, 2 FA Cup, 5 League Cup and 1 UEFA Cup.

### JEEPERS KEEPERS

When Manchester United beat Sunderland 5–0 at Old Trafford on 26 November 1966 David Herd scored four times. Herd's first three goals were scored against three different keepers in the Sunderland goal. He scored his first goal against Montgomery, his second against Hurley and his third (and fourth) against Parke.

### SCOTTISH TRANSFER RECORD

Lou Macari's £200,000 move from Glasgow Celtic to Manchester United on 18 January 1973 set a new Scottish record transfer fee.

### THE LAST MATCH OF THE BABES

On 5 February 1958 Manchester United were in Belgrade for the second leg of their European Cup quarter-final against the Yugoslav champions. United had won the home leg 2–1 a fortnight earlier and were poised to reach their second successive semi-final in the competition. The Busby Babes quietened the intimidating 55,000 home fans with their breathtaking football and were soon 3–0 up on the night and 5–1 ahead on aggregate. The fiercely partisan home crowd then turned on the Babes, which seemed to unnerve the Austrian referee, Karl Kainer. A number of the subsequent reports on the game, particularly that of Henry Rose of *The Daily Express*, questioned a number of the referee's decisions. Two minutes after the interval Red Star scored through Kostic. They were then awarded a bizarre penalty after Foulkes and Tasic tangled in the box. Foulkes fell on top of Tasic as he lay on the grass. Foulkes maintained that Tasic lost his balance and as he was falling brought the United defender down on top of him. However, the penalty stood and was converted by Tasic, sending the crowd into a frenzy. Although Red Star scored again with minutes remaining, United went through 5–4 on aggregate. The next day United's plane home crashed at Munich Airport.

### NEWTON HEATH NICKNAMES

Between 1878 and 1902, the club was known by various nicknames:

The Heathens* ❖ The Coachbuilders ❖ The Newtonians

*\* The Heathens is the one that eventually stuck.*

United clinched their sixth First Division Championship with a 3–1 home win over Arsenal on 26 April 1965 (Law 2, Best). Although there was still one game to play, United were crowned champions at a time when goal average, as opposed to the present system of goal difference, was the rule. United won the title with a narrow margin of 0.686 of a goal over Leeds United. Although United lost their final League game 2–1 away to Aston Villa the result didn't cost them the title.

### *Football League Division 1*
### 1964–65

|  |  | P | W | D | L | F | A | W | D | L | F | A | Pts |
|---|---|---|---|---|---|---|---|---|---|---|---|---|---|
| 1. | MANCHESTER UNITED | 42 | 16 | 4 | 1 | 52 | 13 | 10 | 5 | 6 | 37 | 26 | 61 |
| 2. | Leeds United | 42 | 16 | 3 | 2 | 53 | 23 | 10 | 6 | 5 | 30 | 29 | 61 |
| 3. | Chelsea | 42 | 15 | 2 | 4 | 48 | 19 | 9 | 6 | 6 | 41 | 35 | 56 |
| 4. | Everton | 42 | 9 | 10 | 2 | 37 | 22 | 8 | 5 | 8 | 32 | 38 | 49 |
| 5. | Nottingham Forest | 42 | 10 | 7 | 4 | 45 | 33 | 7 | 6 | 8 | 26 | 34 | 47 |
| 6. | Tottenham Hotspur | 42 | 18 | 3 | 0 | 65 | 20 | 1 | 4 | 16 | 22 | 51 | 45 |
| 7. | Liverpool | 42 | 12 | 5 | 4 | 42 | 33 | 5 | 5 | 11 | 25 | 40 | 44 |
| 8. | Sheffield Wednesday | 42 | 13 | 5 | 3 | 37 | 15 | 3 | 6 | 12 | 20 | 40 | 43 |
| 9. | West Ham United | 42 | 14 | 2 | 5 | 48 | 25 | 5 | 2 | 14 | 34 | 46 | 42 |
| 10. | Blackburn Rovers | 42 | 12 | 2 | 7 | 46 | 33 | 4 | 8 | 9 | 37 | 46 | 42 |
| 11. | Stoke City | 42 | 11 | 4 | 6 | 40 | 27 | 5 | 6 | 10 | 27 | 39 | 42 |
| 12. | Burnley | 42 | 9 | 9 | 3 | 39 | 26 | 7 | 1 | 13 | 31 | 44 | 42 |
| 13. | Arsenal | 42 | 11 | 5 | 5 | 42 | 31 | 6 | 2 | 13 | 27 | 44 | 41 |
| 14. | WBA | 42 | 10 | 5 | 6 | 45 | 25 | 3 | 8 | 10 | 25 | 40 | 39 |
| 15. | Sunderland | 42 | 12 | 6 | 3 | 45 | 26 | 2 | 3 | 16 | 19 | 48 | 37 |
| 16. | Aston Villa | 42 | 14 | 1 | 6 | 36 | 24 | 2 | 4 | 15 | 21 | 58 | 37 |
| 17. | Blackpool | 42 | 9 | 7 | 5 | 41 | 28 | 3 | 4 | 14 | 26 | 50 | 35 |
| 18. | Leicester City | 42 | 9 | 6 | 6 | 43 | 36 | 2 | 7 | 12 | 26 | 49 | 35 |
| 19. | Sheffield United | 42 | 7 | 5 | 9 | 30 | 29 | 5 | 6 | 10 | 20 | 35 | 35 |
| 20. | Fulham | 42 | 10 | 5 | 6 | 44 | 32 | 1 | 7 | 13 | 16 | 46 | 34 |
| 21. | WolverhamptonW | 42 | 8 | 2 | 11 | 33 | 36 | 5 | 2 | 14 | 26 | 53 | 30 |
| 22. | Birmingham City | 42 | 6 | 8 | 7 | 36 | 40 | 2 | 3 | 16 | 28 | 56 | 27 |

### ~~~ FA CUP TREBLE WINNER ~~~

Arthur Albiston was the first Manchester United player to win three FA Cup winner's medals with the club – 1977, 1983 and 1985. Ryan Giggs and Roy Keane have won four FA Cup winner's medals with United since Albiston's achievement, in 1994, 1996, 1999 and 2004.

①
Harry
*GREGG*

②
Jimmy
*NICHOLL*

⑥
Johnny
*CAREY*

⑤
Jackie
*BLANCHFLOWER*

③
Mal
*DONAGHY*

⑦
Trevor
*ANDERSON*

⑧
Sammy
*McILROY*

④
David
*McCREERY*

⑪
Keith
*GILLESPIE*

⑨
Norman
*WHITESIDE*

⑩
George
*BEST*

*Substitutes*
Roy *CARROLL*, Jonny *EVANS*, Tommy *SLOAN*,
Chris *McGRATH*, Tommy *JACKSON*
*Manager*
Bob *BISHOP*

### *Did You Know That?*

Harry Gregg was on the plane returning from United's European Cup game against Red Star Belgrade when it crashed in Munich in 1958. Harry survived and was one of the first to help people from the wreckage as it lay on the runway at Munich Airport.

### ~~~ FIRST SEASON IN THE TOP FLIGHT ~~~

Newton Heath secured Division One football for the 1892–93 season. The club's first ever game in the top flight was against Blackburn Rovers at Ewood Park on 3 September 1892 in a match they lost 4–3. The Heathens finished bottom of Division One at the end of the season, but relegation was not an automatic fate. They had one last chance to retain their status by playing two Test matches against the winners of Division Two, Small Heath, the winners to play Division One football in 1893–94. The first Test match, at Stoke, was drawn 1–1, but the Heathens secured their Division One status with a comfortable 5–2 victory in the second game.

## ⚬⚬⚬ THE FLOWERS OF MANCHESTER ⚬⚬⚬

One cold and bitter Thursday in Munich Germany,
Eight great football stalwarts conceded victory,
Eight men will never play again who met destruction there,
The Flowers of British football, the Flowers of Manchester.

Matt Busby's boys were flying, returning from Belgrade,
This great United family, all masters of their trade,
The pilot of the aircraft, the skipper Captain Thain,
Three times they tried to take off and twice turned back again.

The third time down the runway disaster followed close,
There was slush upon that runway and the aircraft never rose,
It ploughed into the marshy ground, it broke, it overturned
And eight of the team were killed when the blazing wreckage burned.

Roger Byrne and Tommy Taylor who were capped for England's side
And Ireland's Billy Whelan and England's Geoff Bent died,
Mark Jones and Eddie Colman, and David Pegg also,
They lost their lives as it ploughed on through the snow.

Big Duncan he went too, with an injury to his frame,
And Ireland's brave Jack Blanchflower will never play again,
The great Matt Busby lay there, the father of his team,
Three long months passed by before he saw his team again.

The trainer, coach and secretary, and a member of the crew,
Also eight sporting journalists who with United flew,
And one of them Big Swifty, who we will ne'er forget,
The finest English 'keeper that ever graced the net.
Oh, England's finest football team its record truly great,
Its proud successes mocked by a cruel turn of fate.
Eight men will never play again, who met destruction there,
The Flowers of English football, the Flowers of Manchester.

### ⚬⚬⚬ AN EXPENSIVE RAM ⚬⚬⚬

When Johnny Morris left Manchester United to join Derby County
in March 1949 he was sold for a British record fee of £24,500.
Ironically the fee was beaten when Preston North End paid £26,500
to Sheffield Wednesday for the services of Eddie Quigley in
December 1949. Quigley was Morris' Uncle.

"I have found you a genius", were the immortal words of Manchester United's Irish scout, Bill Bishop, to Matt Busby when he first saw George Best play. The young Irishman was a mesmerizing dribbler of the ball who when he was in the mood would beat a defender then do a U-turn just to show the same defender he could do it again. No wonder his team-mate, Pat Crerand, said George had "twisted blood".

Blessed with pace, precision accuracy, immaculate ball control, the ability to see a gap in a defence and exploit it, flair, charisma both on and off the pitch and a vicious body swerve that resembled a Rivelino free-kick, it was Pele who said that George Best was the greatest player in the world.

But football's first superstar, dubbed the Fifth Beatle, George Best had a rollercoaster of a career. He made his Manchester United debut aged just 17 and whereas many of the game's true greats begin to mature and reach their peak as professional footballers in their mid-20s, George packed it all in aged just 26. George once famously said: "I spent a lot of money on booze, birds and fast cars. The rest I just squandered."

Two League Championships medals with United in 1965 and 1967, a European Cup winner's medal in 1968, the same year he was voted European Footballer of the Year and five-times United's top goalscorer, George had the world at his feet. After playing is last game for United on New Year's Day 1974 George turned his back on football.

In his last 30 years George reached some lows: constant battles against alcohol, marriage splits, a liver transplant and a 12-week jail sentence in 1984 for drink-driving and assault. But it is the good times for which that George will be most remembered. His magical performance in 1966 against Benfica in their own backyard when George scored twice in United's 5–1 win, a performance that earned him the nickname *El Beatle*. Or his six goals for United in the FA Cup against Northampton Town, and who will ever forget that night at Wembley on 29 May 1968 when George helped United erase the memory of the Munich Air Disaster some ten years earlier by scoring in the European Cup final in their 4–1 win over Benfica of Portugal.

The shy Belfast boy will forever have a special place in the hearts of every Manchester United fan.

### Did You Know That?

George made his international debut in the same game that Pat Jennings made his. However, whereas Pat went on to win a record 119 caps for his country, George won only 37. Interestingly, George's mother was an international hockey player for Northern Ireland.

Although United experienced early exits in both the FA and League Cups, their League form during 1966–67 was outstanding. The Reds were unbeaten in their last 20 games and they won the Championship on the penultimate Saturday of the season by thrashing West Ham United 6–1 at Upton Park (Law 2, Best, Charlton, Crerand, Foulkes).

### *Football League Division 1*
### 1966–67

| | | P | W | D | L | F | A | W | D | L | F | A | Pts |
|---|---|---|---|---|---|---|---|---|---|---|---|---|---|
| 1. | MANCHESTER UNITED | 42 | 17 | 4 | 0 | 51 | 13 | 7 | 8 | 6 | 33 | 32 | 60 |
| 2. | Nottingham Forest | 42 | 16 | 4 | 1 | 41 | 13 | 7 | 6 | 8 | 23 | 28 | 56 |
| 3. | Tottenham Hotspur | 42 | 15 | 3 | 3 | 44 | 21 | 9 | 5 | 7 | 27 | 27 | 56 |
| 4. | Leeds United | 42 | 15 | 4 | 2 | 41 | 17 | 7 | 7 | 7 | 21 | 25 | 55 |
| 5. | Liverpool | 42 | 12 | 7 | 2 | 36 | 17 | 7 | 6 | 8 | 28 | 30 | 51 |
| 6. | Everton | 42 | 11 | 4 | 6 | 39 | 22 | 8 | 6 | 7 | 26 | 24 | 48 |
| 7. | Arsenal | 42 | 11 | 6 | 4 | 32 | 20 | 5 | 8 | 8 | 26 | 27 | 46 |
| 8. | Leicester City | 42 | 12 | 4 | 5 | 47 | 28 | 6 | 4 | 11 | 31 | 43 | 44 |
| 9. | Chelsea | 42 | 7 | 9 | 5 | 33 | 29 | 8 | 5 | 8 | 34 | 33 | 44 |
| 10. | Sheffield United | 42 | 11 | 5 | 5 | 34 | 22 | 5 | 5 | 11 | 18 | 37 | 42 |
| 11. | Sheffield Wednesday | 42 | 9 | 7 | 5 | 39 | 19 | 5 | 6 | 10 | 17 | 28 | 41 |
| 12. | Stoke City | 42 | 11 | 5 | 5 | 40 | 21 | 6 | 2 | 13 | 23 | 37 | 41 |
| 13. | WBA | 42 | 11 | 1 | 9 | 40 | 28 | 5 | 6 | 10 | 37 | 45 | 39 |
| 14. | Burnley | 42 | 11 | 4 | 6 | 43 | 28 | 4 | 5 | 12 | 23 | 48 | 39 |
| 15. | Manchester City | 42 | 8 | 9 | 4 | 27 | 25 | 4 | 6 | 11 | 16 | 27 | 39 |
| 16. | West Ham United | 42 | 8 | 6 | 7 | 40 | 31 | 6 | 2 | 13 | 40 | 53 | 36 |
| 17. | Sunderland | 42 | 12 | 3 | 6 | 39 | 26 | 2 | 5 | 14 | 19 | 46 | 36 |
| 18. | Fulham | 42 | 8 | 7 | 6 | 49 | 34 | 3 | 5 | 13 | 22 | 49 | 34 |
| 19. | Southampton | 42 | 10 | 3 | 8 | 49 | 41 | 4 | 3 | 14 | 25 | 51 | 34 |
| 20. | Newcastle United | 42 | 9 | 5 | 7 | 24 | 27 | 3 | 4 | 14 | 15 | 54 | 33 |
| 21. | Aston Villa | 42 | 7 | 5 | 9 | 30 | 33 | 4 | 2 | 15 | 24 | 52 | 29 |
| 22. | Blackpool | 42 | 1 | 5 | 15 | 18 | 36 | 5 | 4 | 12 | 23 | 40 | 21 |

~~~ EVENTFUL DEBUT FOR RICARDO ~~~

Manchester United's Spanish goalkeeper Ricardo had an eventful FA Premier League debut. After replacing the injured Fabien Barthez against Blackburn Rovers, his first contribution to the game was to bring down ex-United favourite, Andy Cole for a penalty. Surprisingly he was not sent off and to add insult to injury, he saved David Dunn's spot-kick.

## CHAMPIONSHIP WINNING MANAGERS

Only three men have guided Manchester United to English football's top prize:

| Manager | Dates |
| --- | --- |
| Ernest Mangnall | 1908, 1911 |
| Sir Matt Busby | 1952, 1956, 1957, 1965, 1967 |
| Sir Alex Ferguson | 1993, 1994, 1996, 1997, 1999, 2000, 2001, 2003, 2007, 2008 |

## ATTEMPTED BOYCOTT FAILS

After losing their opening ten games of the 1930–31 season a supporters group set about attempting to organise a boycott of United's home fixture against Arsenal on 18 October 1930. The attempt failed miserably as United's biggest crowd of the season (25,000) turned up at Old Trafford to cheer the team on. United lost the match 2–1.

## REG THE ALL-ROUND SPORTSMAN

In 1950 United paid a British record fee for a goalkeeper when they bought Reg Allen from Queens Park Rangers for £11,000. Reg was an excellent all-round sportsman playing cricket and boxing. During the Second World War Reg was a commando and spent three years as a POW after being captured in North Africa.

## THE UNLUCKY FIVE

Five of the Scotland team that lost 5–1 to England at Wembley on 24 May 1975 were Manchester United players. The United representatives were Martin Buchan, Alex Forsyth, George Graham, Lou Macari and Willie Morgan. No United players played for England in the game.

## SO NEAR YET SO FAR

On the final day of the 1994–95 season United lost their Premiership crown when they failed to beat West Ham United at Upton Park. The Reds' closest rivals, Blackburn Rovers, lost 2–1 at Liverpool but clinched the Championship by a single point. Brian McClair was United's scorer.

### ⚬⚬⚬ LEAGUE FOOTBALL RESUMES ⚬⚬⚬

United's first league game after the Munich Air Disaster was a 1–1 home draw with Nottingham Forest on 22 February 1958. Jimmy Murphy, Matt Busby's right-hand man, assumed charge of team affairs while Matt Busby recovered from the injuries he sustained in the Munich Air Disaster. The attendance of 66,123 at the time set a club record post-war League attendance at Old Trafford.

### ⚬⚬⚬ WARTIME HONOUR ⚬⚬⚬

The only goal of the game from Johnny Carey at Maine Road, United's adopted home, gave United their first ever wartime honour, the Lancashire Cup in 1941. During the game John Breedon in the United goal saved a penalty from Burnley's Brocklebank. United also finished in seventh place in the North Regional League.

### ⚬⚬⚬ GIVE US A KISS ⚬⚬⚬

On 30 July 1994 while playing in a pre-season friendly in Ireland a young girl ran on to the pitch, threw her arms around Ryan Giggs, and kissed him just as he was about to take a corner for Manchester United.

### ⚬⚬⚬ OFF ON THE WRONG FOOT ⚬⚬⚬

Manchester United's 1921–22 League campaign got off to a bad start. They lost 5–0 at Everton on 27 August, the club's worst ever opening day score.

### ⚬⚬⚬ UNITED'S LAY PREACHER ⚬⚬⚬

Herbert Whalley was at Old Trafford as a player from 1935–47 but the Second World War restricted him to only 39 appearances for the club. Bert, a Methodist lay preacher, sadly lost his life in the Munich Air Disaster. Bert actually travelled with United to Belgrade as the deputy for Jimmy Murphy who was on international duty at the time as the manager of Wales.

### ⚬⚬⚬ KIT COMPANIES ⚬⚬⚬

Four companies that have manufactured the Manchester United kit:

Adidas ❖ Admiral ❖ Nike ❖ Umbro

## GOOD AT GAMES

Leonard Langford (goalkeeper 1934–36) was an all round sportsman in his day, winning a middle-weight boxing championship of the Household Brigade along with the championship of Aldershot Command. Leonard also played cricket (wicket-keeper) and won several medals for high-jumping.

## THE MILLION DOLLAR TEAM

In May and June 1950, Manchester United went on a tour of the USA. In one of the games United played the Champions of Mexico, Atlas Club, in the Gilmore Stadium, Los Angeles. The game ended 6–6. The posters put up to advertise the games described United as "The Million Dollar Team".

## A SAD LOSS OF LIFE

Alan Davies, who played for United in the 1983 FA Cup final and replay, committed suicide in Gower, near Swansea on 4 February 1992. He was only 30 years old when he took his own life.

## GLORY GLORY NIGHTS (1)

Many United followers consider this to be the greatest night in the history of the world's most famous football club. Ten years after the Munich Air Disaster, Matt Busby saw his dream fulfilled when his United team were crowned kings of Europe. A Wembley crowd of 100,000 watched United beat the champions of Portugal, Benfica, 4–1 after extra time, with goals from Charlton (2), Best and Kidd.

### EUROPEAN CUP FINAL
*29 May 1968, Wembley Stadium*

MANCHESTER UNITED (0) *4*     *vs*     BENFICA (0) *1 aet*
Charlton (2), Best, Kidd        Graca

*Att. 100,000*

*Manchester United:* Stepney, Brennan, Dunne, Crerand, Foulkes, Stiles, Best, Kidd, Charlton, Sadler, Aston

## TALK OF THE DEVILS (1)

"When you see Eric Cantona brushing up on his skills, you know that no one can be satisfied with their standard."     *Ryan Giggs*

## LOYAL CLUB SECRETARY

Les Olive is remembered more for the 30 years that he spent at United as the club's secretary than for his two League games. He joined the Reds' ground staff from school in 1942 and played in almost every position for all five of United's teams. In 1988 he was made a director of the club and held that position until his death on 20 May 2006. Les Olive made his debut in goal for United in a 2–1 away win at Newcastle United on 11 April 1953, both goals from Tommy Taylor.

## DEVILS VISIT HELL

On 3 November 1993 Manchester United played Galatasaray in their Ali Sam Yen Stadium for the first time. The stadium in Istanbul, Turkey, is commonly known as "Hell". The game ended 0–0.

## INTERNATIONAL MANAGERS

The following Manchester United players went on to become international managers[†]:

| Player | Country |
| --- | --- |
| Noel Cantwell | Republic of Ireland |
| Johnny Giles | Republic of Ireland |
| Mark Hughes | Wales |
| Sammy McIlroy | Northern Ireland |
| Walter Winterbottom | England |

## NOT SO BRIGHT

On 4 October 1958 Manchester United and Wolverhampton Wanderers played in the first ever English Football League Saturday night game under floodlights. The game was played at Molineux with Wolves running out 4–0 winners.

## TALK OF THE DEVILS (2)

"I love pleasing United fans, but I also get a kick out of being on the pitch and having the power to aggravate thousands of opposing fans without them being able to to anything about it."     *Mark Hughes*

[†]*Three Manchester United managers also managed Scotland: Matt Busby, Tommy Docherty and Alex Ferguson.*

## ⚬⚬⚬ ERIC CANTONA ⚬⚬⚬

When Eric Cantona was sensationally transferred from Leeds United to Manchester United in November 1992, some Manchester United fans interviewed on TV questioned the signing, even going as far as to say that they would never sing, "Ooh Aah Cantona". Over the following five seasons, United won four Premier League titles, two FA Cups and two Doubles. Eric almost single-handedly re-wrote the history books of Manchester United. And as for the songs about Eric, well the United faithful are still chanting Eric's name today at Old Trafford even though he left the club in 1997!

Prior to arriving at Old Trafford, Eric had very much been a journeyman footballer, having played for Auxerre, FC Martiques, Olympique Marseille, Bordeaux, Montpellier, Nimes and Leeds United. Sheffield Wednesday passed up on the opportunity of signing Eric when he was on trial with them in 1991.

Sheffield Wednesday's loss was Leeds United's gain as Eric, along with former United great, Gordon Strachan, revitalised the club who won the last-ever First Division Championship in 1992, with Manchester United in runners-up position. However, it was a phone call from Howard Wilkinson to Alex Ferguson that resulted in Eric's move to Old Trafford. Ironically, Howard Wilkinson was inquiring about the availability of Denis Irwin, to which Alex replied the Irishman was not for sale but cheekily asked Wilkinson about Cantona's availability. Within days, Eric had signed for United in a £1 million transfer.

On 6th December 1992, Eric made his United debut as a substitute against Manchester City in a 2–1 home win. Eric's arrival transformed United's fortunes on the pitch with his aura of invincibility, his presence, his Gallic flair, his grace, his skill, his creativity, his vision, his goals and, not forgetting, his turned-up collar. On a number of occasions, Eric's fiery temper got him into trouble both on and off the pitch. In December 1991, Eric appeared before a French Disciplinary Committee and was suspended for calling its members idiots. In January 1995, Eric exacted his own revenge on a Crystal Palace supporter who verbally abused him as he walked off.

However, despite his brushes with authority, Eric will always be remembered for his genius on the pitch in the colours of Manchester United. In the games Eric played for United, they won 66 per cent, drew 23 per cent and lost only 11 per cent. The Frenchman has since translated his passion for football into love of the arts. He once said of Manchester United: "I am in love with Manchester United. It is like finding a wife who has given me the perfect marriage."

## ❧ IDENTITY PARADE ❧

The name of the club has changed twice since it was formed in 1878:

| Date | Name |
| --- | --- |
| 1878–1892 | Newton Heath LRW (Lancashire Railway Workers) |
| 1892–1902 | Newton Heath |
| 1902 to date | Manchester United |

## ❧ BILLY THE WHIZZ ❧

William "Billy" Meredith was born in Chirk, North Wales on 30 July 1874. Billy joined United from neighbours, Manchester City, in May 1906 amidst a bribes and illegal payments scandal that resulted in Billy and several of his City team-mates receiving lengthy suspensions from the Football Association. In 1909 Billy collected an FA Cup winners medal with United and was an important member of their Championship winning sides in 1908 and 1911.

## ❧ SAVING THEIR BLUSHES ❧

United could only manage a draw with non-League Walthamstow Avenue in their FA Cup Fourth Round game at Old Trafford on 31 January 1953. In the replay, played at Arsenal Stadium, United won 5–2.

## ❧ TWO OUT OF THREE AIN'T BAD ❧

In 1994 United narrowly missed out on a unique domestic Treble of League Championship, FA Cup and League Cup when they were beaten 3–1 by Aston Villa in the League Cup final. This was the first time a team had reached the final of both domestic cup competitions and won the League Championship in the same season.

## ❧ 'COS I'M NOT WORTH IT ❧

Elijah Round played two games in goal for United, losing 3–2 at Liverpool on 9 October 1909 and suffering a 7–1 defeat at Aston Villa on 26 February 1910. In May 1912 United transfer listed the hapless Elijah for £25. Round appealed twice to have the fee removed but was unsuccessful on both attempts. Elijah was signed from Charlton Athletic by United to act as an understudy to Harry Moger. Round was a total abstainer and did not smoke.

In their final League game of the 1973–74 season United lost 1–0 at Stoke City and, with other crucial results going against them, were relegated to Division Two. The side recorded only ten League wins out of 42 – the club's post-war record low figure. Their total of 20 League defeats, meanwhile, was a post-war record high. Remarkably every Manchester United player, numbered 1 to 12, scored during the season.

### *Football League Division 1*
### 1973–74

|  |  | P | W | D | L | F | A | W | D | L | F | A | Pts |
|---|---|---|---|---|---|---|---|---|---|---|---|---|---|
| 1. | Leeds United | 42 | 12 | 8 | 1 | 38 | 18 | 12 | 6 | 3 | 28 | 13 | 62 |
| 2. | Liverpool | 42 | 18 | 2 | 1 | 34 | 11 | 4 | 11 | 6 | 18 | 20 | 57 |
| 3. | Derby County | 42 | 13 | 7 | 1 | 40 | 16 | 4 | 7 | 10 | 12 | 26 | 48 |
| 4. | Ipswich Town | 42 | 10 | 7 | 4 | 38 | 21 | 8 | 4 | 9 | 29 | 37 | 47 |
| 5. | Stoke City | 42 | 13 | 6 | 2 | 39 | 15 | 2 | 10 | 9 | 15 | 27 | 46 |
| 6. | Burnley | 42 | 10 | 9 | 2 | 29 | 16 | 6 | 5 | 10 | 27 | 37 | 46 |
| 7. | Everton | 42 | 12 | 7 | 2 | 29 | 14 | 4 | 5 | 12 | 21 | 34 | 44 |
| 8. | QPR | 42 | 8 | 10 | 3 | 30 | 17 | 5 | 7 | 9 | 26 | 35 | 43 |
| 9. | Leicester City | 42 | 10 | 7 | 4 | 35 | 17 | 3 | 9 | 9 | 16 | 24 | 42 |
| 10. | Arsenal | 42 | 9 | 7 | 5 | 23 | 16 | 5 | 7 | 9 | 26 | 35 | 42 |
| 11. | Tottenham Hotspur | 42 | 9 | 4 | 8 | 26 | 27 | 5 | 10 | 6 | 19 | 23 | 42 |
| 12. | Wolverhampton W | 42 | 11 | 6 | 4 | 30 | 18 | 2 | 9 | 10 | 19 | 31 | 41 |
| 13. | Sheffield United | 42 | 7 | 7 | 7 | 25 | 22 | 7 | 5 | 9 | 19 | 27 | 40 |
| 14. | Manchester City | 42 | 10 | 7 | 4 | 25 | 17 | 4 | 5 | 12 | 14 | 29 | 40 |
| 15. | Newcastle United | 42 | 9 | 6 | 6 | 28 | 21 | 4 | 6 | 11 | 21 | 27 | 38 |
| 16. | Coventry City | 42 | 10 | 5 | 6 | 25 | 18 | 4 | 5 | 12 | 18 | 36 | 38 |
| 17. | Chelsea | 42 | 9 | 4 | 8 | 36 | 29 | 3 | 9 | 9 | 20 | 31 | 37 |
| 18. | West Ham United | 42 | 7 | 7 | 7 | 36 | 32 | 4 | 8 | 9 | 19 | 28 | 37 |
| 19. | Birmingham City | 42 | 10 | 7 | 4 | 30 | 21 | 2 | 6 | 13 | 22 | 43 | 37 |
| 20. | Southampton | 42 | 8 | 10 | 3 | 30 | 20 | 3 | 4 | 14 | 17 | 48 | 36 |
| 21. | MANCHESTER UNITED | 42 | 7 | 7 | 7 | 23 | 20 | 3 | 5 | 13 | 15 | 28 | 32 |
| 22. | Norwich City | 42 | 6 | 9 | 6 | 25 | 27 | 1 | 6 | 14 | 12 | 35 | 29 |

### ━ BORN ON THE SAME DAY (1) ━

The following Manchester United people were born on the same day:

21 January......................................Nicky Butt and Phil Neville
1 April.........................................Liam Whelan and Gordon Hill
31 December .........................Sir Alex Ferguson and Steve Bruce

## ⚞ C'MON THE TEN MEN ⚟

Manchester United have been involved in many thrilling games in which they have been reduced to ten men but gone on to record a notable victory. Here are ten to remember:

| Sent off | Competition | Opposition | Score |
|---|---|---|---|
| Nani | FAPL 08/05/2008 | West Ham U *(a)* | 4–1 |
| Paul Scholes | FAPL 03/03/2007 | Liverpool *(a)* | 1–0 |
| Mikael Silvestre | FAPL 01/02/2005 | Arsenal *(a)* | 4–2 |
| Wes Brown | FAPL 15/01/2005 | Liverpool *(a)* | 1–0 |
| Roy Keane | FA Cup 14/04/99 | Arsenal *(n)* | 2–1 *aet* |
| Peter Schmeichel | FA Cup 12/03/94 | Charlton A *(h)* | 3–1 |
| Mark Hughes | FA Cup 09/01/94 | Sheffield U *(a)* | 1–0 |
| Kevin Moran | FA Cup 18/05/85 | Everton *(final)* | 1–0 |
| George Best | D1 18/08/71 | Chelsea *(a)* | 3–2 |
| Denis Law | D1 14/11/64 | Blackpool *(a)* | 2–1 |
| Sandy Turnbull | D1 21/12/07 | Manchester C *(h)* | 3–1 |

## ⚞ TOP DOGS ⚟

Manchester United is one of only eight clubs that have never played in a League lower than what is now the Championship. The other seven – following Leicester City's relegation in 2008, in no particular order, are: Everton, Newcastle United, Arsenal, Tottenham Hotspur, Liverpool, Chelsea and West Ham United.

## ⚞ HAT-TRICK OF LEAGUE WINS AT ANFIELD ⚟

Wayne Rooney's goal against Liverpool on 15 January 2005 gave ten-man Manchester United (Wes Brown was sent off) a historic win over Liverpool at Anfield. The 1–0 victory meant that United had won three successive League games at Anfield for the first time in the club's history.

## ⚞ DRESS REHEARSAL ⚟

In May 1991 Andrei Kanchelskis became the first Manchester United player to make his Old Trafford debut in an international match. He played for the USSR against Argentina and did not make his "proper" home debut until United's opening game of the 1991–92 season (in a 2–0 win over Notts County on 17 August). Andrei left United in the summer of 1995 along with Mark Hughes and Paul Ince.

### FIRST NAME CHANGE

In the 1892–93 season the club made the decision to drop the "Lancashire & Yorkshire Railway" from their name becoming simply known as Newton Heath Football Club. The club's last game as Newton Heath Lancashire & Yorkshire Railway was against Birmingham St George's at home on 9 April 1892.

### UNLUCKY FOR SOME

A paltry 13 spectators turned up at Old Trafford on 7 May 1921 to watch Stockport County play Leicester City in a Division Two game. The Football Association had closed County's ground for disciplinary reasons. And for the unlucky 13 that turned up the game ended scoreless.

### CHIM-CHIMMENY

In the 1895–96 season "Father Bird", a local chimney sweep, often entertained the Newton Heath players at his home with a supper of potato-pie or Lancashire hot-pot, liquid refreshments and a sing-song afterwards.

### FOURTEEN OUT OF FOURTEEN

During the 1904–05 season Manchester United won 14 consecutive League games in Division Two. The run started with a 2–0 home win over Lincoln City on 15 October 1904, ending with a 4–2 away victory at Bolton Wanderers on 3 January 2005.

### FOUR FA CUP TIES IN 27 DAYS

On their way to lifting the FA Cup in 1963, Manchester United played the first four rounds of the competition over 27 days in March (from the 4th to the 30th). A cold snap resulted in the cancellation of many of the early ties.

### GOALS APLENTY

On 25 April 1959 United equalled their record total of 103 for most League goals in a season in their 2–1 away defeat at Leicester City. Warren Bradley was the United goal scorer as United ended the season First Division runners-up.

## ⚬⚬⚬ DENIS LAW ⚬⚬⚬

In July 1962 Matt Busby paid a British record transfer fee of £115,000 to sign Denis Law from the Italian club, Torino. Prior to attempting to make a name for himself in Italy, Denis began his professional career at Huddersfield Town aged 16 and then moved on to Manchester City before trying his luck abroad in 1961. The legendary Bill Shankly signed the young Scot straight from school in Aberdeen for Huddersfield Town in 1956. On his debut for Manchester United he scored in a 2–2 draw with West Bromwich Albion and at the end of his first season at Old Trafford he lifted the FA Cup with United at Wembley in May 1963 scoring in the final.

Denis was the supreme poacher with razor-sharp reflexes. "The King", as the Stretford End affectionately dubbed him, was as brave as a lion, as cunning as a fox and he seemed to possess the ability to leap in the air like a salmon out of water. No Manchester United fan, or indeed football fan that ever saw him play, could ever forget his trademark goal celebration with his right arm raised high in the air clutching his sleeve.

In 1964 Denis was voted European Footballer of the Year but sadly his braveness in battle cost him a place in United's 1968 European Cup final side. Denis was in hospital recovering from a knee operation when United were crowned European champions but make no mistake about it, Denis played a major part in getting them to the final at Wembley.

In 1973 Denis was sensationally placed on the transfer list by United manager, Tommy Docherty, and returned to Manchester City where few will forget his back-heeled goal in the Manchester Derby at Old Trafford on 27 April 1974 that led to a pitch invasion. Denis did not celebrate his goal, merely walking away with his head bowed and shortly afterwards he had to be substituted as the thought that he may have condemned United to the Second Division slowly sunk in and was apparent on his face. The referee abandoned the match with City leading 1–0 and with other results going against United, they were relegated. After the game, Denis never kicked another football in English football again.

George Best once said of Denis: "He's up there with the all-time greats. Electric. He'd snap up any half chance. As a bloke and as a pal, he's a different class. Nobody has a bad word about Denis."

### Did You Know That?
Although Denis missed the European Cup final through injury he got to hold the cup the next day when Matt Busby and his team-mates visited him in hospital.

In the final League game of the 1974–75 season United crushed Blackpool 4–0 at Old Trafford (Pearson 2, Greenhoff, Macari) to claim their second Division Two championship. United were back in the first division after a one-year absence.

### *Football League Division 2*
### 1974–75

|  |  | P | W | D | L | F | A | W | D | L | F | A | Pts |
|---|---|---|---|---|---|---|---|---|---|---|---|---|---|
| 1. | MANCHESTER UNITED | 42 | 17 | 3 | 1 | 45 | 12 | 9 | 6 | 6 | 21 | 18 | 61 |
| 2. | Aston Villa | 42 | 16 | 4 | 1 | 47 | 6 | 9 | 4 | 8 | 32 | 26 | 58 |
| 3. | Norwich City | 42 | 14 | 3 | 4 | 34 | 17 | 6 | 10 | 5 | 24 | 20 | 53 |
| 4. | Sunderland | 42 | 14 | 6 | 1 | 41 | 8 | 5 | 7 | 9 | 24 | 27 | 51 |
| 5. | Bristol City | 42 | 14 | 5 | 2 | 31 | 10 | 7 | 3 | 11 | 16 | 23 | 50 |
| 6. | WBA | 42 | 13 | 4 | 4 | 33 | 15 | 5 | 5 | 11 | 21 | 27 | 45 |
| 7. | Blackpool | 42 | 12 | 6 | 3 | 31 | 17 | 2 | 11 | 8 | 7 | 16 | 45 |
| 8. | Hull City | 42 | 12 | 8 | 1 | 25 | 10 | 3 | 6 | 12 | 15 | 43 | 44 |
| 9. | Fulham | 42 | 9 | 8 | 4 | 29 | 17 | 4 | 8 | 9 | 15 | 22 | 42 |
| 10. | Bolton Wanderers | 42 | 9 | 7 | 5 | 27 | 16 | 6 | 5 | 10 | 18 | 25 | 42 |
| 11. | Oxford United | 42 | 14 | 3 | 4 | 30 | 19 | 1 | 9 | 11 | 11 | 32 | 42 |
| 12. | Leyton Orient | 42 | 8 | 9 | 4 | 17 | 16 | 3 | 11 | 7 | 11 | 23 | 42 |
| 13. | Southampton | 42 | 10 | 6 | 5 | 29 | 20 | 5 | 5 | 11 | 24 | 34 | 41 |
| 14. | Notts County | 42 | 7 | 11 | 3 | 34 | 26 | 5 | 5 | 11 | 15 | 33 | 40 |
| 15. | York City | 42 | 9 | 7 | 5 | 28 | 18 | 5 | 3 | 13 | 23 | 37 | 38 |
| 16. | Nottingham Forest | 42 | 7 | 7 | 7 | 24 | 23 | 5 | 7 | 9 | 19 | 32 | 38 |
| 17. | Portsmouth | 42 | 9 | 7 | 5 | 28 | 20 | 3 | 6 | 12 | 16 | 34 | 37 |
| 18. | Oldham Athletic | 42 | 10 | 7 | 4 | 28 | 16 | 0 | 8 | 13 | 12 | 32 | 35 |
| 19. | Bristol Rovers | 42 | 10 | 4 | 7 | 25 | 23 | 2 | 7 | 12 | 17 | 41 | 35 |
| 20. | Millwall | 42 | 8 | 9 | 4 | 31 | 19 | 2 | 3 | 16 | 13 | 37 | 32 |
| 21. | Cardiff City | 42 | 7 | 8 | 6 | 24 | 21 | 2 | 6 | 13 | 12 | 41 | 32 |
| 22. | Sheffield Wednesday | 42 | 3 | 7 | 11 | 17 | 29 | 2 | 4 | 15 | 12 | 35 | 21 |

—ᴧᴧ— GATES TO BANK STREET LOCKED —ᴧᴧ—

Following the making of a compulsory winding-up order against the club in January 1902 the club was forced into bankruptcy. The bailiffs moved in and took control of the club's offices and assets and locked the gates to their Bank Street ground. Harry Stafford, the Newton Heath captain and full-back, managed to secure an interim ground for the Heathens to play their home games situated at Harpurhey, Manchester.

## ⟿ EUROPEAN MASTERS ⟿

The following players all scored for United in the European Cup, European Cup Winners' Cup and the UEFA Cup (formerly the Fairs Cup):

Bobby Charlton ⁕ David Herd ⁕ Denis Law
Bryan Robson ⁕ Mark Hughes

## ⟿ KEEP IT IN THE FAMILY ⟿

David Herd (Manchester United 1961–68) made his League debut in 1951 when he played for Stockport County. David was just 15 while the 39-year-old player-manager of the team, who he made his League debut alongside, was his father, Alex. It was only the second time that a father-and-son combination had played in the same English League team.

## ⟿ CLICKETY-CLICKS ⟿

On Sir Alex Ferguson's 6,666th day in charge of Manchester United, Roy Keane scored his long awaited 50th goal for the club in their 2–0 Premier League win over Birmingham City at Old Trafford on 5 February 2005. It was Keano's 460th appearance for United.

## ⟿ FROM ANGEL TO DEVIL ⟿

The day that news broke that Wayne Rooney had signed for Manchester United the following somewhat rueful slogan appeared on a wall close to his home in Liverpool: "Born to be an Angel but chose to be a Devil".

## ⟿ ELEVEN DAYS IN HEAVEN ⟿

Day 1: 16 May 1999........................FA Premier League Winners
Day 7: 22 May 1999..........................................FA Cup Winners
Day 11: 26 May 1999.............UEFA Champions League Winners

## ⟿ MATCH PROGRAMME NOT PRINTED ⟿

When the fans turned up at Maine Road for United's "home" game against Blackpool on 22 February 1947 they discovered that there was no match programme. This was due to a printers' strike.

## BARGAIN BUYS

United bought each of the following players during the 1970s for a fee less than £100,000:

| Player | From | Fee |
|---|---|---|
| Gerry Daly | Bohemians | £22,000 |
| Stewart Houston | Brentford | £45,000 |
| Steve Coppell | Tranmere Rovers | £60,000 |
| Gordon Hill | Millwall | £85,000 |
| Jim Holton | Shrewsbury Town | £95,000 |

## THREE DIFFERENT DERBY GAMES

Andrei Kanchelskis was the last player to have played in the Manchester, Merseyside and Old Firm Derbies. He played for both United and City, Everton and Glasgow Rangers.

## SOCCER'S HARDMEN

Sir Alex Ferguson appeared in a video entitled *Soccer's Hardmen* along with Denis Law and Nobby Stiles. The video was hosted by Vinnie Jones who ended up being fined £20,000 by the Football Association, who did not see the funny side of "the ugly side of the game".

## BEST TARGETMAN

George Best is the only player to have been Manchester United's top goalscorer in the League in five consecutive seasons – 1967–68 (28 goals), 1968–69 (19 goals), 1969–70 (15 goals), 1970–71 (18 goals) and 1971–72 (18 goals). Ruud van Nistelrooy came close to emulating his record. In his five seasons at Old Trafford, Ruud was United's top league goalscorer in four of them.

## THE OLD ONION BAG

In season 1890–91 goal-nets are introduced for the first time and all clubs, including Newton Heath, were informed to erect them at their grounds. Nets were first suggested by a Birmingham man but later patented and manufactured by Brodie of Liverpool. The first time they were actually used in a game was during a North vs. South International Trial Match, played at Trent Bridge, Nottingham on 12 January 1891.

In season 1991–92 Manchester United met Leeds United four times. It was the first time since 1904 that Manchester United had played the same team four times in the same season (Small Heath – later called Birmingham City). Ironically, ten years later United played Deportivo La Coruna four times in the 2001–02 UEFA Champions League. In 2004–05, United played Arsenal four times.

## ~~ MANCHESTER UNITED WALES XI ~~

*Substitutes*
Wyn **DAVIES**, John **DOUGHTY**, John **OWEN**, Colin **WEBSTER**,
Alan **DAVIES**, David **WILLIAMS**
*Manager*
Jimmy **MURPHY**

### Did You Know That?

Jimmy Murphy, Manchester United's assistant manager, missed United's trip to Red Star Belgrade on 3 August 1958 because he was required, in his capacity as the manager of the Welsh national team to prepare his countrymen for a forthcoming international against Israel in Cardiff. Jimmy managed United until Matt Busby recovered from the injuries he sustained in the Munich Air Disaster, leading them to the 1958 FA Cup final as well as taking Wales to the 1958 World Cup finals in Sweden.

In 1977, Liverpool, already League champions, were out to emulate the Arsenal team of 1971 by winning the Double of Championship and FA Cup in the same season; they had also reached the final of the European Cup. But this United team were out to prove that the previous year's defeat in the Cup final, at the hands of Southampton, was just a mere blip. While United's Arthur Albiston was making his FA Cup debut, Liverpool's Kevin Keegan was playing his last game for the club before his move to SV Hamburg in West Germany. In the first half Liverpool played their possession game, but they could not break down a United defence marshalled superbly by Martin Buchan. The game came to life in a five-minute period in the second half that brought three goals. Stuart Pearson fired United into the lead only for the old 1970s cliche of "Liverpool are at their most dangerous when they are behind" to come true, Jimmy Case levelling for the Merseysiders. However, thanks to a deflected goal off Jimmy Greenhoff from Lou Macari's shot, United won the Cup. Tommy Docherty's promise to the United fans in May 1976 that United would be back at Wembley the following year to win the Cup was kept. Sadly for many United fans, this was Docherty's last game in charge of the Reds, since he was sacked by the club six weeks later.

### FA CUP FINAL

*21 May 1977, Wembley Stadium*

MANCHESTER UNITED (0) *2*    *vs*    LIVERPOOL (0) *1*
Pearson, J. Greenhoff                  Case

*Att. 100,000*

*Manchester United:* Stepney, Nicholl, Albiston, McIlroy,
B. Greenhoff, Buchan, Coppell, J. Greenhoff, Pearson,
Macari, Hill (McCreery)

### ⚬ MARTIN BUCHAN ⚬

Martin Buchan made his United debut in a 2–0 defeat at Tottenham on 4 March 1972. It was also United's seventh successive defeat. After skippering Aberdeen, Buchan went on to captain United during their revival in the mid-1970s, leading them to the Second Division Championship in 1974–75 and three FA Cup finals between 1976 and 1979. Perhaps his greatest moment came when he became the first player to have captained an FA Cup-winning team in both England and Scotland when United beat Liverpool at Wembley in the 1977 final.

## ⚬ EL BEATLE DESTROYS LISBON EAGLES ⚬

On 9 March 1966 United were in Lisbon with a slender 3–2 advantage from the home Leg of their European Cup quarter-final clash. Before the game kicked off Eusebio was presented on the pitch with his European Player of the Year Award. Benfica were almost invincible at their Stadium of Light but George Best had a night to remember as he tore through the home defence time after time. United were three up after only 16 minutes with Best netting twice and setting up John Connelly for the third. Benfica, the previous season's losing finalists, didn't know what had hit them and even the normally productive Eusebio had a quiet night. Benfica's only goal came from a Shay Brennan own goal but United added two more in the last ten minutes of the game from Paddy Crerand and Bobby Charlton. At the end of the game the home fans hurled cushions on to the pitch in disgust of their side's inept performance.

## ⚬ BROTHERS STRIKE FOR THE HEATHENS ⚬

Brothers, Roger and Jack Doughty, scored in Newton Heath's 9–1 home win over Small Heath (later Birmingham City) in the Football Alliance on 7 April 1890. It was the first and only time that two brothers scored for the club in the same game.

## ⚬ WASHDAY BLUES FOR THE REDS ⚬

All of the club's laundry is done at Old Trafford in a building to the rear of the stadium. On a winter's Monday morning, the laundry team can find themselves having to wash 800 pieces of kit that have been worn by the various teams on the previous Saturday!

## ⚬ NO STOPPING THE BABES ⚬

Manchester United won the first five FA Youth Cup finals. United scored 33 goals in these finals, which were played over two legs, winning three of them by six-goal margins:

| Year | Result |
|---|---|
| 1953 | Manchester United 9, Wolverhampton Wanderers 3 |
| 1954 | Manchester United 5, Wolverhampton Wanderers 4 |
| 1955 | Manchester United 7, West Bromwich Albion 1 |
| 1956 | Manchester United 4, Chesterfield 3 |
| 1957 | Manchester United 8, West Ham United 2 |

### SIR MATT'S THREE TEAMS

Sir Matt Busby managed three different teams during his career:

Manchester United .......................... 1945–1969 and 1970–1971
British Olympic Team ........................................................ 1948
Scotland ......................................................................... 1958

### 300-UP FOR CITY AND UNITED

Billy Meredith is the only player to have played over 300 games for both Manchester clubs. He made 303 appearances for United (1906–21) and 366 for City.

### UNITED'S WORST NIGHT IN EUROPE

United were hopeful of progressing to the semi-final of the 1963–64 European Cup Winners' Cup having won the home leg 4–1. However, in their quarter-final second leg tie in Lisbon on 18 March 1964, United were easily beaten 5–0. The Portuguese side won the tie 6–4 on aggregate.

### SAINTS BEAT DEVILS

At the end of their first season back in the top flight, United made it to Wembley for the FA Cup final against Southampton on 1 May 1976. United were favourites but it was the team from the lower division that won the Cup with a goal late in the game from Bobby Stokes. It was the first time United were beaten at Wembley by a team from a lower division.

### SCOTTISH FOOTBALLERS OF THE YEAR

Three former United players were named Scottish Footballer of the Year prior to moving to Old Trafford:

Martin Buchan .............. Aberdeen ............................... 1971
Gordon Strachan .............. Aberdeen ............................. 1980
Brian McClair .............. Glasgow Celtic ........................ 1987

### TALK OF THE DEVILS (3)

"You just can't win anything with kids."          *Alan Hansen*

### ⚬⚬ HAPPY CHRISTMAS FOR THE HEATHENS ⚬⚬

Newton Heath played two games on Christmas Day. In 1896 they beat Manchester City 2–1 at home in a Division Two game. The following year the Heathens beat Manchester City again, this time 1–0 away in Division Two.

### ⚬⚬ CITY DEFECTORS ⚬⚬

On 16 May 1908 four Manchester City players left Maine Road for Manchester United. The foursome in question were James Bannister, Herbert Burgess, Sandy Turnbull and the legendary Billy Meredith.

### ⚬⚬ BEST IS BEST MAN ⚬⚬

During the early 1960s George Best struck up a friendship with Manchester City's Mike Summerbee[†] that lasted up till George's death in November 2005. George and Mike went into business together opening several boutiques in Manchester in 1966 and 1967. When Mike got married to Tina, who else but George was the best man.

### ⚬⚬ STRANGE FA CUP FACT ⚬⚬

After Barnsley eliminated United from the FA Cup Fourth Round during the 1997–98 season United did not lose their next FA Cup tie until West Ham United's 1–0 win at Old Trafford in the Fourth Round in season 2000–01. However, despite the lengthy unbeaten period, United only won the Cup once during this time. This is because United withdrew from the 1999–2000 FA Cup competition to play in a FIFA World Club Championship in Brazil.

### ⚬⚬ UNIQUE CHAMPIONSHIP HAT-TRICK ⚬⚬

In 1993 Eric Cantona became the first player to win successive English League Championship medals playing for two different teams; Leeds United in 1992 and Manchester United in 1993. Prior to joining Leeds Eric won *Le Championnat* (the French First Division) with Marseilles in 1991. Then in 1994 Eric won his fourth successive Championship medal when Manchester United retained their Premiership crown

---

[†]*Mike Summerbee starred in the 1981 movie,* Escape To Victory, *alongside Michael Caine, Bobby Moore, Pele and Sylvester Stallone. Mike played Syd Harmer.*

## FELLOWS PARK FIASCO

Third Division Walsall dumped United out of the FA Cup in 1974–75. Three days earlier Walsall drew 0–0 at Old Trafford in the third round but won the replay 3–2 after extra time.

## SEMI-FINALISTS SUPREME

When United met Crystal Palace in the semi-final of the FA Cup in 1995 it was their 20th appearance at that stage of the competition. Everton, also semi-finalists in 1995, were the clear leaders with 23 appearances at the same stage. Since then, however, United have pulled level with the Toffees with 25 semi-finals apiece. United have played an FA Cup semi-final at ten different grounds:

*Bramall Lane:* ............................................................ 1909, 1926
*Hillsborough:* 1948, 1949, 1957, 1962, 1964, 1965, 1970, 1976, 1977
*Villa Park:* ... 1958, 1963, 1970 *(replay)*, 1983, 1995, 1995 *(replay)*, 1996, 1999, 1999 *(replay)*, 2004, 2007
*Highbury:* ............................................................ 1958 *(replay)*
*City Ground:* ........................................................ 1965 *(replay)*
*Burnden Park:* ................................ 1966, 1970 *(second replay)*
*Maine Road:* ........................ 1979, 1985 *(replay)*, 1990, 1990 *(replay)*, 1994 *(replay)*
*Goodison Park:* .................... 1949 *(replay)*, 1979 *(replay)*, 1985
*Wembley:* ........................................................................ 1994
*Millennium Stadium:* ........................................................ 2005

## LE KING OF THE FA CUP

Eric Cantona played in 14 FA Cup games for Manchester United, two of them finals. He scored in the 1994 and 1996 finals and was serving his ban for the 1995 final. Manchester United never lost an FA Cup game when Eric played.

## BOTH SIDES OF THE BORDER

Sir Alex Ferguson is one of only two men who have managed English and Scottish FA Cup winning teams. Sir Alex led Aberdeen to Scottish FA Cup victories in 1983, 1984 and 1986 and Manchester United to FA Cup victories in 1990, 1994, 1996, 1999 and 2004. Meanwhile Jimmy Cochrane managed Kilmarnock to victory in 1929 and Sunderland in 1937.

On paper this was a mismatch. To many it seemed that the south coast side, managed by Jimmy Melia, were there merely to enjoy the occasion. However, the underdogs took the lead with a headed goal from Gordon Smith and held their 1–0 advantage to half-time. Early in the second half Stapleton brought United level, and then with only minutes remaining Ray Wilkins scored one of the greatest ever FA Cup final goals when he curled a 30-yard shot past Moseley in the Brighton goal. But the Seagulls gave it everything they had at the end of the game, and Gary Stevens scored an equalizer to force the game into extra time. In the last minute of extra time Gary Bailey made a miraculous save from Gordon Smith to secure a replay.

### FA CUP FINAL

*21 May 1983, Wembley Stadium*
MANCHESTER UNITED (1) *2 vs* BRIGHTON & HOVE ALBION (1) *2*
Stapleton, Wilkins     Smith, Stevens
*Att. 100,000*
*Manchester United:* Bailey, Duxbury, Albiston, Wilkins, Moran,
McQueen, Robson, Muhren, Stapleton, Whiteside, Davies

---

### ~~~ REPLAY ~~~

Bryan Robson opened the scoring for the Reds, and a few minutes later Norman Whiteside added a second to become the only player to have scored in both the League Cup final and FA Cup final in the same season. Just before the end of the first half, Robson scored again to put the Reds 3–0 up at the interval. In the second half Arnold Muhren added a fourth for United from the penalty spot.[†] The 4–0 winning scoreline equalled the best ever final score.

### FA CUP FINAL REPLAY

*26 May 1983, Wembley Stadium*
MANCHESTER UNITED (3) *4 vs* BRIGHTON & HOVE ALBION (0) *0*
Robson (2), Whiteside,
Muhren (pen)
*Att. 92,000*
*Manchester United:* Bailey, Duxbury, Albiston, Wilkins, Moran,
McQueen, Robson, Muhren, Stapleton, Whiteside, Davies

---

[†]*Arnold Muhren became the first foreign player to score in an FA Cup final when he scored from the spot for United.*

United players who later became managers:

| Player | Team managed |
| --- | --- |
| Trevor Anderson | Linfield, Northern Ireland |
| Frank Barson | Hartlepool United |
| William Behan | Drumcondra, Ireland |
| Shay Brennan | Waterford, Ireland |
| Steve Bruce | Birmingham City, Wigan Athletic |
| Martin Buchan | Burnley |
| Francis Burns | Italia FC, Australia |
| Noel Cantwell | Coventry City |
| Johnny Carey | Blackburn Rovers |
| Bobby Charlton | Preston North End |
| Allenby Chilton | Grimsby Town* |
| Steve Coppell | Crystal Palace, Reading |
| Pat Crerand | Northampton Town |
| Peter Davenport | Bangor City |
| Tony Dunne | Steinjker, Norway |
| Darren Ferguson | Peterborough United |
| Bill Foulkes | Viking Stavanger, Norway |
| Johnny Giles | West Bromwich Albion |
| Billy Garton | Salford City* |
| George Graham | Arsenal |
| Harry Gregg | Carlisle United |
| David Herd | Lincoln City |
| Clarence "Lal" Hilditch | Manchester United* |
| Gordon Hill | Northwich Victoria |
| Mark Hughes | Blackburn Rovers, Man City |

| Player | Team managed |
| --- | --- |
| Paul Ince | Macclesfield T, MK Dons, Blackburn R |
| Joe Jordan | Bristol City |
| Roy Keane | Sunderland |
| Brian Kidd | Blackburn Rovers |
| Lou Macari | Swindon Town |
| Neil McBain | Ayr United |
| Jim McCalliog | Halifax Town |
| Wilf McGuinness | Manchester United |
| Sammy McIlroy | Northern Ireland |
| George McLachlan | Queen of the South |
| Gordon McQueen | Airdrieonians |
| Charlie Mitten | Newcastle United |
| Kenny Morgans | Cwmbran Town* |
| Jimmy Nicholl | Raith Rovers* |
| Andy Ritchie | Oldham, Barnsley, Huddersfield |
| Bryan Robson | Middlesbrough, Sheffield United |
| Alex Stepney | Altrincham |
| Nobby Stiles | Preston North End |
| Ian Storey-Moore | Shepshed Charterhouse |
| Gordon Strachan | Coventry, Southampton, Celtic |
| Chris Turner | Hartlepool United |
| Dennis Viollet | Crewe Alexandra |
| Ray Wilkins | Fulham |
| Walter Winterbottom | England |

* Player-manager.

## OUTPOSTS OF EMPIRE

According to research conducted by the pollsters MORI, Manchester United has a worldwide fan base of 75 million. Overseas branches of the supporters' club keep the Red Flag flying high in the following locations:

Evergem, Belgium ❖ Toronto, Canada ❖ Limassol, Cyprus ❖ Geroldsgrün, Germany ❖ Krefeld, Germany ❖ Zarrentin, Germany ❖ Gibraltar ❖ Larisa, Greece ❖ Den Haag, Holland ❖ Hong Kong ❖ Reykjavik, Iceland ❖ Tokyo, Japan ❖ Luxembourg ❖ Malta ❖ Mauritius ❖ Sutherland, New South Wales ❖ Auckland, New Zealand ❖ Bergan, Norway ❖ Gauteng, South Africa ❖ Ingle Farm, South Australia ❖ Singapore ❖ Wettingen, Switzerland ❖ Huntington, NY, USA ❖ Camberwell, Victoria ❖ Perth, Western Australia

## ARGY-BARGY

In the second leg of their World Club Championship clash with Estudiantes de la Plata at Old Trafford, United could only manage a 1–1 draw that wasn't good enough to see them crowned as World Club Champions. As with the first game in Argentina, the match was littered with late tackles and countless off-the-ball incidents. George Best was sent off along with Medina while Willie Morgan scored for the Reds. A crowd of 63,500 packed Old Trafford for the game on 16 October 1968.

## THE GREAT ESCAPE

On 29 September 2001 Manchester United made their way to the changing rooms at White Hart Lane 3–0 down to Tottenham Hotspur. Whatever the United team were given at half-time, apart from a tongue lashing from Sir Alex Ferguson, worked as United tore the Spurs defence apart in the second half winning the game 5–3. Some 91 years earlier United had found themselves 3–0 down to Newcastle United only to make an equally spirited fight-back and win 4–3.

## ROY OF THE ROVERS

Four famous Manchester United players can be found in this famous football comic strip's Hall of Fame. They are:

Duncan Edwards ❖ Bobby Charlton ❖ George Best ❖ Denis Law

## FOULKES' FA CUP RUN

On 9 January 1954 Bill Foulkes played the first of his 61 FA Cup ties for United. United lost 5–3 away to Burnley in their third-round tie. Remarkably, all 61 appearances were made consecutively.

## WE'RE PART OF THE UNION

In 1898 the first Players' Union movement was formed. The Spread Eagle Hotel, Manchester was the venue for the meeting to form the "Union of Professional Football Players". Many Newton Heath players were in attendance and some were invited to address the audience at the meeting. The ultimate aim of the players was to achieve better pay and conditions from their employers, the clubs.

## UP FOR THE CUP (6)

Everton, the FA Cup holders, were at Wembley attempting to win not only the League and Cup Double but also possibly a historic Treble of FA Cup, First Division Championship and European Cup Winners' Cup (indeed they had already won the latter two trophies). In 1977 United had ended Liverpool's hopes of the Double by defeating them in the FA Cup final, and on 18 May 1985 the Reds did the same thing to Liverpool's Merseyside neighbours. Although United won the game 1–0 thanks to a superb strike from Norman Whiteside, the game will be remembered more for Kevin Moran's sending-off. Moran became the first player to be dismissed in an FA Cup final when retired police inspector Peter Willis brandished the red card following a tackle on Peter Reid. Moran was inconsolable as his team-mates battled on without him.[†] The game ended 0–0 after 90 minutes, but in the 110th minute Norman Whiteside curled a magnificent shot past Neville Southall in the Everton goal to give United the Cup.

### FA CUP FINAL
*18 May 1985, Wembley Stadium*
MANCHESTER UNITED (1) *1*   *vs*   EVERTON (0) *0 aet*
Whiteside

*Att. 100,000*
*Manchester United:* Bailey, Gidman, Albiston (Duxbury), Whiteside, McGrath, Moran, Robson, Strachan, Hughes, Stapleton, Olsen

[†]*Moran was not awarded his winner's medal after the game and had to wait several days before the FA agreed that he should receive it.*

Over the years Manchester United footballers have played for a number of North American Soccer League teams including:

| | |
|---|---|
| Atlanta Chiefs | New York Arrows |
| California Surf | Portland Timbers |
| Chicago Sting | San Jose Earthquakes |
| Detroit Express | Seattle Sounders |
| Fort Lauderdale Strikers | Tacoma Stars |
| Jacksonville Tea Men | Tampa Bay Rowdies |
| Kansas Comets | Toronto Blizzard |
| Los Angeles Aztecs | Tulsa Roughnecks |
| Miami Toros | Vancouver Whitecaps |
| Montreal Manic | |
| New England Tea Men | |

## ～ FA CUP HEROES RECEIVE CIVIC RECEPTION ～

When the Manchester United team returned home from London after beating Bristol City in the 1909 FA Cup final, they were met at Manchester's Central Station by a horse drawn carriage and taken to the Town Hall where a civic reception was held in their honour.

## ～ TALK OF THE DEVILS (4) ～

"An artist, in my eyes, is someone who can lighten up a dark room. I have never and will never find the difference between the pass from Pele to Carlos Alberto in the final of the World Cup in 1970 and the poetry of the young Rimbaud, who stretches cords from steeple to steeple and from window to window. There is in each of these human manifestations an expression of beauty which touches us and gives us a feeling of eternity."                                    *Eric Cantona*

## ～ RULER OF THE REDS AND THE BLUES ～

Ernest Mangnall[†] holds the distinction of being the only man to have managed both United and City. He managed United from 1902 to 1912 and City from 1912 to 1924. Sadly he died in January 1932.

---

[†]*Ernest Mangnall was also the secretary of Manchester United from 1903 to 1912 and was succeeded as secretary by J.J. Bentley (1912–16). Mangnall and Bentley played in the same Lancashire County team.*

## SIR BOBBY CHARLTON, CBE

Bobby Charlton was born on 11 October 1937 in the mining village of Ashington, Northumberland. Bobby's genes dictated that he would be a footballer as his mother, Cissie, was the cousin of Jackie Milburn ("Wor Jackie") the legendary Newcastle United and England centre-forward. Added to this, his grandfather and four other uncles were all professional footballers (his uncles George, Jack and Jim played for Leeds United while his uncle Stan played for Leicester City).

On 9 February 1953 the Manchester United scout, Joe Armstrong, watched Bobby Charlton play and speaking of the game Joe said: "I had to peer through a mist, but what I saw was enough. This boy is going to be a world-beater." In the region of 18 teams wanted to sign him, but Bobby had committed his future to Matt Busby's Manchester United. A member of the famous Busby Babes, Bobby played in Manchester United's successful FA Youth Cup winning sides in 1954, 1955 and 1956. On 6 October 1956 he made his Manchester United debut against Charlton Athletic at Old Trafford, scoring twice in a 4–2 victory.

Bobby won everything there was to win in the game; an FA Cup winner's medal, three League Championship winner's medals, a European Cup winner's medal and he was voted European Player of the Year in 1966. On top of all that he played 106 times for England, scoring a record 49 goals, and he won the World Cup in 1966. He also played in four World Cup finals for England (1958, 1962, 1966 and 1970). The great Sir Matt Busby once said of Bobby: "He has broken all records and won everything possible that there is to win. Yet he has remained completely unspoiled."

Whereas George Best possessed the style and Denis Law was flamboyant, Bobby Charlton was a football machine. He possessed superb skills, had tremendous balance and grace, he was athletic and he possessed a cannon of a shot from as far out as 35 yards. From the very moment Bobby made his United debut he was the ultimate professional. Always a gentleman on the pitch he never complained about crunching tackles and he never questioned the referee's decisions. He was the consummate professional footballer.

In 1973 when Bobby left Old Trafford after more than 750 appearances for the club he took up the role of player-manager at Preston North End.

Roy of the Rovers was the complete footballer who won everything with his team but whereas Roy Race was a comic book hero, Bobby Charlton was the real thing.

## ⟿ BRYAN ROBSON ⟿

On 7 October 1981 Bryan Robson made his debut for United in their 1–0 League Cup second round 2, first leg defeat at the hands of Spurs at White Hart Lane. Robson began his professional playing career with West Bromwich Albion. In his early days at the Hawthorns he was so skinny that the training staff put him on a diet of raw eggs and Guinness. The diet certainly worked because he grew into one of England's fiercest midfield competitors. In 1981 Ron Atkinson, his boss at West Bromwich Albion, paid a British transfer record fee of £1.5 million to shape his Manchester United team around him. In 13 seasons with United Robson gave 110% every time he pulled on a United shirt or the white shirt of England. With the Reds he became the first player to captain three FA Cup winning sides (1983, 1985 and 1990), he captained United to a European Cup Winners' Cup success in 1991 and helped United to two Premier League titles (1993 and 1994). Robson's place in the United history books is assured.

## ⟿ KIND INVITATION ⟿

When Wolverhampton Wanderers were crowned Champions in season 1957–58, UEFA issued United with an invitation to participate in the 1958–59 European Cup despite United finishing 9th in the League. It was a gesture of respect from European football's governing body for the sorrow felt for United by all football fans following the Munich Air Disaster. However, the Football League refused United permission to participate, perhaps exercising some form of twisted revenge for Matt Busby's defiance in leading United into Europe in season 1956–57 against their wishes. But Matt got his revenge a decade later when United were crowned Champions of Europe.

## ⟿ FOURFOURTWO AWARDS ⟿

The football magazine, *FourFourTwo*, conducted a poll in March 1995 to find the 100 greatest footballers of all time. The judges included Sepp Blatter, Michel Platini and Gordon Taylor. No fewer than 13 Manchester United players made the Top 100 with George Best the highest placed in third position. The others were:

Eric Cantona ❖ Bobby Charlton ❖ Duncan Edwards
Ryan Giggs ❖ Mark Hughes ❖ Andrei Kanchelskis ❖ Denis Law
Arnold Muhren ❖ Jesper Olsen ❖ Albert Quixall
Bryan Robson ❖ Gordon Strachan

## GEORGE'S CLUBS

George Best played for 11 different teams during his career:

AFC Bournemouth ❖ Brisbane Lions ❖ Cork ❖ Dunstable Town ❖
Fort Lauderdale Strikers ❖ Fulham ❖ Hibernian ❖ Los Angeles Aztecs
❖ Manchester United ❖ San Jose Earthquakes ❖ Tobermore United

## SAVIOUR OF UNITED

When Newton Heath subsequently became Manchester United in April 1902, John H. Davies was elected the new President. Over the next 25 years he was the club's saviour in times of financial crisis and along with manager, Ernest Mangnall, John H. Davies brought success to Manchester United. He was also instrumental in the club moving to Old Trafford in 1910. Sadly he died on 24 October 1927, but his place in the club's history is guaranteed.

## LEEDS DOUBLE-HEADER

During the 1991–92 season United were drawn away to Leeds United, their closest rivals for the First Division Championship, in the fifth round of the League Cup. United won the game 3–1 with goals from Blackmore, Kanchelskis and Giggs. It was the only time all season that Leeds lost at home, with United going all the way to Wembley to win the Cup while Leeds pipped them to the Championship.

## UNITED MANAGER SUSPENDED

On 8 October 1926 the Football Association issued a letter to Manchester United informing them that their secretary-manager, John Chapman, was suspended from all involvement with the club because of alleged improper conduct concerning management irregularities. Clarence "Lal" Hilditch was promoted to caretaker player-manager until Herbert Bamlett was appointed Manchester United's new manager on 13 April 1927.

## TOP TEENAGER

The BBC Young Sports Personality of the Year award, first made in 2001 and is awarded to sports figures aged under 17 as voted by a panel of expert judges. Wayne Rooney, who only turned 17 on 24 October 2002, was the second winner of the award in 2002.

Crystal Palace, the semi-final conquerors of Liverpool, took the lead in the 18th minute with a goal from Gary O'Reilly, only for Bryan Robson to pull United level in the 35th minute. Mark Hughes twisted and scored with a bullet-like shot from inside the area to put United 2–1 ahead after 62 minutes, then former Old Trafford hero Steve Coppell, the Crystal Palace manager, sent on Ian Wright, who scored within three minutes of taking the field. After 90 minutes the scores were tied at 2–2 and so the game went into extra time. Wright sent the Palace fans into a frenzy when he scored his second, and Palace's third, goal of the game two minutes into extra time. But there was still another twist to come, and in the 117th minute Mark Hughes drew the Reds level with another stunning goal. The match ended 3–3.

### FA CUP FINAL
*12 May 1990, Wembley Stadium*
MANCHESTER UNITED (3) *3*   *vs*   CRYSTAL PALACE (1) *3*
Robson, Hughes (2)      O'Reilly, Wright (2)

*Att. 80,000*
*Manchester United:* United: Leighton, Ince, Martin (Blackmore), Bruce, Phelan, Pallister (Robins), Robson, Webb, McClair, Hughes, Wallace

—— REPLAY ——

United finally saw off Crystal Palace in the 1990 FA Cup final replay with a strike from Lee Martin – only his second ever goal for the club. Alex Ferguson sensationally dropped goalkeeper Jim Leighton for the replay, preferring Les Sealey, who became the first ever on-loan player to play in an FA Cup final and was making his FA Cup debut for United into the bargain. The victory meant that Ferguson became the first manager since the war to have won both the FA Cup and the Scottish Cup (he won the latter with Aberdeen in 1982, 1983, 1984 and 1986).

### FA CUP FINAL REPLAY
*17 May 1990, Wembley Stadium*
MANCHESTER UNITED (0) *1*   *vs*   CRYSTAL PALACE (0) *0*
Martin

*Att. 80,000*
*Manchester United:* Sealey, Ince, Martin, Bruce, Phelan, Pallister, Robson, Webb, McClair, Hughes, Wallace

## ⚬⚬⚬ CANTONA RETIRES ⚬⚬⚬

The entire football world was stunned into silence when Manchester United called a press conference at Old Trafford on Sunday 18 May 1997 and Eric Cantona announced that he was retiring from the game. Even as the news broke stunned fans could not quite believe that the man they called "Le King" was leaving Old Trafford. Football fans, not just those of United, would no longer witness the genius of the man who won four FA Carling Premiership titles, two FA Cups (completing the Double, twice) and three Charity Shields during his four and a half years at Old Trafford.

## ⚬⚬⚬ MANCHESTER UNITED/LEEDS UNITED XI ⚬⚬⚬

*Substitutes*
Mickey *THOMAS*, Jimmy *GREENHOFF*, Andy *RITCHIE*, Alan *SMITH*
*Player-Manager*
Gordon *STRACHAN OBE*

### *Did You Know That?*
Johnny Giles won an FA Cup winners' medal with Manchester United in 1963 and an FA Cup winners' medal with Leeds United in 1972. Gordon Strachan won an FA Cup winners' medal with Manchester United in 1985 and the First Division Championship with Leeds United in 1992.

## REDS IN WHITE

Manchester United have played in white shirts in seven cup finals:

| Year | Competition | Result |
|------|-------------|--------|
| 1909 | FA Cup | Manchester United 1, Bristol City 0 |
| 1957 | FA Cup | Manchester United 1, Aston Villa 2 |
| 1958 | FA Cup | Manchester United 0, Bolton Wanderers 2 |
| 1983 | League Cup | Manchester United 1, Liverpool 2 *aet* |
| 1990 | FA Cup | Manchester United 3, Crystal Palace 3 |
| 1991 | Euro Cup Winners' Cup | Manchester United 2, Barcelona 1 |
| 2003 | League Cup | Manchester United 0, Liverpool 2 |

## FORMER REFEREE APPOINTED

On 13 April 1927 Herbert Bamlett succeeded Clarence "Lal" Hilditch as manager of Manchester United. Bamlett took charge of United when they were struggling in Division One and under him things didn't improve. He had been one of the country's top referees prior to becoming involved in management. In 1914, aged 32, he became the youngest man to referee an FA Cup final when he refereed the Burnley vs. Liverpool game. Prior to his appointment as United manager he also managed Oldham Athletic, Wigan Borough and Middlesbrough.

## YO YEOVIL!

Jack Rowley scored five of United's eight goals as they crushed Yeovil Town 8–0 at Maine Road in the fifth round of the 1948–49 FA Cup. At the time it was United's best ever FA Cup victory. The crowd of 81,565 is United's highest ever "home" attendance and the largest crowd to watch a non-League team in an FA Cup tie.

## THE GOAL THAT NEVER WAS

Playing for Northern Ireland against England George Best scored the goal that never was in a Home International game at Windsor Park, Belfast on 15 May 1971. As the legendary Gordon Banks tossed the ball in the air to kick it upfield, Best nudged the ball away from him while it was in mid-air and then took it around Banks to score. However, and to the amazement of the crowd, the referee disallowed the goal for an obstruction on the goalkeeper. Northern Ireland lost the game 1–0.

## GLORY GLORY NIGHTS (2)

On their way to their 2–1 victory over the mighty Barcelona in the final of the 1991 European Cup Winners' Cup, United won all four of their away leg matches. They beat Pecsi Munkas 1–0, Wrexham 2–0, Montpellier 2–0 and Legia Warsaw 3–1. Mark Hughes, playing against the side that considered him a flop, scored both United goals in the final. With this success, United became the first English club to have won both the European Cup and the European Cup Winners' Cup. The game was played in Feyenoord's stadium in Rotterdam, Holland.

### EUROPEAN CUP WINNERS' CUP FINAL
*15 May 1991, Feyenoord Stadion*
MANCHESTER UNITED (0) *2*  *vs*  BARCELONA (0) *1*
Hughes (2)  Koeman
*Att. 45,000*
*Manchester United:* Sealey, Irwin, Blackmore, Bruce, Phelan, Pallister, Robson, Ince, McClair, Hughes, Sharpe

## VICTORIAN BOO-BOYS

When Newton Heath were beaten 2–1 by New Brighton Tower on 18 March 1899 a group of supporters ran on to the pitch and surrounded the referee as he attempted to walk off the field. The fans started to boo and jeer the referee but thankfully he was not hurt as club officials and a few policemen escorted the referee to the safety of the dressing-room. During the game the referee made several dubious decisions in favour of the opposition while the loss seriously damaged any hopes of Newton Heath's promotion chances to Division One at the end of the season. They finished fourth in Division Two.

## THRILLER AT THE VILLA

United beat Aston Villa 6–4 at Villa Park when the two sides met in the third round of the FA Cup in 1948. Villa scored first with a goal after only 13 seconds but then United hit back and were cruising 5–1 at the interval. In the second half Villa put up a tremendous fight in the mud and rain to trail 4–5 but Stan Pearson scored his second goal of the game to give United a 6–4 victory. The other United goalscorers were Johnny Morris (2), Jimmy Delaney and Jack Rowley. United went all the way to Wembley defeating Blackpool 4–2 in the final.

## EURO 96 MATCHES AT OLD TRAFFORD

### *Germany vs. Czech Republic*

Germany defeated the Czech Republic 2–0 at Old Trafford in a Euro 96 Group C game in front of 37,300 fans on 9 June 1996.

### *Germany vs. Russia*

On 16 June 1996 Germany beat Russia 3–0 at Old Trafford in a Group C Euro 96 game in front of a crowd of 50,760.

### *France vs. Czech Republic (Semi-Final)*

On 26 June 1996 France and the Czech Republic drew 0–0 after extra-time in the semi-final of Euro 96 at Old Trafford. However, the Czechs booked their place in the final winning the penalty shoot-out 6–5.[†]

## NOT-SO-LUCKY LUCKY LOSERS

When Manchester United, the FA Cup holders, elected not to participate in the FA Cup during the 1999–2000 season, the FA decided that United's place in the third round of the competition should go to a "Lucky Loser" from the second round. Darlington were drawn out of the hat as the FA Cup's lucky losers and handed an away tie at Aston Villa. The Third Division side came out first in a draw of 20 clubs who had lost second round ties. Darlington had lost 3–1 to Gillingham in their second round tie on 20 November, while Aston Villa beat them 2–1 in the third round.

## A VERY RARE PROGRAMME

Plymouth Argyle visited Old Trafford on 5 January 1974 for an FA Cup Third Round tie. Plymouth had a programme printed for a replay against United, but no replay was needed as United won the game 1–0 with a Lou Macari goal. Plymouth took the precaution of printing the programme in advance in case there were power cuts during the Three-Day Week.

## COLOURS USED IN UNITED KITS

Red ❖ White ❖ Black ❖ Yellow ❖ Green ❖ Blue
Gold ❖ Grey ❖ Pink ❖ Silver ❖ Purple

---

[†]*On 29 June 1996 Simply Red, M People, Madness and Dodgy appeared in front of 62,000 fans at Old Trafford at a concert to mark the close of Euro 96.*

## REDS IN THE EMERALD ISLE

There are 1.3 million people in Ireland who support Manchester United, which amounts to a third of the combined population of the island North and South. Few Irish fans have to travel very far to find their local branch of the supporters' club:

Abbeyfeale & District ❖ Antrim Town ❖ Arklow & South Leinster
Ballycastle ❖ Ballyclare ❖ Ballymena ❖ Banbridge ❖ Bangor
Bray ❖ Bundoran ❖ Carlingford Louth ❖ Carlow
Carrickfergus ❖ Carryduff ❖ Castledawson ❖ Castlepollard
Castlewellan ❖ Cavehill ❖ City of Derry ❖ Clara ❖ Clonmel
Coleraine ❖ Comber ❖ Cookstown ❖ County Cavan ❖ County
Longford ❖ County Monaghan ❖ County Roscommon
County Tipperary ❖ County Waterford ❖ Craigavon ❖ Donegal
Dublin ❖ Dundalk ❖ Dungannon ❖ Ennis ❖ Fermanagh
Foyle ❖ Galway ❖ Glenowen ❖ Hilltown ❖ Kilkeel ❖ Kilkenny
Killaloe & Roscrea ❖ Killarney ❖ Killmallock ❖ Laois ❖ Larne
Limavady ❖ Limerick ❖ Lisburn ❖ Listowel ❖ Lurgan ❖ Mayo
Meath ❖ Muckamore Abbey ❖ Newry ❖ Nias ❖ North Down
Omagh ❖ Portadown ❖ Portaferry ❖ Portavogie ❖ Portrush
Portstewart ❖ Rostrevor ❖ Sion Mills ❖ Sligo ❖ Stewartstown
Strabane ❖ Tallaght ❖ Tipperary Town ❖ Tralee ❖ Warrenpoint

## JUDGMENT NIGHT AT OLD TRAFFORD

Nigel Benn fought Chris Eubank at Old Trafford on 9 October 1993 in a contest that was dubbed "Judgment Night".

## PFA PLAYER OF THE YEAR AWARD

Six Manchester United players have won the Professional Footballers' Association Player of the Year Award, two of them – Mark Hughes and Cristiano Ronaldo – twice:

| Year | Recipient |
|------|-----------|
| 1989/1991 | Mark Hughes |
| 1992 | Gary Pallister |
| 1994 | Eric Cantona |
| 2000 | Roy Keane |
| 2001 | Teddy Sheringham |
| 2002 | Ruud van Nistelrooy |
| 2007/2008 | Cristiano Ronaldo |

## ⚬⚬⚬ DOUBLE HAT-TRICK STAR ⚬⚬⚬

Christopher Taylor played for United from 1925–30. In 28 League appearances he scored six goals but the remarkable fact about his tally is that they were two hat-tricks. On 21 April 1925 he scored his first hat-trick in a 5–1 home win over Sunderland and ten days later he kept the match ball again following his second hat-trick in United's 3–2 win over West Bromwich Albion at Old Trafford.

## ⚬⚬⚬ RETURN OF THE KING ⚬⚬⚬

Following his eight-month ban from football, Eric Cantona made his long awaited comeback in a Premier League game versus Liverpool at Old Trafford on 1 October 1995. Nicky Butt fired the Reds ahead in the second minute thanks to a marvellous through ball from the French genius. Robbie Fowler looked set to spoil Eric's return by putting the Merseysiders 2–1 ahead with goals either side of half-time. But the stage was set for Eric and after Ryan Giggs was pulled down in the penalty area, Eric stepped up and very coolly placed his spot-kick past an outstretched David James. Eric could not hide his delight and ran to the fans behind the goal to celebrate, where he was engulfed in embraces from his team-mates.

## ⚬⚬⚬ GETTING TO KNOW YOU ⚬⚬⚬

During the 1964–65 season United played a team in the FA Cup that they had played in the League the previous Saturday on three occasions:

| | | | |
|---|---|---|---|
| 23 Jan | Stoke City | Division One | 1–1 |
| 30 Jan | Stoke City | FA Cup fourth round | 0–0 |
| 13 Feb | Burnley | Division One | 3–2 *win* |
| 20 Feb | Burnley | FA Cup fifth round | 2–1 *win* |
| 27 Feb | Wolves | Division One | 3–0 *win* |
| 6 Mar | Wolves | FA Cup sixth round | 5–3 *win* |

## ⚬⚬⚬ A CHANGE OF COLOURS ⚬⚬⚬

Following the change of name from Newton Heath to Manchester United on 26 April 1902 it was also decided to change the colour of the club's kit. Out went the green and gold shirts with white shorts and in came red shirts with white shorts. The club's first ever game in their new colours was a friendly played at Preston North End on 1 September 1902.

## ⟶ DUNCAN EDWARDS ⟵

There have been many polls over the last decade asking United fans "who is the greatest Manchester United player of all-time?" Legends such as Eric Cantona, Denis Law and George Best regularly appear in the Top 10 of fans' choices. However, to many United supporters the greatest player ever to pull on the red shirt of United was Duncan Edwards. Jimmy Murphy, assistant manager to Matt Busby, when asked about Duncan simply responded: "When I used to hear Muhammad Ali proclaim to the world that he was the greatest, I used to smile. You see the greatest of them all was an English footballer named Duncan Edwards."

Duncan made his Manchester United debut when he was aged just 16 years and 185 days, the youngest ever player in the English First Division at the time. He made his England debut in a 7–2 win over Scotland on 2 April 1955 at Wembley aged 18 years, 183 days becoming the youngest ever England international in the twentieth century, a record he held until 1998 when Michael Owen made his debut.

A young Duncan Edwards was first spotted when he played for his local team, Dudley Boys. Many teams were seeking Duncan's signature, but with the astute work of Jimmy Murphy and Matt Busby, Duncan signed for Manchester United as an amateur in June 1952. He was only 15 when he signed but already a giant of a man both in physical presence and stature. Duncan had it all; he had presence, power, grace on the ball, composure, the ability to pass a ball that would make an Olympic archer hang his head in disbelief, he scored goals (21 for United and 5 for England) but above all else, Duncan was a gentleman. Speaking in July 2001 Sir Bobby Charlton said of Duncan: "Duncan Edwards is the one person who, even today, I really felt inferior to. I've never known anybody so gifted and strong and powerful with the presence that he had."

Who knows what Duncan, and indeed Manchester United, would have achieved had the Munich Air Disaster on 6 February 1958 not tragically claimed his life and those of seven of his team-mates. But the final words surely belong to Duncan himself. Despite a host of clubs clambering for his signature it turned out that Matt Busby and Jimmy Murphy did not need to use much persuasion to lure Duncan to Old Trafford. In his autobiography Matt Busby recalled Duncan saying to him: "I think Manchester United is the greatest team in the world. I'd give anything to play for you." Duncan was true to his word, he did give everything to United, including his life.

## BAD LIGHT STOPS PLAY

The kick-off to the Manchester United vs. West Ham United Premier League game at Old Trafford on 10 January 1999 was delayed due to a power failure in the Trafford area of Manchester. The 45 minutes extra waiting time clearly did not affect United as they ran out 4–1 winners with two goals from Andy Cole and one each from Ole Gunnar Solskjaer and Dwight Yorke.

## THE PFA MERIT AWARD

Seven current or former Manchester United players or officials have received the PFA Merit Award, first presented in 1974:

| Year | Recipient |
| --- | --- |
| 1974 | Bobby Charlton |
| 1974 | Denis Law |
| 1980 | Sir Matt Busby |
| 1995 | Gordon Strachan |
| 1997 | Peter Beardsley |
| 2006 | George Best |
| 2007 | Sir Alex Ferguson |

## UP FOR THE CUP (8)

In April 1992, United were pushing for the First Division title and for success in the League Cup (then known as the Rumbelows League Cup), having exited the FA Cup in the fourth round. In this their third final in the competition, United overcame a strong Nottingham Forest side thanks to a 14th-minute goal from Brian McClair. The victory made up for the defeat to Sheffield Wednesday in the 1991 final. Although United first entered the League Cup competition in 1960–61, this was the first time the club had won it. On their way to lifting the trophy, United remained unbeaten in the competition, even though they played home and away legs in the second round.

### LEAGUE CUP FINAL
*12 April 1992, Wembley Stadium*
MANCHESTER UNITED (1) *1*    *vs*    NOTTINGHAM FOREST (0) *0*
McClair
*Att. 76,810*
*Manchester United:* Schmeichel, Parker, Irwin, Bruce, Phelan, Pallister, Kanchelskis (Sharpe), Ince, McClair, Hughes, Giggs

| Nickname | Player |
|---|---|
| Apache | Carlos Tevez |
| Baby-Faced Assassin | Ole Gunnar Solskjaer |
| Bamber | Alan Gowling |
| Berry | Robert Beresford Brown |
| Big Al | Alex Stepney |
| Billy | Liam Whelan |
| Black Pearl of Inchicore | Paul McGrath |
| Black Prince | Alex Dawson |
| Bogota Bandit | Charlie Mitten |
| Boom Boom | Duncan Edwards |
| Busby | Paul Parker |
| Cario | Johnny Carey |
| Charlie | Clatworthy Rennox |
| Choccy | Brian McClair |
| Cowboy | Bill Foulkes |
| Daisy | Gary Pallister |
| Dolly | Steve Bruce |
| El Beatle | George Best |
| Fabs | Fabien Barthez |
| Ghost | Charlie Roberts |
| Giggsy | Ryan Giggs |
| Gunner | Jack Rowley |
| Happy | Nobby Stiles |
| Jap | Danny Wallace |
| Judge | Lou Macari |
| Keano | Roy Keane |
| King | Denis Law |
| Knocker | Enoch West |
| Larry White | Laurent Blanc |
| Le King | Eric Cantona |
| Merlin | Gordon Hill |
| Mr Soccer | Joe Spence |
| Pancho | Stuart Pearson |
| Pocket Hercules | Herbert Burgess |
| Robbo | Bryan Robson |
| Rocket Ronaldo | Cristiano Ronaldo |
| Roonaldo | Wayne Rooney |
| Shark | Joe Jordan |
| Sharpey | Lee Sharpe |
| Shay | Seamus Anthony Brennan |
| Smudger | Alan Smith |
| Snake Hips | Eddie Colman |
| Sparky | Mark Hughes |
| Stroller | George Graham |
| Sunbed | Clayton Blackmore |
| Tank | Duncan Edwards |
| Turnbull the Terrible | Sandy Turnbull |
| Welsh Wizard/Old Skinny | Billy Meredith |

### ⚬ MORE TEA VICAR? ⚬

When George Best arrived at Old Trafford in 1961 he wasn't allowed to sign as an apprentice for United under Irish and Scottish League rules. The two countries had complained about the way the big English Football League clubs were poaching their best young players, and so he had to sign as an amateur. Because he was an amateur George had to get a job and he worked as a clerk at the Manchester Ship Canal. George complained bitterly about not being able to train more than two days per week and said he did not come to Manchester to make tea.

### ⚬ DIGS AT MRS FULLAWAY'S ⚬

When George Best arrived in Manchester from Belfast in 1961 the club placed him in digs with a club landlady named Mrs Mary Fullaway in Aycliffe Avenue, Chorlton-cum-Hardy, Manchester. George did not settle in Manchester in those early days he spent away from his family and even returned home to Belfast through homesickness. However, he was persuaded to return to United by Matt Busby and spent many wonderful and happy years at Mrs Fullaway's who had more than her fair share of admiring girls to contend with.

### ⚬ PEDEN HAT-TRICK FOR IRELAND ⚬

John Peden[†], Newton Heath forward 1893–94, scored a hat-trick for Ireland against Wales in Belfast on 5 April 1893. Ireland won the game 4–3. Although English based players were not introduced into the Irish side until season 1898–99, Peden was technically a Newton Heath player when he turned out for Ireland as his registration for the Heathens was dated 23 February 1893 despite the fact that he did not play for Newton Heath until 2 September 1893.

### ⚬ THEY SHALL NOT PASS ⚬

On 22 April 1925 United conceded their 23rd and final League goal of the 1924–25 season (Division Two) in a 1–1 home draw with Southampton. It is the fewest goals conceded by United in a single season.

[†]*John Peden was the first Irish player to play League football for the club.*

## OLD TRAFFORD CLOSED BY THE FA

As a result of a knife-throwing incident during a League game at Old Trafford against Newcastle United on 27 February 1971, the Football Association closed Old Trafford at the start of the following season, 1971–1972.[†]

## DRAMATIC COMEBACK THWARTED

Arsenal took the lead after only 12 minutes of the 1979 FA Cup final through Brian Talbot. Then just before the interval, Stapleton scored to put the Gunners 2–0 up. The Reds were still 2–0 down with four minutes of the match remaining, and then a remarkable sequence of events unfolded. Gordon McQueen pulled a goal back for United. It seemed merely a consolation until Sammy McIlroy wove his way through the Arsenal defence to place his shot past Pat Jennings and bring the two sides level with less than a minute on the clock. But victory was snatched from United's grasp when Alan Sunderland scored for Arsenal in the dying seconds of the game.

## FA CUP FINALS AT OLD TRAFFORD

### 1911 FA Cup Final
Just over one year after it was officially opened, Old Trafford was chosen as the venue for the 1911 FA Cup final. Bradford City beat Newcastle United.

### 1915 FA Cup Final
In 1915 Old Trafford played host to its second FA Cup final in only four years. Sheffield United lifted the Cup after a 3–0 victory over Newcastle United. The final was dubbed "The Khaki Final" because of the very large number of servicemen among the spectators.

### 1970 FA Cup Final Replay
In 1970 Old Trafford staged its third FA Cup final and its first for 65 years. Eighteen days after drawing 2–2 at Wembley on 18 April 1970, Chelsea and Leeds United battled it out in the FA Cup final replay at Old Trafford. The Londoners won the game 2–1.

---

[†]*Manchester United have played a "home" game at six grounds other than their own ground. The venues are: Anfield (Liverpool), Goodison Park (Liverpool), Home Park (Plymouth), Leeds Road (Huddersfield), Maine Road (Manchester) and the Victoria Ground (Stoke).*

United rounded off the season as true champions by winning 2–1 (Ince, Robson) against Wimbledon at Selhurst Park on 9 May 1993. The win meant that United equalled their best ever finish to a season, seven successive wins, first set in 1980–81. United were champions by a margin of ten points over their nearest challengers, Aston Villa.

### Premiership
### 1992–93

| | | P | W | D | L | F | A | W | D | L | F | A | Pts |
|---|---|---|---|---|---|---|---|---|---|---|---|---|---|
| 1. | MANCHESTER UNITED | 42 | 14 | 5 | 2 | 39 | 14 | 10 | 7 | 4 | 28 | 17 | 84 |
| 2. | Aston Villa | 42 | 13 | 5 | 3 | 36 | 16 | 8 | 6 | 7 | 21 | 24 | 74 |
| 3. | Norwich City | 42 | 13 | 6 | 2 | 31 | 19 | 8 | 3 | 10 | 30 | 46 | 72 |
| 4. | Blackburn Rovers | 42 | 13 | 4 | 4 | 38 | 18 | 7 | 7 | 7 | 30 | 28 | 71 |
| 5. | QPR | 42 | 11 | 5 | 5 | 41 | 32 | 6 | 7 | 8 | 22 | 24 | 63 |
| 6. | Liverpool | 42 | 13 | 4 | 4 | 41 | 18 | 3 | 7 | 11 | 21 | 37 | 59 |
| 7. | Sheffield Wednesday | 42 | 9 | 8 | 4 | 34 | 26 | 6 | 6 | 9 | 21 | 25 | 59 |
| 8. | Tottenham Hotspur | 42 | 11 | 5 | 5 | 40 | 25 | 5 | 6 | 10 | 20 | 41 | 59 |
| 9. | Manchester City | 42 | 7 | 8 | 6 | 30 | 25 | 8 | 4 | 9 | 26 | 26 | 57 |
| 10. | Arsenal | 42 | 8 | 6 | 7 | 25 | 20 | 7 | 5 | 9 | 15 | 18 | 56 |
| 11. | Chelsea | 42 | 9 | 7 | 5 | 29 | 22 | 5 | 7 | 9 | 22 | 32 | 56 |
| 12. | Wimbledon | 42 | 9 | 4 | 8 | 33 | 23 | 5 | 8 | 8 | 24 | 32 | 54 |
| 13. | Everton | 42 | 7 | 6 | 8 | 26 | 27 | 8 | 2 | 11 | 27 | 28 | 53 |
| 14. | Sheffield United | 42 | 10 | 6 | 5 | 33 | 19 | 4 | 4 | 13 | 21 | 34 | 52 |
| 15. | Coventry City | 42 | 7 | 4 | 10 | 29 | 28 | 6 | 9 | 6 | 23 | 29 | 52 |
| 16. | Ipswich Town | 42 | 8 | 9 | 4 | 29 | 22 | 4 | 7 | 10 | 21 | 33 | 52 |
| 17. | Leeds United | 42 | 12 | 8 | 1 | 40 | 17 | 0 | 7 | 14 | 17 | 45 | 51 |
| 18. | Southampton | 42 | 10 | 6 | 5 | 30 | 21 | 3 | 5 | 13 | 24 | 40 | 50 |
| 19. | Oldham Athletic | 42 | 10 | 6 | 5 | 43 | 30 | 3 | 4 | 14 | 20 | 44 | 49 |
| 20. | Crystal Palace | 42 | 6 | 9 | 6 | 27 | 25 | 5 | 7 | 9 | 21 | 36 | 49 |
| 21. | Middlesbrough | 42 | 8 | 5 | 8 | 33 | 27 | 3 | 6 | 12 | 21 | 48 | 44 |
| 22. | Nottingham Forest | 42 | 6 | 4 | 11 | 17 | 25 | 4 | 6 | 11 | 24 | 37 | 40 |

~~~ RED AND RAW ~~~

United has been drawn to play Liverpool more times, twelve, than any other club in the FA Cup. Perhaps the three most memorable ties for United fans were United's 1977 and 1996 FA Cup final wins and the dramatic 1999 fourth round tie at Old Trafford when United were trailing 1–0 with seconds remaining only for United to win the game 2–1 and go on to win the Treble.

## —— HONOURED BY THE QUEEN ——

These Manchester United players and officials have received honours:
David Beckham, OBE
Sir Matt Busby, CBE
Sir Bobby Charlton, CBE, OBE
Sir Alex Ferguson, CBE
Ryan Giggs, OBE
Mark Hughes, CBE
Sammy McIlroy, MBE
Bryan Robson, OBE
Teddy Sheringham, MBE
Nobby Stiles, MBE
Gordon Strachan, OBE
Ray Wilkins, MBE
Sir Walter Winterbottom, CBE

## —— A HAT-TRICK OF PENALTIES ——

Charlie Mitten scored three penalties for United in a 7–0 First Division home win over Aston Villa on 8 March 1950. Charlie also netted a fourth goal in the game.

## —— BUSBY AND FOULKES SAY FAREWELL ——

On 15 May 1969 Sir Matt Busby managed his last European game, and Bill Foulkes played his last game in European competition, as United beat AC Milan 1–0 in the second leg of their European Cup semi-final tie at Old Trafford. Foulkes appearance was his 52nd in Europe for the club, a record at the time. Trailing 2–0 from the first leg United pulled one goal back then, with 13 minutes remaining the Reds thought they had equalised on aggregate when Pat Crerand's cross appeared to cross the line. The goal was not given, which led to a section of the Stretford End throwing missiles onto the pitch. AC Milan's Cudicini was hit by a stone. Following this incident UEFA ordered United to erect screens behind the goals at Old Trafford for future European games. Ironically it was eight years before United qualified for European football again.

## —— WORLD CUP MATCHES AT OLD TRAFFORD ——

In the 1966 World Cup, Old Trafford provided the venue for the Pool B games of Portugal, Hungary, Bulgaria and Brazil.

## ᜱ TWO STINTS IN THE HOT SEAT ᜱ

Two men have managed Manchester United in two separate spells: Walter Crickmer (1931–32 and 1937–45) and Sir Matt Busby (1945–69 and 1970–71).

## ᜱ USE YOUR LOAF ᜱ

United fans teased their French counterparts by throwing bread at them during United's 1–1 draw with Saint Etienne in the First Round, first leg, European Cup Winners' Cup encounter on 14 September 1977. There was a bakers' strike on in France at the time. United's penalty? UEFA banned United from playing the return match at Old Trafford and stated that they had to play the tie at the furthest English ground from Old Trafford. United played at Plymouth Argyle's Home Park ground and goals from Gordon Hill and Lou Macari were enough to put United into the second round. A case of tough "dough" for the French.

## ᜱ VIOLLET'S GOALSCORING RECORD ᜱ

Dennis Viollet scored his last league goal of the season in United's 4–2 defeat at Sheffield Wednesday on 30 March 1960. Viollet ended the season as United's, and the First Division's, top goalscorer with 32 goals from 36 games. Viollet's 32-goal haul was a United record in the League.

## ᜱ LORDS OF THE WING ᜱ

United have been blessed with some exceptional wingers over the years. Here are some to remember:

| Winger | Dates | Winger | Dates |
|---|---|---|---|
| Billy Meredith | 1906–21 | Gordon Hill | 1975–78 |
| Charlie Mitten | 1946–50 | Mickey Thomas | 1978–81 |
| Johnny Berry | 1951–58 | Alan Davies | 1981–84 |
| David Pegg | 1952–58 | Laurie Cunningham | 1982–83 |
| Liam Whelan | 1954–58 | Peter Barnes | 1983–85 |
| Eddie Colman | 1955–58 | Arthur Graham | 1983–85 |
| George Best | 1963–74 | Ryan Giggs | 1991 to date |
| John Aston Jr | 1964–72 | Andrei Kanchelskis | 1991–95 |
| Willie Morgan | 1968–75 | David Beckham | 1992–2003 |
| Steve Coppell | 1974–83 | Cristiano Ronaldo | 2003 to date |

After winning the inaugural FA Premier League in season 1992–93, United went one better the following year when they retained their Premiership crown. A crowd of 44,717 filled Old Trafford and applauded the Champions in their final game of the season, a 0–0 draw with Coventry City. The following week, United lifted the FA Cup after a 4–0 win over Chelsea at Wembley to clinch their first ever domestic Double. United notched up a record 92 points from their 42 League games, a record that lasted until Chelsea beat it in 2004–05 (38 games).

### *Premiership* 1993–94

|     |                       | P  | W  | D  | L  | F  | A  | W  | D  | L  | F  | A  | Pts |
| --- | --------------------- | -- | -- | -- | -- | -- | -- | -- | -- | -- | -- | -- | --- |
| 1.  | MANCHESTER UNITED     | 42 | 14 | 6  | 1  | 39 | 13 | 13 | 5  | 3  | 41 | 25 | 92  |
| 2.  | Blackburn Rovers      | 42 | 14 | 5  | 2  | 31 | 11 | 11 | 4  | 6  | 32 | 25 | 84  |
| 3.  | Newcastle United      | 42 | 14 | 4  | 3  | 51 | 14 | 9  | 4  | 8  | 31 | 27 | 77  |
| 4.  | Arsenal               | 42 | 10 | 8  | 3  | 25 | 15 | 8  | 9  | 4  | 28 | 13 | 71  |
| 5.  | Leeds United          | 42 | 13 | 6  | 2  | 37 | 18 | 5  | 10 | 6  | 28 | 21 | 70  |
| 6.  | Wimbledon             | 42 | 12 | 5  | 4  | 35 | 21 | 6  | 6  | 9  | 21 | 32 | 65  |
| 7.  | Sheffield Wednesday   | 42 | 10 | 7  | 4  | 48 | 24 | 6  | 9  | 6  | 28 | 30 | 64  |
| 8.  | Liverpool             | 42 | 12 | 4  | 5  | 33 | 23 | 5  | 5  | 11 | 26 | 32 | 60  |
| 9.  | QPR                   | 42 | 8  | 7  | 6  | 32 | 29 | 8  | 5  | 8  | 30 | 32 | 60  |
| 10. | Aston Villa           | 42 | 8  | 5  | 8  | 23 | 18 | 7  | 7  | 7  | 23 | 32 | 57  |
| 11. | Coventry City         | 42 | 9  | 7  | 5  | 23 | 17 | 5  | 7  | 9  | 20 | 28 | 56  |
| 12. | Norwich City          | 42 | 4  | 9  | 8  | 26 | 29 | 8  | 8  | 5  | 39 | 32 | 53  |
| 13. | West Ham United       | 42 | 6  | 7  | 8  | 26 | 31 | 7  | 6  | 8  | 21 | 27 | 52  |
| 14. | Chelsea               | 42 | 11 | 5  | 5  | 31 | 20 | 2  | 7  | 12 | 18 | 33 | 51  |
| 15. | Tottenham Hotspur     | 42 | 4  | 8  | 9  | 29 | 33 | 7  | 4  | 10 | 25 | 26 | 45  |
| 16. | Manchester City       | 42 | 6  | 10 | 5  | 24 | 22 | 3  | 8  | 10 | 14 | 27 | 45  |
| 17. | Everton               | 42 | 8  | 4  | 9  | 26 | 30 | 4  | 4  | 13 | 16 | 33 | 44  |
| 18. | Southampton           | 42 | 9  | 2  | 10 | 30 | 31 | 3  | 5  | 13 | 19 | 35 | 43  |
| 19. | Ipswich Town          | 42 | 5  | 8  | 8  | 21 | 32 | 4  | 8  | 9  | 14 | 26 | 43  |
| 20. | Sheffield United      | 42 | 6  | 10 | 5  | 24 | 23 | 2  | 8  | 11 | 18 | 37 | 42  |
| 21. | Oldham Athletic       | 42 | 5  | 8  | 8  | 24 | 33 | 4  | 5  | 12 | 18 | 35 | 40  |
| 22. | Swindon Town          | 42 | 4  | 7  | 10 | 25 | 45 | 1  | 8  | 12 | 22 | 55 | 30  |

~~~ THE HEATHENS' LAST GAME ~~~

The Heathens played their last game on 27 April 1902, beating Manchester City 2–1 in the Manchester Senior Cup. The following season Newton Heath became Manchester United.

United, the Premier League champions, went into the 1994 FA Cup final knowing that a win would ensure their place in history, since they would become only the sixth team to win English football's coveted Double. Chelsea had already defeated the Reds home and away in the League during the season, but the day belonged to United and Eric Cantona, who scored two second-half penalties. Goals from Mark Hughes and Brian McClair gave United a thumping 4–0 win, their eighth in the FA Cup. More importantly it was their first ever Double.

### FA CUP FINAL

*14 May 1994, Wembley Stadium*

MANCHESTER UNITED (0) *4*     *vs*     CHELSEA (0) *0*
Cantona (2) (2 pens),
Hughes, McClair

*Att. 79,634*

*Manchester United:* Schmeichel, Parker, Irwin (Sharpe), Bruce, Kanchelskis (McClair), Pallister, Cantona, Ince, Keane, Hughes, Giggs

—— PFA YOUNG PLAYER OF THE YEAR ——

Six Manchester United players have received the Professional Footballers' Association Young Player of the Year Award. Cristiano Ronaldo finished second to Cesc Fabregas of Arsenal in 2008.

| Year | Young Player of the Year |
|---|---|
| 1985 | Mark Hughes |
| 1991 | Lee Sharpe |
| 1992, 1993 | Ryan Giggs |
| 1997 | David Beckham |
| 2005, 2006 | Wayne Rooney |
| 2007 | Cristiano Ronaldo |

—— MAGNIFICENT SEVEN FOR KEANE ——

When Roy Keane captained Manchester United in the 2005 FA Cup final he set a modern day record by appearing in his seventh FA Cup final. Keane's first FA Cup final appearance was for Nottingham Forest in 1991 and he also played for United in the finals of 1994, 1995, 1996, 1999 and 2004. Lord Kinnaird played in nine of the first 11 finals in the 1870s and 1880s.

## ENGLAND CAPTAINS

Six Manchester United players have captained England: Bobby Charlton, Bryan Robson, Ray Wilkins, Paul Ince, David Beckham and Rio Ferdinand.

## A LESS THAN HAPPY REUNION

In United's first League game of the 1994–95 season Paul Parker was sent off against his former club Queens Park Rangers. The Reds won 2–0.

## SHARPE'S HAT-TRICK IN THE BOOK

When Lee Sharpe was shown the yellow card in United's 1–0 defeat at Sheffield Wednesday on 8 October 1994, it was the third successive time he had been cautioned in a game. In his next match, against West Ham United, he was booked again!

## THIS IS YOUR LIFE

Prior to the Manchester Derby game at Old Trafford on 12 December 1970 Sir Matt Busby and the City manager, Joe Mercer, were presented with mementos on the pitch prior to the game. Sir Matt Busby received a further surprise when Eamonn Andrews crept up on him with an invitation for a second appearance on the TV show *This Is Your Life*. United lost the game 4–1.

## FA CUP FOOTBALL RETURNS

On 8 January 1949 United, the FA Cup holders, played their first FA Cup fixture in ten years at Old Trafford when they thrashed Bournemouth 6–0 in front of 55,012 fans. United's previous FA Cup fixture at Old Trafford took place on 11 January 1939 when West Bromwich Albion beat them 5–1 in a third round replay.

## MEN IN BLACK

United have played in two Cup finals wearing an all-black kit, losing both. Aston Villa beat them 3–1 in the 1994 League Cup final and Arsenal beat them on penalties in the 2005 FA Cup Final. Eric Cantona did not have a lucky time in United's black kit. He was sent off three times while wearing it, including that fateful night at Selhurst Park in January 1995 when he jumped into the crowd.

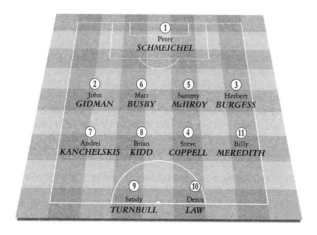

| | |
|---|---|
| **①** Peter *SCHMEICHEL* | |

| **②** John *GIDMAN* | **⑥** Matt *BUSBY* | **⑤** Sammy *McILROY* | **③** Herbert *BURGESS* |
|---|---|---|---|

| **⑦** Andrei *KANCHELSKIS* | **⑧** Brian *KIDD* | **④** Steve *COPPELL* | **⑪** Billy *MEREDITH* |
|---|---|---|---|

| **⑨** Sandy *TURNBULL* | **⑩** Denis *LAW* |
|---|---|

*Substitutes*
Tony *COTON*, Wyn *DAVIES*, Peter *BARNES*, James *BANNISTER*
*Manager*
Ernest *MANGNALL*

### Did You Know That?

Sir Matt Busby won the FA Cup three times, once as a player and twice as a manager. In 1934, when he was a player with Manchester City, he won a winners' medal when United's neighbours beat Portsmouth 2–1. Then in 1948 and again in 1963, he led United to FA Cup glory with Wembley wins over Blackpool (4–2) and Leicester City (3–1).

### A LONG SEASON

During the 1993–94 season Manchester United played an amazing 63 first-team games, comprising 42 FA Premier League games, 9 League Cup ties (including the final), 7 FA Cup ties (including the final), 4 European Cup fixtures and the FA Charity Shield.

### TALK OF THE DEVILS (5)

"This team never loses. They just run out of time."    *Steve McClaren*

On the last day of the 1995–96 season, Newcastle United had to beat Tottenham Hotspur at St James' Park and hope that Middlesbrough could beat United in order for the Geordies to pip the Reds for the title. But United were in Championship form and easily beat Middlesbrough 3–0 at the Riverside Stadium (May, Cole, Giggs) while Newcastle United could only manage a draw. The victory put United on course for a record second Double.

### Premiership
### 1995–96

| | | P | W | D | L | F | A | W | D | L | F | A | Pts |
|---|---|---|---|---|---|---|---|---|---|---|---|---|---|
| 1 | MANCHESTER UNITED | 38 | 15 | 4 | 0 | 36 | 9 | 10 | 3 | 6 | 37 | 26 | 82 |
| 2 | Newcastle United | 38 | 17 | 1 | 1 | 38 | 9 | 7 | 5 | 7 | 28 | 28 | 78 |
| 3 | Liverpool | 38 | 14 | 4 | 1 | 46 | 13 | 6 | 7 | 6 | 24 | 21 | 71 |
| 4 | Aston Villa | 38 | 11 | 5 | 3 | 32 | 15 | 7 | 4 | 8 | 20 | 20 | 63 |
| 5 | Arsenal | 38 | 10 | 7 | 2 | 30 | 16 | 7 | 5 | 7 | 19 | 16 | 63 |
| 6 | Everton | 38 | 10 | 5 | 4 | 35 | 19 | 7 | 5 | 7 | 29 | 25 | 61 |
| 7 | Blackburn Rovers | 38 | 14 | 2 | 3 | 44 | 19 | 4 | 5 | 10 | 17 | 28 | 61 |
| 8 | Tottenham Hotspur | 38 | 9 | 5 | 5 | 26 | 19 | 7 | 8 | 4 | 24 | 19 | 61 |
| 9 | Nottingham Forest | 38 | 11 | 6 | 2 | 29 | 17 | 4 | 7 | 8 | 21 | 37 | 58 |
| 10 | West Ham United | 38 | 9 | 5 | 5 | 25 | 21 | 5 | 4 | 10 | 18 | 31 | 51 |
| 11 | Chelsea | 38 | 7 | 7 | 5 | 30 | 22 | 5 | 7 | 7 | 16 | 22 | 50 |
| 12 | Middlesbrough | 38 | 8 | 3 | 8 | 27 | 27 | 3 | 7 | 9 | 8 | 23 | 43 |
| 13 | Leeds United | 38 | 8 | 3 | 8 | 21 | 21 | 4 | 4 | 11 | 19 | 36 | 43 |
| 14 | Wimbledon | 38 | 5 | 6 | 8 | 27 | 33 | 5 | 5 | 9 | 28 | 37 | 41 |
| 15 | Sheffield Wednesday | 38 | 7 | 5 | 7 | 30 | 31 | 3 | 5 | 11 | 18 | 30 | 40 |
| 16 | Coventry City | 38 | 6 | 7 | 6 | 21 | 23 | 2 | 7 | 10 | 21 | 37 | 38 |
| 17 | Southampton | 38 | 7 | 7 | 5 | 21 | 18 | 2 | 4 | 13 | 13 | 34 | 38 |
| 18 | Manchester City | 38 | 7 | 7 | 5 | 21 | 19 | 2 | 4 | 13 | 12 | 39 | 38 |
| 19 | Queens Park Rangers | 38 | 6 | 5 | 8 | 25 | 26 | 3 | 1 | 15 | 13 | 31 | 33 |
| 20 | Bolton Wanderers | 38 | 5 | 4 | 10 | 16 | 31 | 3 | 1 | 15 | 23 | 40 | 29 |

~~~ FRANKLY REMARKABLE ~~~

Frank Stapleton is the only player to have played in and scored in two FA Cup finals for two different teams. He scored for Arsenal in their 3–2 win over United in 1979 and four years later he scored in United's 4–0 FA Cup final replay win over Brighton & Hove Albion. Frank was also an FA Cup runner-up with Arsenal in 1978 and 1980 while he collected his third FA Cup winners' medal with United in 1985.

## I FOUGHT THE LAW, AND THE LAW WON

On 15 December 1962, only four days after Denis Law got married, he played for United in a 3–0 away defeat at West Bromwich Albion. However, the game will be remembered more for what happened in the days after the game. Denis claimed that throughout the game the referee, Mr Gilbert Pullin, was abusive towards him for no apparent reason. Denis was so hurt by the official's remarks that he informed Matt Busby what had happened. Matt was incensed and reported the incident to the FA. The FA's disciplinary hearing found in favour of Denis and Mr Pullin, refusing to accept the FA's findings, resigned his status as a Football League referee.

## CHAMPIONS OF THE WORLD

In 1999, United became the first British club to be crowned World Club champions after beating South America's champions, Palmeiras of Brazil, 1–0 (Roy Keane scoring) in the Olympic Stadium, Tokyo.

## UNITED PLAYERS WHO DIED IN WORLD WAR II

| Name | Circumstances |
| --- | --- |
| Ben Carpenter | In the retreat to Dunkirk |
| George Curless | On a bombing raid in Germany |
| Bert Redwood | As a civilian after being invalided out of the Army |

## UP FOR THE CUP (10)

What most people remember about this final is the Liverpool players parading the Wembley pitch prior to the game in cream suits. A drab final was won with a strike from, who else but Eric Cantona, with only a few minutes of the game remaining. United's 1–0 victory made them the first team in history to win English football's domestic Double twice.

**FA CUP FINAL**
*11 May 1996, Wembley Stadium*
MANCHESTER UNITED (0) *1*     *vs*     LIVERPOOL (0) *0*
Cantona
*Att. 79,007*
*Manchester United:* Schmeichel, Irwin, P. Neville, May,
Keane, Pallister, Cantona, Beckham (G. Neville), Cole (Scholes),
Butt, Giggs

United players appearing in television commercials:

|  |  |
|---|---|
| David Beckham | Adidas Predator boots |
| David Beckham | Brylcream |
| David Beckham | Gillette Razor Blades/Shaving Gel |
| David Beckham | Pepsi |
| David Beckham | Police Sunglasses |
| George Best | Cookstown Sausages |
| George Best | Egg Marketing Board |
| George Best | Fore Aftershave |
| George Best | Great Universal Stores |
| George Best | Stylo Boots |
| George Best | Tyne-tex Anoraks |
| Steve Bruce | Sure deodorant |
| Eric Cantona | Eurostar |
| Eric Cantona | Nike |
| Sir Bobby Charlton | Kirin Beer* |
| Sir Bobby Charlton | Mastercard |
| Andy Cole | Reebok |
| Ryan Giggs | Fuji Film |
| Ryan Giggs | ITV Digital |
| Ryan Giggs | Quorn Burgers |
| Ryan Giggs | Reebok |
| Rio Ferdinand | Anti-bullying campaign |
| Rio Ferdinand | Stand-up, Speak-up** |
| Sir Alex Ferguson | Barclays Bank |
| Sir Alex Ferguson & United team | Nike |
| Sir Alex Ferguson & United team | UNICEF |
| Roy Keane | Diadora |
| Roy Keane | Kit Kat |
| Roy Keane | Walker's Crisps |
| Gary & Phil Neville | Vodafone |
| Joe Jordan | Heineken |
| Ruud van Nistelrooy | Coca-Cola |
| Ruud van Nistelrooy | Nike |
| Ruud van Nistelrooy | Stand-up, Speak-up** |
| Cristiano Ronaldo | Fuji Xerox |
| Cristiano Ronaldo | Pepe Jeans |
| Cristiano Ronaldo | Suzuki Jeep |
| Wayne Rooney | Coc Zero |
| Wayne Rooney | Powerade |
| Wayne Rooney | Nike |
| Louis Saha | Nike |
| Peter Schmeichel | Danepak Bacon |
| Peter Schmeichel | Reebok |
| Peter Schmeichel | Sugar Puffs |
| Gordon Strachan | Barclays Bank |
| Paul Scholes | Nike |
| Ole Gunnar Solskjaer | Nike |
| Carlos Tevez | Joga Bonito Nike |
| Ray Wilkins | Tango (*voice-over*) |

*Shown only in Japan. ** Campaign against racism.*

## ⚬⚬⚬ LAST MATCH AT BANK STREET ⚬⚬⚬

On 22 January 1910 Manchester United played their last game at their Bank Street home, just before moving to Old Trafford. Tottenham Hotspur were the visitors for this historic occasion, with United winning 5–0.

## ⚬⚬⚬ SCHOLES'S DYNAMIC DEBUT ⚬⚬⚬

When Paul Scholes scored twice against Port Vale in the 1994–95 League Cup in his first game for United, he became the first United player to notch two goals on his debut since Bobby Charlton in 1956.

## ⚬⚬⚬ GLOBAL ENTERTAINMENT ⚬⚬⚬

United's Champions League home game against Barcelona on 19 October 1994 was beamed live to 80 million people in 107 countries. The worldwide audience were treated to a thrilling 2–2 draw.

## ⚬⚬⚬ FOOTBALL WRITERS' TRIBUTE AWARD ⚬⚬⚬

| Year | Player |
|---|---|
| 1989 | Bobby Charlton |
| 1994 | Denis Law |
| 1996 | Alex Ferguson |
| 2000 | George Best |
| 2001 | Teddy Sheringham |

## ⚬⚬⚬ KEEPING OUT OF THE RAIN ⚬⚬⚬

The 2001 Charity Shield match between Manchester United and Liverpool was the first ever top-flight game in British football to be played indoors. United lost 2–1 to Liverpool in Cardiff's Millennium Stadium, whose retractable roof had been closed for the game because of a forecast of poor weather conditions. The game marked the debut of Ruud van Nistelrooy, who scored United's goal.

## ⚬⚬⚬ STEPNEY'S WINNING SPOT-KICK ⚬⚬⚬

Alex Stepney, the United goalkeeper, scored from the penalty spot to give the Reds a 1–0 league win over Birmingham City at Old Trafford on 20 October 1973. It was Stepney's second goal of the season having scored a penalty against Leicester City in September.

### HOME GAME AT GOODISON PARK

Although United were drawn at home for their FA Cup Fourth Round tie against Liverpool scheduled for 24 January 1948, the game had to be played at Everton's Goodison Park. Old Trafford had not yet recovered from bomb damage, and Maine Road, where United were playing their home games in the interim, was not available because Manchester City were also drawn at home in the Cup. In the event, United beat Liverpool 3–0.

### YOUR COUNTRY NEEDS YOU

The 1914–15 season was the last Football League programme before the intervention of the Great War. From 1915 until 1919 Wartime Regional Leagues were introduced. United played in the Lancashire Section, with a highest ever finish of seventh in 1916–17. Sadly United's Sandy Turnbull, scorer of their 1909 FA Cup winning goal, was killed in action at Arras, France, on 3 May 1917.

### TRAINSPOTTERS

During the 1930s the London & North Eastern Railway Company built a steam locomotive engine and named it *Manchester United*. The engine was one of twenty-four Class B17s that were given the name of a famous football team. The engine was built at a factory in Darlington, and when it was scrapped in 1960 its number plate was presented to the club. Today the plate is on display in the Manchester United Museum at Old Trafford.

### NADIR UNDER SIR MATT

Despite reaching Wembley for the FA Cup final, season 1962–63 resulted in United's lowest ever League position under Matt Busby. Following a 3–2 defeat (scorers: Giles and Herd) away at Nottingham Forest on 20 May 1963 the Reds finished the season in 19th place and were now the underdogs to beat Leicester City in the Cup Final in five days time. Their nine defeats at home equalled an unwanted club record set in season 1930–31.

### MISTER CONTINUITY

James West is the only man to have managed both Newton Heath (1900–02) and Manchester United (1902–03).

United lifted their fourth FA Carling Premier League Championship in five seasons after a 2–0 home win over West Ham United in the last game of the 1996–97 season. At the end of the game, a unique event was witnessed by the 55,249-strong crowd and the millions watching on television. United's four teams paraded the four league trophies they had won: the FA Carling Premiership, the Pontins League Premier Division, the Lancashire League Division One and Lancashire League Division Two trophies. It was the club's first ever clean sweep of championships. However, the win over West Ham United proved to be Eric Cantona's last competitive game for the Reds before he announced his retirement from the game.

### Premiership
### 1996–97

| | | P | W | D | L | F | A | W | D | L | F | A | Pts |
|---|---|---|---|---|---|---|---|---|---|---|---|---|---|
| 1. | MANCHESTER UNITED | 38 | 12 | 5 | 2 | 38 | 17 | 9 | 7 | 3 | 38 | 27 | 75 |
| 2. | Newcastle United | 38 | 13 | 3 | 3 | 54 | 20 | 6 | 8 | 5 | 19 | 20 | 68 |
| 3. | Arsenal | 38 | 10 | 5 | 4 | 36 | 18 | 9 | 6 | 4 | 26 | 14 | 68 |
| 4. | Liverpool | 38 | 10 | 6 | 3 | 38 | 19 | 9 | 5 | 5 | 24 | 18 | 68 |
| 5. | Aston Villa | 38 | 11 | 5 | 3 | 27 | 13 | 6 | 5 | 8 | 20 | 21 | 61 |
| 6. | Chelsea | 38 | 9 | 8 | 2 | 33 | 22 | 7 | 3 | 9 | 25 | 33 | 59 |
| 7. | Sheffield Wednesday | 38 | 8 | 10 | 1 | 25 | 16 | 6 | 5 | 8 | 25 | 35 | 57 |
| 8. | Wimbledon | 38 | 9 | 6 | 4 | 28 | 21 | 6 | 5 | 8 | 21 | 25 | 56 |
| 9. | Leicester City | 38 | 7 | 5 | 7 | 22 | 26 | 5 | 6 | 8 | 24 | 28 | 47 |
| 10. | Tottenham Hotspur | 38 | 8 | 4 | 7 | 19 | 17 | 5 | 3 | 11 | 25 | 34 | 46 |
| 11. | Leeds United | 38 | 7 | 7 | 5 | 15 | 13 | 4 | 6 | 9 | 13 | 25 | 46 |
| 12. | Derby County | 38 | 8 | 6 | 5 | 25 | 22 | 3 | 7 | 9 | 20 | 36 | 46 |
| 13. | Blackburn Rovers | 38 | 8 | 4 | 7 | 28 | 23 | 1 | 11 | 7 | 14 | 20 | 42 |
| 14. | West Ham United | 38 | 7 | 6 | 6 | 27 | 25 | 3 | 6 | 10 | 12 | 23 | 42 |
| 15. | Everton | 38 | 7 | 4 | 8 | 24 | 22 | 3 | 8 | 8 | 20 | 35 | 42 |
| 16. | Southampton | 38 | 6 | 7 | 6 | 32 | 24 | 4 | 4 | 11 | 18 | 32 | 41 |
| 17. | Coventry City | 38 | 4 | 8 | 7 | 19 | 23 | 5 | 6 | 8 | 19 | 31 | 41 |
| 18. | Sunderland | 38 | 7 | 6 | 6 | 20 | 18 | 3 | 4 | 12 | 15 | 35 | 40 |
| 19. | Middlesbrough* | 38 | 8 | 5 | 6 | 34 | 25 | 2 | 7 | 10 | 17 | 35 | 39 |
| 20. | Nottingham Forest | 38 | 3 | 9 | 7 | 15 | 27 | 3 | 7 | 9 | 16 | 32 | 34 |

*Middlesbrough deducted 3 points for failing to fulfil fixture.

—⁓— TALK OF THE DEVILS (6) —⁓—

"Football, eh! Bloody hell!"                    *Alex Ferguson, Nou Camp 1999*

## UNITED'S PLAYER-MANGER

Clarence George "Lal" Hilditch was born in Hartford, Cheshire on 2 June 1894. In October 1926, after John Chapman had been sacked, Hilditch became the first and only player-manager in Manchester United's history. United looked to the half-back to bring back the glory days. Hilditch had joined Manchester United from Altrincham during the First World War and went on to play for United for 16 seasons, making a total of 322 appearances. When Hilditch was appointed it was made clear to him that it was only a temporary measure. Nevertheless, Hilditch was in charge until the end of the 1926–27 season, when he handed over power to Herbert Bamlett, although he continued to play for United until he retired in 1932.

## FOUR DEBUTS, FOUR GOALS

Neil Webb scored only four goals for Manchester United in 104 appearances, but remarkably he scored for the club on his debuts in four different competitions: the League, the Football League Cup, the European Cup Winners' Cup and the FA Cup.

## UNITED'S FIRST SHIRT SPONSORSHIP DEAL

Manchester United's first ever shirt sponsorship deal was with Sharp Electronics in 1982. The sum was £250,000 over three years.

## KNIGHT COMMANDER

In 1972 Pope Paul VI made Sir Matt Busby a Knight Commander of Saint Gregory. The award is given for conspicuous service to the church and society, regardless of religious allegiance.

## THE FOOTBALL WRITERS' CHOICE

Seven Manchester United players have won the Football Writers' Footballer of the Year Award. In 2008 Cristiano Ronaldo emulated Arsenal's Thierry Henry by winning the award in consecutive seasons.

| Year | Player | Year | Player |
|------|--------|------|--------|
| 1949 | Johnny Carey | 2000 | Roy Keane |
| 1966 | Bobby Charlton | 2001 | Teddy Sheringham |
| 1968 | George Best | 2007 | Cristiano Ronaldo |
| 1996 | Eric Cantona | 2008 | Cristiano Ronaldo |

### — MARATHON FA CUP TIE —

On 11 January 1904 Manchester United ended their most lengthy FA Cup tie when they beat Small Heath (later renamed Birmingham City) 3–1 at Hyde Road. The two clubs played four times, encompassing three replays and over seven hours of football (scorers: Arkesden (2) and Grassam). United's reward for winning the marathon tie was their name being put in the hat to play a tie in the first round!

### — SNOWFALL HELPS UNITED TO THE CUP —

In their 1909 FA Cup quarter-final tie with Burnley, United were trailing 1–0 with only 18 minutes of the game remaining when a heavy snowfall resulted in the referee, Herbert Bamlett, abandoning the match. Four days later United won the replay 3–2 and went on to win the Cup. Bamlett managed United from 1927–1931.

### — FATHER AND SON —

John Aston Sr won the League Championship with United in 1952. Fifteen years later his son, John Aston Jr, won the Championship with the club. They are the only father-and-son combination to win the English First Division Championship with the same club.

### — STOKE'S DOUBLE —

In the 1971–72 season, Stoke City knocked United out of the FA Cup (sixth round) and the Football League Cup (fourth round).

### — DOUBLE NOT TO BE —

Five days before the 1957 FA Cup final the Reds lifted the First Division Championship and looked set to become the first team to win the Double in the twentieth century. Ironically, United's opponents, Aston Villa, were the last side to do the Double. Six minutes into the game United's goalkeeper, Ray Wood, was stretchered off after a collision with Villa's Peter McParland. Jackie Blanchflower took Wood's place in goal as there were no substitutes allowed in 1957 and United were by far the best team in the first half. However, United's Double dream vanished in the second half when McParland scored twice. Tommy Taylor pulled a goal back for the Reds and when Wood returned after treatment he played on the wing. United even had a late equalizer ruled out for offside and so the Cup went to the Midlanders.

After going head-to-head with Arsenal all season, the Championship came down to the final day. United just had to beat Spurs to regain their trophy from their London rivals. A crowd of 55,189 packed Old Trafford and was stunned into silence when Les Ferdinand put the visitors in front. Arsenal fans put their dislike of their North London rivals to one side for the day and were ecstatic with joy when United fell behind. However, a David Beckham drive from the edge of the area put United level at the interval and in the second half, Andy Cole, who came on as a substitute for Teddy Sheringham, lobbed a delicate chip over Ian Walker to give United Championship glory. United had claimed the first leg of the illustrious Treble, their fifth Premiership crown.

### *Premiership* 1998–99

|    |                       | P  | W  | D | L | F  | A  | W | D | L  | F  | A  | Pts |
|----|-----------------------|----|----|---|---|----|----|---|---|----|----|----|-----|
| 1. | MANCHESTER UNITED     | 38 | 14 | 4 | 1 | 45 | 18 | 8 | 9 | 2  | 35 | 19 | 79  |
| 2. | Arsenal               | 38 | 14 | 5 | 0 | 34 | 5  | 8 | 7 | 4  | 25 | 12 | 78  |
| 3. | Chelsea               | 38 | 12 | 6 | 1 | 29 | 13 | 8 | 9 | 2  | 28 | 17 | 75  |
| 4. | Leeds United          | 38 | 12 | 5 | 2 | 32 | 9  | 6 | 8 | 5  | 30 | 25 | 67  |
| 5. | West Ham United       | 38 | 11 | 3 | 5 | 32 | 26 | 5 | 6 | 8  | 14 | 27 | 57  |
| 6. | Aston Villa           | 38 | 10 | 3 | 6 | 33 | 28 | 5 | 7 | 7  | 18 | 18 | 55  |
| 7. | Liverpool             | 38 | 10 | 5 | 4 | 44 | 24 | 5 | 4 | 10 | 24 | 25 | 54  |
| 8. | Derby County          | 38 | 8  | 7 | 4 | 22 | 19 | 5 | 6 | 8  | 18 | 26 | 52  |
| 9. | Middlesbrough         | 38 | 7  | 9 | 3 | 25 | 18 | 5 | 6 | 8  | 23 | 36 | 51  |
| 10. | Leicester City       | 38 | 7  | 6 | 6 | 25 | 25 | 5 | 7 | 7  | 15 | 21 | 49  |
| 11. | Tottenham Hotspur    | 38 | 7  | 7 | 5 | 28 | 26 | 4 | 7 | 8  | 19 | 24 | 47  |
| 12. | Sheffield Wednesday  | 38 | 7  | 5 | 7 | 20 | 15 | 6 | 2 | 11 | 21 | 27 | 46  |
| 13. | Newcastle United     | 38 | 7  | 6 | 6 | 26 | 25 | 4 | 7 | 8  | 22 | 29 | 46  |
| 14. | Everton              | 38 | 6  | 8 | 5 | 22 | 12 | 5 | 2 | 12 | 20 | 35 | 43  |
| 15. | Coventry City        | 38 | 8  | 6 | 5 | 26 | 21 | 3 | 3 | 13 | 13 | 30 | 42  |
| 16. | Wimbledon            | 38 | 7  | 7 | 5 | 22 | 21 | 3 | 5 | 11 | 18 | 42 | 42  |
| 17. | Southampton          | 38 | 9  | 4 | 6 | 29 | 26 | 2 | 4 | 13 | 8  | 38 | 41  |
| 18. | Charlton Athletic    | 38 | 4  | 7 | 8 | 20 | 20 | 4 | 5 | 10 | 21 | 36 | 36  |
| 19. | Blackburn Rovers     | 38 | 6  | 5 | 8 | 21 | 24 | 1 | 9 | 9  | 17 | 28 | 35  |
| 20. | Nottingham Forest    | 38 | 3  | 7 | 9 | 18 | 31 | 4 | 2 | 13 | 17 | 38 | 30  |

### ⟶ TALK OF THE DEVILS (7) ⟶

"Managing this club can become an obsession."     *Sir Alex Ferguson*

## —— UP FOR THE CUP (11) ——

Six days after recapturing their Premiership crown from Arsenal, United were at Wembley to face Newcastle United for the second leg of the historic Treble they were chasing in 1999. Despite Roy Keane suffering an early injury and having to leave the field, United ran out 2–0 winners with goals from Scholes and Sheringham. It was United's tenth FA Cup victory.

### FA CUP FINAL
*22 May 1999, Wembley Stadium*
MANCHESTER UNITED (1) *2*      *vs*      NEWCASTLE UNITED (0) *0*
Sheringham, Scholes

*Att. 79,101*
*Manchester United:* Schmeichel, G. Neville, May, Johnsen, P. Neville, Beckham, Scholes (Stam), Keane (Sheringham), Giggs, Cole (Yorke), Solskjaer

## —— GLORY GLORY NIGHTS (3) ——

On a balmy Spanish night Manchester United met Bayern Munich in the UEFA Champions League final at Barcelona's famous Nou Camp Stadium. Only five days earlier United had beaten Newcastle United in the FA Cup final at Wembley to clinch their third domestic Double. Now all that stood between United and a historic Treble was the German Champions, Bayern Munich, who ironically had been in the same group as United in the early stages of the competition. Indeed, Bayern were chasing the second leg of their own Treble having already won the Bundesliga and being due to face Kaiserslautern in the German Cup final. Despite conceding an early goal to a Mario Basler free-kick and surviving numerous close calls during the course of the game, United won the Cup in dramatic fashion with late injury-time goals from Teddy Sheringham and Ole Gunnar Solskjaer.

### EUROPEAN CUP FINAL
*26 May 1999, Nou Camp Stadium, Barcelona*
MANCHESTER UNITED (0) *2*      *vs*      BAYERN MUNICH (1) *1*
Sheringham, Solskjaer              Basler

*Att. 90,000*
*Manchester United:* Schmeichel, G. Neville, Irwin, Johnsen, Stam, Blomqvist (Sheringham), Butt, Giggs, Beckham, Cole (Solskjaer), Yorke

## ⚬⚬⚬ ALL STITCHED-UP ⚬⚬⚬

On 26 April 1965 Matt Busby ordered Denis Law to play against Arsenal at Old Trafford despite the fact that Law had stitches in a knee wound. Denis scored twice (Best also scored) in a 3–1 win, and United were crowned League champions.

## ⚬⚬⚬ SCORING DEBUTANTS ⚬⚬⚬

Since Newton Heath were formed in 1878 (and renamed Manchester United in 1902), there have been many instances of a player scoring on his debut for the club. Here are ten to remember:

| Player | Competition | Opposition | Score |
|--------|-------------|------------|-------|
| Gabriel Heinze | FAPL 09/11/04 | Bolton W *(a)* | 2–2 |
| Ruud van Nistelrooy | CS 2001 | Liverpool *(n)* | 1–2 |
| Ole Gunnar Solskjaer | FAPL 25/08/96 | Blackburn R *(h)* | 2–2 |
| Paul Scholes (2) | LC 21/09/94 | Port Vale *(a)* | 2–1 |
| Gordon Strachan | D1 25/08/84 | Watford *(h)* | 1–1 |
| Lou Macari | D1 20/01/73 | West Ham U *(h)* | 2–2 |
| Sammy McIlroy | D1 06/11/71 | Manchester C *(a)* | 3–3 |
| Denis Law | D1 18/08/62 | WBA *(h)* | 2–2 |
| Bobby Charlton (2) | D1 06/10/56 | Charlton A *(h)* | 4–2 |
| Tommy Taylor (2) | D1 07/03/53 | Preston NE *(h)* | 5–2 |

## ⚬⚬⚬ SUPERSUB ⚬⚬⚬

On 22 February 1975 Ron Davies made his tenth appearance for United. It was his last game for the club and he never played a full game – all ten appearances were made as a substitute.

## ⚬⚬⚬ THE LAST BUSBY BABE ⚬⚬⚬

On 21 January 1971 Sir Matt Busby's last signing, Sammy McIlroy, played for United, at the tender age of 16 years and 172 days, in a friendly against Bohemians in Dublin. However, he did not make his League debut for a further ten months.

## ⚬⚬⚬ CHARLTON JOINS CELTIC FOR A PENNY ⚬⚬⚬

In order for Bobby Charlton's testimonial against Glasgow Celtic to go ahead, the United and England legend had to sign for the Glasgow giants for one old penny.

## UNITED'S FIRST LEAGUE CUP GAME

Manchester United's first ever game in the League Cup competition, a first round match away at Exeter City, resulted in a 1–1 draw (Dawson). The game was played on 19 October 1960.

## A BODY OF EVIDENCE

During an operation on his knee, Denis Law had a quantity of loose material removed from the joint. Denis had the particles placed in a bottle and labelled it "They said they were in my mind". The Scottish forward had been complaining to the club doctor and physio for a long time about problems with the joint, only for it to be suggested that they were the result of his imagination.

## HOME-GROWN REDS

Only two of the twelve players named in Manchester United's 1968 European Cup final team were bought by the club: Paddy Crerand from Glasgow Celtic and Alex Stepney from Chelsea.

## FIRST DISMISSAL

Sandy Turnbull became the first Manchester United player to be sent off when he received his marching orders against Manchester City on 21 December 1907.

## CAPTAIN MARVEL

Bryan Robson was the only player to captain three FA Cup winning teams in the twentieth century (1983, 1985 and 1990). He was still at United when they lifted the FA Cup (and Double) in 1994 but missed out on a Cup final appearance.

## BABES SET FOREST ATTENDANCE RECORD

On 12 October 1957 Nottingham Forest opened their new East Stand at their City Ground with benches to seat 2,500 fans at a cost of £40,000. The Busby Babes were the visitors and won the game 2–1 thanks to goals from Dennis Viollet and Liam Whelan. The ball used in the game was signed by both sets of players and can be currently viewed in Nottingham Forest's trophy room. The crowd of 47,804 was a Forest club record at the time.

## VISITORS GET A MENTION

Manchester United's game against Portsmouth at Old Trafford on 21 October 1950 marked the occasion when an opposing team's name appeared on the front cover of the *United Review* for the first time. The match ended 0–0.

## GORDON MCQUEEN

On 25 February 1978 Gordon McQueen made his Manchester United debut in a 3–1 loss at Liverpool. Dave Sexton brought McQueen to Old Trafford a month after his close friend, and former team-mate at Leeds United, Joe Jordan had arrived. McQueen cost United £450,000, a record English League transfer fee at the time, and over the following seven years he was a rock in the Reds' defence.

## THE THREE KINGS OF EUROPE

Three Manchester United players have been voted European Footballer of the Year:

| Year | Player |
|------|--------|
| 1964 | Denis Law |
| 1966 | Bobby Charlton |
| 1968 | George Best |

## MR VERSATILE

Following an injury to goalkeeper Ray Wood, captain Johnny Carey was called upon to play the entire game in goal when United visited Roker Park for a First Division game against Sunderland on 18 February 1953. Carey helped United to a 2–2 draw. During his career with United, the versatile Carey played for the club in every position except outside-left.

## ROBSON PASSES UP CUP FINAL HAT-TRICK

In the 1983 FA Cup final replay Bryan Robson had the chance to score his third goal of the match when United were awarded a penalty against Brighton & Hove Albion. Only one player had previously scored an FA Cup final hat-trick at Wembley, but Robson passed up the opportunity and insisted that Arnold Muhren, United's regular penalty specialist, take the spot kick. Muhren scored and United won 4–0.

United lifted their sixth Premier League Championship in only eight seasons with an exhilarating end-of-season Championship winning run. After some poor performances in February, United won their last 11 FA Premier League games that included a 7–1 home win over West Ham United. United scored 97 goals in their 38 League games, conceding 45.

### *Premiership* 1999–2000

| | | P | W | D | L | F | A | W | D | L | F | A | Pts |
|---|---|---|---|---|---|---|---|---|---|---|---|---|---|
| 1. | MANCHESTER UNITED | 38 | 15 | 4 | 0 | 59 | 16 | 13 | 3 | 3 | 38 | 29 | 91 |
| 2. | Arsenal | 38 | 14 | 3 | 2 | 42 | 17 | 8 | 4 | 7 | 31 | 26 | 73 |
| 3. | Leeds United | 38 | 12 | 2 | 5 | 29 | 18 | 9 | 4 | 6 | 29 | 25 | 69 |
| 4. | Liverpool | 38 | 11 | 4 | 4 | 28 | 13 | 8 | 6 | 5 | 23 | 17 | 67 |
| 5. | Chelsea | 38 | 12 | 5 | 2 | 35 | 12 | 6 | 6 | 7 | 18 | 22 | 65 |
| 6. | Aston Villa | 38 | 8 | 8 | 3 | 23 | 12 | 7 | 5 | 7 | 23 | 23 | 58 |
| 7. | Sunderland | 38 | 10 | 6 | 3 | 28 | 17 | 6 | 4 | 9 | 29 | 39 | 58 |
| 8. | Leicester City | 38 | 10 | 3 | 6 | 31 | 24 | 6 | 4 | 9 | 24 | 31 | 55 |
| 9. | West Ham United | 38 | 11 | 5 | 3 | 32 | 23 | 4 | 5 | 10 | 20 | 30 | 55 |
| 10. | Tottenham Hotspur | 38 | 10 | 3 | 6 | 40 | 26 | 5 | 5 | 9 | 17 | 23 | 53 |
| 11. | Newcastle United | 38 | 10 | 5 | 4 | 42 | 20 | 4 | 5 | 10 | 21 | 34 | 52 |
| 12. | Middlesbrough | 38 | 8 | 5 | 6 | 23 | 26 | 6 | 5 | 8 | 23 | 26 | 52 |
| 13. | Everton | 38 | 7 | 9 | 3 | 36 | 21 | 5 | 5 | 9 | 23 | 28 | 50 |
| 14. | Coventry City | 38 | 12 | 1 | 6 | 38 | 22 | 0 | 7 | 12 | 9 | 32 | 44 |
| 15. | Southampton | 38 | 8 | 4 | 7 | 26 | 22 | 4 | 4 | 11 | 19 | 40 | 44 |
| 16. | Derby County | 38 | 6 | 3 | 10 | 22 | 25 | 3 | 8 | 8 | 22 | 32 | 38 |
| 17. | Bradford City | 38 | 6 | 8 | 5 | 26 | 29 | 3 | 1 | 15 | 12 | 39 | 36 |
| 18. | Wimbledon | 38 | 6 | 7 | 6 | 30 | 28 | 1 | 5 | 13 | 16 | 46 | 33 |
| 19. | Sheffield Wednesday | 38 | 6 | 3 | 10 | 21 | 23 | 2 | 4 | 13 | 17 | 47 | 31 |
| 20. | Watford | 38 | 5 | 4 | 10 | 24 | 31 | 1 | 2 | 16 | 11 | 46 | 24 |

—— GIGGS & CO. WIN FA YOUTH CUP ——

Following their 3–1 away win in the first leg of the FA Youth Cup final, United lifted the trophy with a 3–2 home win over Crystal Palace on 5 May 1992. Ryan Giggs proudly collected the trophy at Old Trafford. Also in the team were Gary Neville, David Beckham, Nicky Butt, Ben Thornley and Keith Gillespie, who came on as a substitute. It was United's sixth success in the competition, but their first since 1957.

## MANCHESTER UNITED YOUTH TEAM XI

*Substitutes*

Gary **WALSH**, Lee **MARTIN**, Phil **NEVILLE**, Nicky **BUTT**, Sammy **MCILROY**,

Keith **GILLESPIE**, David **BECKHAM**

*Manager*

Eric **HARRISON**

### *Did You Know That?*

Manchester United began to develop their youth scheme in the 1930s. MUJAC (Manchester United Junior Athletic Club) was the brainchild of club secretary Walter Crickmer. Players such as John Aston Sr, Charlie Mitten, Johnny Morris, Stan Pearson and Joseph Walton were all MUJAC graduates.

### AWAY DAY SPECIAL

During the 1986–87 season United won only one away fixture. Remarkably it came on Boxing Day, when they beat Liverpool 1–0 at Anfield thanks to a Norman Whiteside goal.

### NEW FACES

When Manchester United played Aston Villa in a Worthington Cup tie on 13 October 1999, not one player from the previous game against Chelsea started the cup game for the Reds.

## 14–0 WIN CHALKED OFF

On 9 March 1895 Newton Heath beat Walsall Town Swifts 14–0 at Bank Street. However, the visitors complained to the Football League about the extremely poor state of the pitch. Their appeal was upheld and a rematch was ordered. In the rearranged game, on 2 April 1895, Walsall Town Swifts were soundly beaten 9–0, Robert Donaldson scoring a hat-trick.

## BIRTH OF THE BUSBY BABES

On 24 November 1951 the term "Busby Babes" was used for the first time when it appeared in an article in the *Manchester Evening News* concerning United's goalless First Division match with Liverpool at Anfield. The game marked the debuts of Roger Byrne and Jackie Blanchflower.

## BLACK CATS JINXED

Manchester United have been drawn to meet Sunderland in five cup ties – four in the FA Cup and one in the Football League Cup. All four of the FA Cup ties went to a replay, with one tie needing a second replay. The only time the two sides were drawn together in the Football League Cup a second replay was required. In total the two teams have played each other in 12 cup matches, with United remaining unbeaten in all of them:

| *FA Cup* | *Round* | *Result* |
|---|---|---|
| 1925–26 | 5th Round | Sunderland 3, United 3 |
| 1925–26 | 5th Round *(r)* | United 2, Sunderland 1 |
| 1963–64 | 6th Round | United 3, Sunderland 3 |
| 1963–64 | 6th Round *(r)* | Sunderland 2, United 2 *aet* |
| 1963–64 | 6th Round 2nd *(r)* | United 5, Sunderland 1   * |
| 1985–86 | 4th Round | Sunderland 0, United 0 |
| 1985–86 | 4th Round *(r)* | United 3, Sunderland 0 |
| 1995–96 | 3rd Round | United 2, Sunderland 2 |
| 1995–96 | 3rd Round *(r)* | Sunderland 1, United 2 |

| *League Cup* | *Round* | *Result* |
|---|---|---|
| 1976–77 | 3rd Round | United 2, Sunderland 2 |
| 1976–77 | 3rd Round *(r)* | Sunderland 2, United 2 *aet* |
| 1976–77 | 3rd Round 2nd *(r)* | United 1, Sunderland 0 ** |

* *Venue – Leeds Road.* ** *Venue – Old Trafford.*

## ⚜ END OF A LANDMARK ⚜

On 4 May 1992 the famous Stretford End at Old Trafford was pulled down to make way for an all-seater two-tier stand. This marked the end of the famous Stretford End "wave" when United scored.

## ⚜ UNITED'S FASTEST EVER GOAL ⚜

Ryan Giggs scored United's fastest ever goal, in their 4–1 home win over Southampton on 18 November 1995. He scored after only 15 seconds.

## ⚜ FA CUP WINNING MANAGERS ⚜

Five men have guided United to FA Cup glory:

| Manager | Winning year(s) |
| --- | --- |
| Ernest Mangnall | 1909 |
| Sir Matt Busby | 1948, 1963 |
| Tommy Docherty | 1977 |
| Ron Atkinson | 1983, 1985 |
| Sir Alex Ferguson | 1990, 1994, 1996, 1999, 2004 |

## ⚜ HE WEARS SHORT SHORTS ⚜

Charlie Roberts (Manchester United 1903–13) defied FA orders that all players had to wear shorts that covered their knees. Roberts, a rebel in many respects, wore his shorts, short. He was also a pioneer in the Players' Union, becoming its chairman and later the leader of United's famous band of "Outcasts".

## ⚜ CHAPMAN SUSPENSION MYSTERY ⚜

Following the resignation as manager of John Robson, United appointed John A. Chapman as his successor on 31 October 1921. Chapman was a Scot who had been manager of Airdrieonians for 15 years before moving to Old Trafford. At the end of his first season in charge, United finished bottom of the First Division and remained in the Second Division until 1925. In October 1926 Chapman was suspended by the Football Association for alleged improper conduct, and the United board felt they had no option but to sack him. However, to this day the reasons for Chapman's suspension by the FA remain a mystery.

In season 2000–01 United were just simply too good for the rest of the pack. United rarely moved out of third gear all season and when Arsenal visited Old Trafford on 24 February, they were sent packing on the end of a 6–1 demolition. United won their third consecutive FA Premier League title, their seventh overall, at a canter.

### *Premiership* 2000–01

|  |  | P | W | D | L | F | A | W | D | L | F | A | Pts |
|---|---|---|---|---|---|---|---|---|---|---|---|---|---|
| 1. | MANCHESTER UNITED | 38 | 15 | 2 | 2 | 49 | 12 | 9 | 6 | 4 | 30 | 19 | 80 |
| 2. | Arsenal | 38 | 15 | 3 | 1 | 45 | 13 | 5 | 7 | 7 | 18 | 25 | 70 |
| 3. | Liverpool | 38 | 13 | 4 | 2 | 40 | 14 | 7 | 5 | 7 | 31 | 25 | 69 |
| 4. | Leeds United | 38 | 11 | 3 | 5 | 36 | 21 | 9 | 5 | 5 | 28 | 22 | 68 |
| 5. | Ipswich Town | 38 | 11 | 5 | 3 | 31 | 15 | 9 | 1 | 9 | 26 | 27 | 66 |
| 6. | Chelsea | 38 | 13 | 3 | 3 | 44 | 20 | 4 | 7 | 8 | 24 | 25 | 61 |
| 7. | Sunderland | 38 | 9 | 7 | 3 | 24 | 16 | 6 | 5 | 8 | 22 | 25 | 57 |
| 8. | Aston Villa | 38 | 8 | 8 | 3 | 27 | 20 | 5 | 7 | 7 | 19 | 23 | 54 |
| 9. | Charlton Athletic | 38 | 11 | 5 | 3 | 31 | 19 | 3 | 5 | 11 | 19 | 38 | 52 |
| 10. | Southampton | 38 | 11 | 2 | 6 | 27 | 22 | 3 | 8 | 8 | 13 | 26 | 52 |
| 11. | Newcastle United | 38 | 10 | 4 | 5 | 26 | 17 | 4 | 5 | 10 | 18 | 33 | 51 |
| 12. | Tottenham Hotspur | 38 | 11 | 6 | 2 | 31 | 16 | 2 | 4 | 13 | 16 | 38 | 49 |
| 13. | Leicester City | 38 | 10 | 4 | 5 | 28 | 23 | 4 | 2 | 13 | 11 | 28 | 48 |
| 14. | Middlesbrough | 38 | 4 | 7 | 8 | 18 | 23 | 5 | 8 | 6 | 26 | 21 | 42 |
| 15. | West Ham United | 38 | 6 | 6 | 7 | 24 | 20 | 4 | 6 | 9 | 21 | 30 | 42 |
| 16. | Everton | 38 | 6 | 8 | 5 | 29 | 27 | 5 | 1 | 13 | 16 | 32 | 42 |
| 17. | Derby County | 38 | 8 | 7 | 4 | 23 | 24 | 2 | 5 | 12 | 14 | 35 | 42 |
| 18. | Manchester City | 38 | 4 | 3 | 12 | 20 | 31 | 4 | 7 | 8 | 21 | 34 | 34 |
| 19. | Coventry City | 38 | 4 | 7 | 8 | 14 | 23 | 4 | 3 | 12 | 22 | 40 | 34 |
| 20. | Bradford City | 38 | 4 | 7 | 8 | 20 | 29 | 1 | 4 | 14 | 10 | 41 | 26 |

### ━ OLD TRAFFORD REWIRED ━

On 11 May 1987, after a 30-year career, the floodlight towers at Old Trafford were dismantled. The new lighting system was housed along the roof of the stadium and is still in existence today.

### ━ ERIC RULES ENGLAND ━

In 1994 Eric Cantona became the first foreign player to win the PFA Player of the Year Award.

### SPLASHING OUT

When United signed Reg Allen from Queens Park Rangers during the 1950–51 season he became the first goalkeeper to command a five-figure sum, £11,000.

### BEEB AWARD FOR BECKS

David Beckham won the BBC Sports Personality of the Year Award, awarded for "capturing the imagination of the Nation", in 2002.

### BLESSED BY THE POPE

On 21 March 1973 the Manchester United squad and officials had an audience with Pope Paul VI prior to their Anglo-Italian Tournament match with Lazio in Rome.

### THAT'S GRAND

When Manchester United beat Stoke City 1–0 away on 3 September 1983, it was their 1000th victory in the first division. Arnold Muhren scored the goal.

### UNITED FEELING BLUE

Manchester United have won three cup finals in a blue kit:

1948.............................FA Cup final
1968.....................European Cup final
1992.......................League Cup final

### PFA AWARD "DOUBLE"

In 1991 Mark Hughes was voted PFA Player of the Year while his young team-mate Lee Sharpe won the PFA Young Player of the Year Award. It was the first time a club had won the "Double" of senior and junior PFA awards in the same season. It was also the first time that a player had won the senior award twice.

### BEST BEATS UNITED

On 5 August 1973 George Best played for Dunstable Town against Manchester United Reserves. United's Reserves lost the game 3–2.

## Sport

| | |
|---|---|
| Wasim Akram | cricketer |
| Michael Atherton | cricketer |
| Ainsley Bingham | boxer |
| Darren Campbell | athlete |
| Colin Croft | cricketer |
| Ken Doherty | snooker player |
| Neil Fairbrother | cricketer |
| Jarkko Nieminen | tennis player |
| Martin Offiah | rugby player |
| John Virgo | snooker player |

## Music

| | |
|---|---|
| Paul "Bonehead" Arthurs | guitarist |
| Richard Ashcroft | lead singer |
| Victoria Beckham | singer |
| Melanie Blatt | singer |
| Ian Brown | lead singer |
| Tim Burgess | lead singer |
| Larry Gott | guitarist |
| Black Grape | band |
| Terry Hall | lead singer |
| Mick Hucknall | lead singer |
| Kerry Katona | singer |
| Kym Marsh | singer |
| Cerys Matthews | lead singer |
| Morrissey | lead singer |
| Mani Mounfield | guitarist |
| Ed O'Brien | guitarist |
| New Order | band |
| John Squire | guitarist |
| Supergrass | band |
| Malcolm Treece | guitarist |
| Russell Watson | opera singer |
| Thom Yorke | lead singer |

## Entertainment and media

| | |
|---|---|
| Steven Arnold | actor |
| Zoe Ball | radio/TV presenter |
| Chris Bisson | actor |
| Edith Bowman | radio/TV presenter |
| Gordon Burns | TV presenter |
| Mark Chapman | sports reporter |
| Mark Charnock | actor |
| Terry Christian | TV presenter |
| Steve Coogan | actor |
| Jimmy Cricket | comedian |
| Angus Deayton | actor/presenter |
| John Dyson | TV presenter |
| Christopher Ecclestone | actor |
| Jez Edwards | TV presenter |
| Alan Halsall | actor |
| Eamonn Holmes | TV presenter |
| Ulrika Jonsson | TV personality |
| Patrick Kielty | comedian |
| Terry Kiely | actor |
| Mark Lamarr | radio/TV presenter |
| Michael Le Vell | actor |
| Ralf Little | actor |
| Steve McFadden | actor |
| Ian McShane | actor |
| Justin Moorhouse | comedian/radio presenter |
| Nemone | radio DJ |
| James Nesbitt | actor |
| Robert Powell | actor |
| Gary Rhodes | TV chef |
| Lisa Riley | actor |
| Shane Ritchie | actor |
| Jennifer Saunders | actress/comedienne |
| Andrew Whyment | actor |
| Richard Wilson | actor |
| Sean Wilson | actor |

## Politics

| | |
|---|---|
| Bertie Ahern | Irish Prime Minister |
| Tony Lloyd | politician |

## TOP 12 RECORD INCOMING TRANSFERS

| Player | Fee |
|---|---|
| Rio Ferdinand | £29.1m from Leeds United |
| Juan Sebastian Veron | £28.1m from SS Lazio |
| Wayne Rooney | £27m from Everton |
| Ruud van Nistelrooy | £19m from PSV Eindhoven |
| Anderson | £18m from FC Porto |
| Owen Hargreaves | £17m from Bayern Munich |
| Nani | £14m from Sporting Lisbon |
| Michael Carrick | £14m from Tottenham Hotspur |
| Louis Saha | £12.8m from Fulham |
| Dwight Yorke | £12.6m from Aston Villa |
| Cristiano Ronaldo | £12.24m from Sporting Lisbon |
| Jaap Stam | £10.75m from PSV Eindhoven |

## NIGHTMARE START

Tommy Breen made his debut in goal for Manchester United at Leeds United on 28 November 1936. Without even having touched the ball he conceded a goal in the first minute of the game. United lost 2–1.

## FIRST UNITED PLAYER CAPPED BY IRELAND

On 10 February 1912 Michael Hamill became the first Manchester United player to be capped by Ireland. Born in Belfast (it was an all-Ireland side in those days), Hamill made his international debut in the 6–1 defeat by England in Dublin, scoring the Irish goal.

## FIERCE RIVALRY BEGINS

On 3 October 1891 Newton Heath (later to become Manchester United) beat Ardwick (who subsequently became Manchester City) 5–1 (Farman 2, Doughty, Sneddon, Edge). This FA Cup first qualifying round game was the first ever Manchester derby.

## UNITED'S FIRST BLACK PLAYER

On 20 May 1963 Dennis Walker made his Manchester United debut in the 3–2 defeat away at Nottingham Forest, becoming the first black player to appear for United's first team. Walker, a product of United's youth scheme, never played for the Reds again and was transferred to York City in April 1964.

"We Got Our Trophy Back" was the song being sung by United fans at Goodison Park on the final day of the season. In what was a long and hard season United rose to the top at the end to claim their eighth Premiership crown in 12 seasons after a titanic battle with Arsenal. However, United's home form was exceptional, winning 16, drawing 2 and losing only 1 (0–1 to Bolton Wanderers) of their 19 League games, scoring 42 goals and conceding only 12.

### *Premiership* 2002–2003

|  |  | P | W | D | L | F | A | W | D | L | F | A | Pts |
|---|---|---|---|---|---|---|---|---|---|---|---|---|---|
| 1. | MANCHESTER UNITED | 38 | 16 | 2 | 1 | 42 | 12 | 9 | 6 | 4 | 32 | 22 | 83 |
| 2. | Arsenal | 38 | 15 | 2 | 2 | 47 | 20 | 8 | 7 | 4 | 38 | 22 | 78 |
| 3. | Newcastle United | 38 | 15 | 2 | 2 | 36 | 17 | 6 | 4 | 9 | 27 | 31 | 69 |
| 4. | Chelsea | 38 | 12 | 5 | 2 | 41 | 15 | 7 | 5 | 7 | 27 | 23 | 67 |
| 5. | Liverpool | 38 | 9 | 8 | 2 | 30 | 16 | 9 | 2 | 8 | 31 | 25 | 64 |
| 6. | Blackburn Rovers | 38 | 9 | 7 | 3 | 24 | 15 | 7 | 5 | 7 | 28 | 28 | 60 |
| 7. | Everton | 38 | 11 | 5 | 3 | 28 | 19 | 6 | 3 | 10 | 20 | 30 | 59 |
| 8. | Southampton | 38 | 9 | 8 | 2 | 25 | 16 | 4 | 5 | 10 | 18 | 30 | 52 |
| 9. | Manchester City | 38 | 9 | 2 | 8 | 28 | 26 | 6 | 4 | 9 | 19 | 28 | 51 |
| 10. | Tottenham Hotspur | 38 | 9 | 4 | 6 | 30 | 29 | 5 | 4 | 10 | 21 | 33 | 50 |
| 11. | Middlesbrough | 38 | 10 | 7 | 2 | 36 | 21 | 3 | 3 | 13 | 12 | 23 | 49 |
| 12. | Charlton Athletic | 38 | 8 | 3 | 8 | 26 | 30 | 6 | 4 | 9 | 19 | 26 | 49 |
| 13. | Birmingham City | 38 | 8 | 5 | 6 | 25 | 23 | 5 | 4 | 10 | 16 | 26 | 48 |
| 14. | Fulham | 38 | 11 | 3 | 5 | 26 | 18 | 2 | 6 | 11 | 15 | 32 | 48 |
| 15. | Leeds United | 38 | 7 | 3 | 9 | 25 | 26 | 7 | 2 | 10 | 33 | 31 | 47 |
| 16. | Aston Villa | 38 | 11 | 2 | 6 | 25 | 14 | 1 | 7 | 11 | 17 | 33 | 45 |
| 17. | Bolton Wanderers | 38 | 7 | 8 | 4 | 27 | 24 | 3 | 6 | 10 | 14 | 27 | 44 |
| 18. | West Ham United | 38 | 5 | 7 | 7 | 21 | 24 | 5 | 5 | 9 | 21 | 35 | 42 |
| 19. | WBA | 38 | 3 | 5 | 11 | 17 | 34 | 3 | 3 | 13 | 12 | 31 | 26 |
| 20. | Sunderland | 38 | 3 | 2 | 14 | 11 | 31 | 1 | 5 | 13 | 10 | 34 | 19 |

### ~~~ COLLECTION OF CUSTODIANS ~~~

In 1952–53 United used a club record-equalling five different goalkeepers during the season: Reg Allen, Johnny Carey, Jack Crompton, Les Olive and Ray Wood. Fifty-seven years earlier, Newton Heath used five different goalkeepers in season 1895–96: William Douglas, George Perrins, Joseph Ridgway, Richard Smith and Walter Whittaker.

## BUSBY FIELDS EIGHT RESERVES

On 22 April 1957 Matt Busby decided to rest the bulk of his first team and played eight reserves in a League match against Burnley at Old Trafford. Despite nine of the players not having appeared in the previous first-team game two days earlier, United won 2–0 (Dawson, Webster). Matt was resting his first team in preparation for the second leg of their European Cup semi-final against Real Madrid at Old Trafford three days later.

## UNLUCKY CHARLTON

Bobby Charlton made his debut for Manchester United against Charlton Athletic at Old Trafford on 6 October 1956 and scored twice in a 4–2 win. Later that same season, on 18 February 1957, he scored his first hat-trick for United – against Charlton Athletic at The Valley as United won 5–1.

## LOWEST EVER FA CUP HOME CROWD

Their days as Newton Heath aside, Manchester United recorded their lowest ever home gate for an FA Cup tie on 16 January 1909. A crowd of only 8074 watched them beat Brighton & Hove Albion 1–0 in the first round of the Cup with a goal from Harold Halse. United went all the way that year and won the Cup for the first time in the club's history, beating Bristol City 1–0 in the final.

## BYRNE KEEPS HIS PROMISE

Following United's 1957 FA Cup final defeat to Aston Villa, Roger Byrne, the United captain, promised the fans that they would be back at Wembley the following year. Byrne was true to his word, but sadly he never made the final. He lost his life in the Munich Air Disaster, three months before United stepped out at Wembley to face Bolton Wanderers.

## GOING DUTCH

When United signed Edwin van der Sar in June 2005, he became United's sixth Dutch signing (following Jordi Cruyff, Arnold Muhren, Raimond van der Gouw, Ruud van Nistelrooy and Jaap Stam). Muhren (Ajax 1971), Stam (United 1999) and van der Sar (Ajax 1995 and United 2008) have all won Europe's top club prize, the European Cup.

## 20 FAMOUS FREE EXITS

| Player | Destination and date |
|---|---|
| David May | Released May 2003 |
| Ronnie Wallwork | West Bromwich Albion, July 2002 |
| Ronny Johnsen | Aston Villa, June 2002 |
| Denis Irwin | Wolverhampton Wanderers, June 2002 |
| Jesper Blomqvist | Everton, July 2001 |
| Teddy Sheringham | Tottenham Hotspur, May 2001 |
| Mark Bosnich | Chelsea, January 2001 |
| Jordi Cruyff | Alaves, July 2000 |
| Peter Schmeichel | Sporting Lisbon, June 1999 |
| Brian McClair | Motherwell, June 1998 |
| Steve Bruce | Birmingham City, June 1996 |
| Paul Parker | Released June 1996 |
| Bryan Robson | Middlesbrough, May 1994 |
| Clayton Blackmore | Middlesbrough, May 1994 |
| Viv Anderson | Sheffield Wednesday, January 1991 |
| Kevin Moran | Sporting Gijon, August 1988 |
| Martin Buchan | Oldham Athletic, August 1983 |
| George Best | Released August 1974 |
| Tony Dunne | Bolton Wanderers, August 1973 |
| Denis Law | Manchester City, July 1973 |

## CHARLTON'S HUNDREDTH IS KIDD'S FIRST

On 27 April 1970 Brian Kidd made his England debut against Northern Ireland at Wembley, with his United team-mate Bobby Charlton making his 100th appearance for his country alongside him. Charlton was made England captain for the game and was among the scorers in a 3–1 England win (George Best scored for Northern Ireland).

## MATT BUSBY ARRIVES HOME

On 18 April 1958 Matt Busby arrived back at his home in Kings Road, Chorlton, 71 days after the Munich Air Disaster. A huge crowd turned out to welcome him back.

## YOUNGEST BABES

The Manchester United team that won the First Division Championship in 1955–56 had an average age of only 22.

## —— UP FOR THE CUP (12) ——

This game was one of the most one-sided FA Cup finals ever played. From the very first minute Millwall simply appeared to be only too happy to actually be in the final, safe in the knowledge that regardless of the result they would be playing European football at the Den the following season as United had already qualified for the UEFA Champions League. Ronaldo opened the scoring in the first half for United with van Nistelrooy adding a second just before half-time. In the second half United took their foot off the pedal but still managed to score a third goal when van Nistelrooy found the net a second time.

### FA Cup Final

*22 May 2004, Millennium Stadium, Cardiff*
Manchester United (1) *3*    *vs*    Millwall (0) *0*
Ronaldo,
Van Nistelrooy 2 (1 pen)
*Att. 72,350*
*Manchester United:* Howard (Carroll), G. Neville, O'Shea, Brown, Silvestre, Ronaldo (Solskjaer), Fletcher (Butt), van Nistelrooy, Scholes, Giggs

## —— UNITED TELEVISION ——

In August 1998 Manchester United launched its own television channel. MUTV broadcasts six hours a day, seven days a week from a studio at Old Trafford. The channel is available through subscription and shows live youth and reserve team games and friendlies but not FA Premier League matches.

## —— HUMBLE BEGINNINGS ——

Manchester United began life in 1878, when a group of railway workers from the Lancashire & Yorkshire Railway formed a football team and named it Newton Heath. In the early days the players used the nearby pub, The Three Crowns Inn, for changing facilities before taking the short walk to the pitch in North Road, off Monsall Road, Newton Heath.

## —— HAT-TRICK OF HAT-TRICKS ——

During the 1959–60 season Alex Dawson scored a hat-trick in three consecutive games for Manchester United Reserves.

## 26-YEAR WAIT ENDS

On 2 May 1993 United became the inaugural winners of the FA Carling Premiership when their nearest rivals, Aston Villa, lost 1–0 at home to Oldham Athletic. This was United's first Championship success in English football's top flight since 1967.

## FAREWELL BOBBY

Prior to United's last home League game of the 1972–73 season, a guard of honour comprising the players of United and Sheffield United lined up on the pitch to pay tribute to Bobby Charlton in his last game at Old Trafford. The visitors then proceeded to take a little of the shine off the occasion by beating United 2–1.

## UNITED HIT THE AIRWAVES

On 5 March 1994 Manchester United Radio was officially launched. Fans could now – and still can – listen to games from Old Trafford on 1413 AM. Mind you, the station's first broadcast of a game, United against Chelsea, left the team in the studio a little red-faced as the Londoners spoiled the party by winning 1–0.

## BAILEY'S GOLDEN GLOVES

In 1981–82 United goalkeeper Gary Bailey won the inaugural Golden Gloves trophy after conceding only 22 goals in 39 matches.

## TOP 12 RECORD OUTGOING TRANSFERS

| Player | Fee |
| --- | --- |
| David Beckham | £24.25m to Real Madrid |
| Jaap Stam | £15.25m to SS Lazio |
| Juan Sebastian Veron | £15m to Chelsea |
| John Obi Mikel | £12m to Chelsea |
| Ruud van Nistelrooy | £10.2m to Real Madrid |
| Andy Cole | £7.5m to Blackburn Rovers |
| Paul Ince | £7m to Inter Milan |
| Andrei Kanchelskis | £5m to Everton |
| Lee Sharpe | £4.5m to Leeds United |
| Eric Djemba-Djemba | £3.5m to Aston Villa |
| Diego Forlan | £3m to Villareal |
| Phil Neville | £3m to Everton |

| Date | Player | Fee | From |
|---|---|---|---|
| 1900, Jan | Gilbert Godsmark | £40 | Ashford FC |
| 1903, Jan | Alexander Bell | £700 | Ayr Parkhouse |
| 1904, Apr | Charlie Roberts | £750 | Grimsby Town |
| 1914, Mar | George Hunter | £1300 | Chelsea |
| 1922, Aug | Frank Barson | £5000 | Aston Villa |
| 1951, Aug | Johnny Berry | £15,000 | Birmingham City |
| 1953, Mar | Tommy Taylor | £29,999 | Barnsley |
| 1958, Sept | Albert Quixall | £45,000 | Sheffield Weds |
| 1962, July | Denis Law | £115,000 | Torino |
| 1972, Feb | Martin Buchan | £120,000 | Aberdeen |
| 1972, Mar | Ian Storey-Moore | £200,000 | Nottingham Forest |
| 1978, Jan | Joe Jordan | £350,000 | Leeds United |
| 1978, Feb | Gordon McQueen | £495,000 | Leeds United |
| 1979, Aug | Ray Wilkins | £825,000 | Chelsea |
| 1980, Oct | Garry Birtles | £1.25m | Nottingham Forest |
| 1981, Oct | Bryan Robson | £1.5m | WBA |
| 1988, July | Mark Hughes | £1.6m | Barcelona |
| 1989, Aug | Gary Pallister | £2.3m | Middlesbrough |
| 1989, Sept | Paul Ince | £2.4m | West Ham United |
| 1993, July | Roy Keane | £3.75m | Nottingham Forest |
| 1995, Jan | Andy Cole | £7m | Newcastle United |
| 1998, July | Jaap Stam | £10.75m | PSV Eindhoven |
| 1998, Aug | Dwight Yorke | £12.6m | Aston Villa |
| 2001, Apr | Ruud van Nistelrooy | £19m | PSV Eindhoven |
| 2002, July | Juan Sebastian Veron | £28.1m | SS Lazio |
| 2002, July | Rio Ferdinand | £30m | Leeds United |

—— CAUGHT ON CCTV ——

Manchester United's 1–1 draw with Arsenal at Old Trafford on 3 March 1967 was the first Division One game to be televised on closed-circuit television. John Aston Jr was the United goalscorer.

—— THE FIRST EVER PENALTY SHOOT-OUT ——

United took part in the first-ever penalty shoot-out in English football. On 5 August 1970, United drew 1–1 with Hull City at Hull in the Watney Cup. The game was decided on penalties, with United progressing to the final with a 4–3 win. In the final, United were beaten 4–1 by Derby County at the Baseball Ground (scorer: Best).

## OLDEST HAT-TRICK SCORER

Teddy Sheringham's hat-trick for Manchester United against Southampton on 28 October 2000 gave him the distinction, at 34 years, 6 months and 26 days, of being the oldest player to score a hat-trick for the club.

## MAN FOR ALL STADIUMS

Billy Meredith is the only player to have played at Manchester City's Hyde Road and Maine Road grounds and at Manchester United's Bank Street and Old Trafford grounds.

## QUIXALL QUICK ON THE DRAW

On 8 August 1959 Manchester United played Bayern Munich away in a pre-season friendly. When the referee started the second half, Dennis Viollet passed the ball to Albert Quixall, who shot at goal from 48 yards and scored – only four seconds of the half had elapsed. In a far from friendly game that United won 2–1, both Quixall and Joe Carolan were sent off for United.

## ANYONE FOR TENNIS?

On 15 July 1927 the famous stage impresario of the era, C.B. Cochran, organized a tennis tournament at Old Trafford. Despite the appearance of Suzanne Lenglen, six-times Wimbledon Ladies Singles Champion, and Bill Tilden, twice Wimbledon Men's Singles Champion, the event was a financial disaster.

## PHILOSOPHY FOOTBALL

"When seagulls follow the trawler, it is because they think sardines will be thrown into the sea. Merci." Eric Cantona gives an enigmatic statement at the end of a Press conference in March 1995 after having his two-week prison sentence for common assault reduced on appeal to 120 hours community service following the "kung-fu" incident at Selhurst Park.

"My lawyer and the officials wanted me to speak. So I said that. It was nothing, it did not mean anything. I could have said: 'The curtains are pink but I love them.'" Cantona "explains" his famous sardines quote.

"I'd crawl all the way from Norwich to Manchester for the chance to play for United."                                                    *Steve Bruce*

## ‑‑‑ THE FIFTH BEATLE ‑‑‑

On 9 March 1966 George Best scored twice as Manchester United beat Benfica 5–1 in their European Cup quarter-final tie at Lisbon's Stadium of Light. When George stepped off the aircraft on the team's arrival back in Manchester, he was pictured wearing a huge sombrero-style hat. Fleet Street quickly dubbed him "El Beatle", and from that moment on he became football's first true superstar. Companies flocked to the doorstep of the "Fifth Beatle", seeking endorsement of their products, ranging from clothes to aftershave to sausages to football boots. And George did not let his superstar image down, driving to and from his three boutiques and his nightclub in a white E-type Jaguar; he even had a luxury bachelor pad built for himself that had curtains activated by sunlight, hot-air heating pumped underfloor by a large boiler, a television that disappeared into the chimney, a sunken bath, and intercom security.

## ‑‑‑ LOSING THE LOTTERY ‑‑‑

The 2005 FA Cup final, the penultimate to be played at the Millennium Stadium during Wembley"s rebuilding, between Manchester United and Arsenal made history by becoming the first ever FA Cup final to be settled in a penalty shoot-out. Despite United dominating the game, and creating the most chances, the score remained 0–0 at the end of 120 minutes play. United won the toss and elected to take the spot kicks in front of their fans. However, it was Arsenal who triumphed winning the shoot-out by a score of 5–4. This is how the shoot-out unfolded:

| 1. | Van Nistelrooy | scored | 1–0 |
|----|----------------|--------|-----|
| 2. | *Lauren* | scored | 1–1 |
| 3. | Ronaldo | scored | 2–1 |
| 4. | *Ljungberg* | scored | 2–2 |
| 5. | Scholes | missed | 2–2 |
| 6. | *Van Persie* | scored | 2–3 |
| 7. | Rooney | scored | 3–3 |
| 8. | *Cole* | scored | 3–4 |
| 9. | Keane | scored | 4–4 |
| 10. | *Vieira* | scored | 4–5 |

**1**
Edwin
*VAN DER SAR*
Holland

**2**
Gary
*NEVILLE*
England

**6**
Rio
*FERDINAND*
England

**5**
Mikael
*SILVESTRE*
France

**3**
Gabriel
*HEINZE*
Argentina

**8**
Michael
*CARRICK*
England

**4**
Nemanja
*VIDIC*
Serbia-Montenegro

**11**
Park
*JI-SUNG*
South Korea

**7**
Cristiano
*RONALDO*
Portugal

**9**
Wayne
*ROONEY*
England

**10**
Ruud
*VAN NISTELROOY*
Holland

*Substitutes*

Fabien *BARTHEZ* (France), Dwight *YORKE* (Trinidad & Tobago), Louis *SAHA* (France),
David *BECKHAM* (England), Karel *POBORSKI* (Czech Republic).

*Manager*

Steve *McClaren*

### Did You Know That?

The five substitutes are all former United players who appeared at
the 2006 World Cup finals. At the time of the tournament, however,
van Nistelrooy was still a United player and Carrick had yet to
sign.

—— FERGUSON PULLS RANK ON FA ——

Wayne Rooney's MRI scan that the English football fans were
holding their breath over took place at a BUPA hospital in
Manchester on 7 June 2006, just three days before England's
opening game against Paraguay. However, the inspection of the
fourth metatarsal bone of his right foot was carried out without a
Football Association official in the room. Manchester United did not
invite any of Sven-Goran Eriksson's medical staff, instead opting to
make their own assessment of the 20-year-old's progress before they
released the results. However, the hopes of all England fans were
lifted when the inspection showed that his bone had healed.

Wayne Rooney was born on 24 October 1985 in Liverpool. Wayne grew up in Croxteth on Merseyside supporting his boyhood heroes, Everton, and his dream came true when he made his debut for The Toffees. In October 2002, Rooney became the youngest ever goalscorer in the history of the FA Premier League when he fired a long-range effort in against Arsenal at Goodison Park. He was just 16 years and 360 days old. Rooney's instant impact on domestic football won him the 2002 BBC Sports Young Personality of the Year Award.

His performances for Everton earned Rooney international recognition when the England coach, Sven-Goran Erikkson, made him the youngest player to be capped by England when he made his international debut against Australia on 12 February 2003, aged 17 years and 11 days (since surpassed by Theo Walcott). At Euro 2004 in Portugal he burst on to the world stage, and when he scored for England he became the youngest ever player to score in the finals, although this was subsequently surpassed by Johan Vonlanthen (for Switzerland just four days after Rooney's strike).

Following intense interest from a number of top clubs in the aftermath of his outstanding displays for England at Euro 2004, Rooney joined Manchester United in a deal worth approximately £31 million (£49 million including wages). He signed on the dotted line just hours before the 2004–05 transfer window closed to become the most expensive teenage footballer ever; he was 18 at the time. On 28 September 2004, following recovery from the foot injury he sustained during Euro 2004, Rooney made his Manchester United debut in front of a packed Old Trafford crowd against Fenerbahce in a UEFA Champions League group stage game. The Manchester United faithful immediately took the young Liverpudlian to their hearts when he scored a hat-trick and laid on a goal in United's 6–2 thrashing of the Turkish side. Rooney and Ruud van Nistelrooy spearheaded the United attack in season 2004–05 and drove the team to the FA Cup final where they lost out on penalties to Arsenal in a game totally dominated by the Reds. However, In February 2006, Wayne won his first winner's medal as a professional when United took Wigan Athletic apart in the 2006 Carling Cup final at the Millennium Stadium, Cardiff. His two goals in a 4–0 win for United earned him the Man of the Match award.

Prior to the 2006 World Cup finals in Germany Wayne broke a metatarsal bone in his right foot, and over the next six weeks a heated debate ensued between United's and England's medical advisors about the speed of his recuperation. However, Wayne recovered in time to make his World Cup finals debut against Trinidad and Tobago, but his tournament ended controversially when he was sent off against Portugal in the quarter-finals. On the field Rooney and his United team-mate, Cristiano Ronaldo, appeared to square up to one another when Ronaldo waved an imaginary card in the referee's direction. However, all hard been forgiven by the time the two United men embarked on the new FA Premier League campaign for their club side.

### Did You Know That?
Rooney is the youngest England goalscorer ever. Aged 17 years and 317 days he got on the scoresheet in the game against Macedonia on 6 September 2003.

## ⸺ HARGREAVES JOINS UNITED ⸺

In August 2006, Owen Hargreaves of Bayern Munich made it clear to his German employers that he wished to move to Manchester United.[†] However, he came under attack for expressing his opinion from the Bundesliga club's Chief Executive, Uli Hoeness, who fined Hargreaves a week's wages (£18,000). It was reported that Hoeness openly criticised Hargreaves in front of his team-mates at a Bayern training session, saying: "I am incredibly disappointed in you. You are prostituting yourself for Manchester United." Hargreaves was voted the best England player at the 2006 World Cup finals in Germany. In July 2007 the deal was done and Hargreaves joined United.

## ⸺ CELEBRITY FRIENDS ⸺

Whereas former Old Trafford favourite David Beckham, and his wife Victoria, held a lavish pre-2006 World Cup party at their "Beckingham Palace" home prior to the 2006 finals, the 1966 side including Bobby Charlton and Nobby Stiles visited Hendon Town Hall for tea and sandwiches. For their pre-2006 World Cup party, the Beckhams persuaded Graham Norton to host a charity auction, celebrity chef Gordon Ramsey to prepare the food, and James Brown and Robbie Williams to provide the musical entertainment.

---

[†]*Up until the end of the 2006 World Cup finals, Owen Hargreaves was unique in being the only England international who has neither lived nor played club football in England.*

The 2008 UEFA Champions League Final, in rainy Moscow, was the first all-English contest for Europe's biggest prize. On a night of high tension, it was Manchester United who came out on top beating Chelsea 6–5 on penalties after the teams had been level at 1–1 after 45, 90 and 120 minutes. The Reds had the better of the first half, and took the lead after 26 minutes when Cristiano Ronaldo headed home his 42nd goal of the season. Frank Lampard equalised for Chelsea just before half-time and the Blues were on top after the break, with both Lampard and Didier Drogba hitting the woodwork. The drama continued in extra-time and it exploded when Drogba was sent off for striking Nemanja Vidic. United couldn't take advantage of their extra player, so it went to penalties. Petr Cech saved Ronaldo's attempt, United's first, and Chelsea would have won the Cup if skipper John Terry had not slipped and missed his effort. It went to sudden death and after Ryan Giggs – on his record-setting 759th United appearance – had converted his try, Edwin van der Sar saved from Nicolas Anelka to give United their third European Cup.

### EUROPEAN CUP FINAL
*22 May 2008, Luzhniki Stadium, Moscow*
MANCHESTER UNITED (1) *1*　　*vs*　　CHELSEA (1) *1*
Cristiano Ronaldo　　　　Lampard
*United won 6–5 on penalties after extra time*
*Att. 69,552*
*Manchester United:* Van der Sar, Brown (Anderson), Ferdinand, Vidic, Evra, Hargreaves, Scholes (Giggs), Carrick, Ronaldo, Tevez, Rooney (Nani)
*Subs:* Kuszczak, O'Shea, Fletcher, Silvestre

—— CARRICK'S OFFICIAL DEBUT ——

On 23 August 2006, Michael Carrick made his official Manchester United debut coming on as a second half substitute in the Reds' 3–0 win over Charlton Athletic at the Valley.[†] Carrick had played for United in the Amsterdam Tournament over the summer, a competition United won. It was United's second consecutive win of the 2006–07 Premiership campaign keeping them top of the table on six points with a goal difference of +7.

[†]*Michael Carrick scored his first senior goal against Charlton Athletic when he was on loan at Swindon Town from West Ham United.*

## ~~~ BECKHAM DROPPED ~~~

When Steve McClaren announced his first squad as England manager on 11 August 2006, to much surprise, he omitted David Beckham, who had resigned as England captain five weeks earlier. The former skipper had won 96 caps over the previous 10 years, but vowed to win back his place. Wayne Rooney was also excluded from McClaren's squad, following his sending off in England's previous match, the 2006 World Cup quarter-final exit against Portugal.

## ~~~ TALK OF THE DEVILS (9) ~~~

"I want to say absolutely categorically that I did not intentionally put my foot down on Carvalho."                                                *Wayne Rooney*

## ~~~ UNITED'S SOUR TASTE OF VICTORY ~~~

Manchester United won the 2006 LG Amsterdam Tournament after defeating hosts Ajax 1–0 in front of a full house at the Amsterdam ArenA on 5 August.[†] It was the first time that the Reds won the competition and Sir Alex Ferguson was pleased with United's performances. United ended the competition with 10 points – three for each victory over Porto and Ajax, plus one bonus point for each goal they scored (three against Porto and one against Ajax). However, United's success was tarnished when Wayne Rooney and Paul Scholes were both sent off in the 3–1 win over Porto. Both players received three match bans which carried over into the Premier League.

## ~~~ THE GIRL IN WAYNE'S WORLD ~~~

Coleen McLoughlin, the wife of Wayne Rooney, was born in Liverpool in 1986. Wayne first met Coleen when she was 12 years old and she was deputy head prefect of her Roman Catholic girl's school, St John Bosco. When Coleen left school she appeared in the Channel 4 TV show *Hollyoaks*. In 2005, Coleen was named the British Retail Consortium's Celebrity Shopper of 2005, and in September 2006, she became the "face" of Asda's new women's fashion collection for the autumn, securing a £3 million contract in the process. Coleen, along with many other "Wags" attended England's World Cup games in Germany 2006. Wayne and Coleen were married in Rome on 12 June 2008.

[†]*Edwin van der Sar was voted the Player of the Tournament.*

Manchester United met FA Premier League newcomers, Wigan Athletic, in the 2006 Carling Cup final. It was United's sixth appearance in the Final following defeats to Liverpool (1983), Sheffield Wednesday (1991), Aston Villa (1994) and Liverpool (2003) and their victory over Nottingham Forest in the 1992 Final. In contrast their Lancashire neighbours were making their first appearance in a major final. En route to the final United disposed of Barnet, West Bromwich Albion, Birmingham City and Blackburn Rovers. The final turned out to be one of the most one-sided FA Cup finals since United defeated Brighton and Hove Albion 4–0 at Wembley Stadium in 1983. United's 4–0 win over the Latics was the biggest margin of victory in the final in the history of the competition. Not surprisingly, Wayne Rooney, the scorer of two goals, was named the Man of the Match.

### CARLING CUP FINAL
*26 February 2006, Millennium Stadium, Cardiff*
MANCHESTER UNITED (1) *4*    *vs*    WIGAN ATHLETIC (0) *0*
Rooney (2), Saha, Ronaldo

*Att. 66,866*
*Manchester United:* Van der Sar, Neville, Brown (Vidic), Ferdinand, Silvestre (Evra), Ronaldo (Richardson), O'Shea, Giggs, Park, Saha, Rooney.
*Subs (not used):* Howard, van Nistelrooy.

—ᴡᴡ— BRITAIN'S MOST WATCHED FOOTBALLER —ᴡᴡ—

Sir Bobby Charlton may have been watched by more people than any other British footballer ever. In his 757-match Manchester United first-team career the combined atendance was 33,293,159; with England, 7,322,287 spectators were at his 106 matches, while his brief spell at Preston North End attracted 477,612. Excluding the FA Charity Shield, Football League representative games, plus those for England schools, youth and Under-23s, 41,093,058 fans were at matches where Sir Bobby appeared. Ryan Giggs, however, is closing fast.

—ᴡᴡ— TALK OF THE DEVILS (10) —ᴡᴡ—

"I am not a referee and I don't have the power to send off a player."
*Cristiano Ronaldo*

## A FITTING TRIBUTE

Manchester United's 2008 UEFA Champions League victory came in the same year the club marked the 50th anniversary of the Munich Air Disaster and the 40th anniversary of the Reds' first European Cup win.

## FIGHTING SPIRIT

Dave Sexton managed Manchester United from 1977 to 1981, some years after his playing career had ended.[†] Sexton started out as a professional footballer with West Ham United in 1948 where he was a useful inside-forward, and then enjoyed spells at Luton Town, Leyton Orient, Brighton & Hove Albion and Crystal Palace. In season 1957-58, he won the Division Three South Championship with Brighton & Hove Albion.

## UNITED'S GREATEST EVER GOAL

In a poll conducted among Manchester United fans to find out United's best ever goal there was only going to be one clear winner, Ryan Giggs. The goal in question was scored in the FA Cup semi-final replay 2–1 win after extra time against Arsenal, when Giggs picked up Vieira's pass and beat four Gooners, Lee Dixon twice, to rifle the ball high into the Arsenal goal beyond a despairing David Seaman. Giggsy's celebration is still talked about by United fans as he removed his shirt and ran down the touchline at Villa Park waving it in the air as the United faithful went completely berserk in the stands.

## BUCCANEER AT THE HELM

Malcolm Irving Glazer was born in Rochester, New York, USA in 1928. He is a businessman who is the President and Chief Executive Officer of First Allied Corporation, a holding company for many of his various business interests including ownership of Manchester United and the Tampa Bay Buccaneers, an American Football team. Malcolm Glazer's takeover of United in 2005 cost £790 million with a huge slice of this amount funded from borrowing. His takeover of United was fiercely opposed by many Manchester United fans who formed Shareholders United and a football team named FC United.

[†]*Dave Sexton is the son of the former professional boxer, Archie Sexton*

## A DEVIL NOW IN HEAVEN

George Best died on 25 November 2005 following a long battle against liver disease. On 3 December 2005, Belfast and Manchester came to a standstill when George's funeral took place. Tens of thousands of mourners lined the streets from his home in the Cregagh estate of East Belfast to Stormont Castle to show their appreciation of his genius on the football pitch. Bestie's one final wish was that he hoped the people would remember him for his football. His countrymen did not disappoint him on that overcast day as fans from all walks of life said a tearful farewell to a legend. All along the funeral route fans threw flowers and scarves at the cortege as it made its way to Stormont for George's funeral service. One man in the crowd stood still, silent in his respect holding aloft a banner which summed George Best up as a footballer: "Maradona good, Pele better, George Best". At the funeral service, hosted solemnly by Eamonn Holmes, Brian Kennedy and Peter Corry sang songs in tribute to George whilst sporting stars, including Sir Alex Ferguson and the Manchester United team, attended the service. On 22 May 2006, the George Best Carryduff Manchester United Supporters Club held a gala dinner in Belfast City Hall to raise monies in aid of The George Best Foundation on the day George would have celebrated his 60th birthday. The gala dinner was hosted by the Lord Mayor of Belfast and was attended by Sir Alex Ferguson, David Gill and Paddy Crerand as well as a host of other sporting stars, friends of family of the "Genius".

## CROWD PLEASERS

United kicked off the 2006–07 FA Premier League campaign with a scintillating 5–1 win over Fulham at Old Trafford on 20 August 2006. Following the construction of two additional sections of the stadium named The Quadrants, a new record FA Premier League crowd of 75,115 fans attended the game.

## ALEX IS GOD

At the end of the 2005–06 season United's shirt sponsorship deal with Vodafone came to an end and the Reds quickly moved to sign a contract with American Insurance Group (AIG). AIG is the largest underwriters of commercial and industrial insurance in the USA. United fans were quick off the mark themselves claiming that AIG actually stood for "Alex Is God".

## THE MOST EFFECTUAL TOP CAT

On 28 August 2006, Roy Keane, who retired from playing professional football on 12 June 2006, became the new manager of Sunderland when he signed a three-year deal following their 2–0 win over West Bromwich Albion, managed by United legend Bryan Robson, at the Stadium of Light. Keane shook hands with the Black Cats' chairman Niall Quinn, a former Republic of International team-mate with whom he had a disagreement at the Irish squad's training camp in Saipan prior to the 2002 World Cup finals in Japan and South Korea. Keano was sent home by manager Mick McCarthy, who later became the manager of Sunderland himself, following criticism by United's fiery captain of the facilities laid on for the Irish squad. After Keano's shock departure he stated how unhappy he was about Niall Quinn and Steve Staunton siding with McCarthy and not him. Keane speaking about Quinn said: "And Niall Quinn? Who is he? Mother Theresa?" In Keane's first game in charge of Sunderland he led them to a 2–1 victory at Derby County on 9 September 2006.[†]

## WHEN IRISH EYES ARE SMILING

Manchester United's Liam Miller scored for the Republic of Ireland in their 3–0 win over Sweden at Lansdowne Road on 1 March 2006 in what was Steve Staunton's first game in charge of the Irish national team.

## THE IMPOSSIBLE DREAM

In September 2006, Sir Alex Ferguson decided Old Trafford needed an anthem and so he commissioned one on behalf of the fans. Sir Alex wanted to recreate the atmosphere at arch-rivals Liverpool where the crowd raises the roof at Anfield with their anthem "You'll Never Walk Alone". Vince Miller, a friend of Sir Alex, was asked to record the 1972 Andy Williams classic "The Impossible Dream". The song was used in early 2006 in Honda's "Power of Dreams" TV ads.

## RED LIONS SEE RED MIST

Only three England players have been sent off in World Cup Finals games and they are all United players; Ray Wilkins (Mexico 1986), David Beckham (France 1998) and Wayne Rooney (Germany 2006).

[†]*Keane's first signing for Sunderland was his former Manchester United team-mate, Dwight Yorke.*

## ⚬⚬⚬ QUIDS IN FOR BESTIE SHIRT ⚬⚬⚬

The Manchester United shirt worn by George Best when he scored six goals against Northampton Town in an FA Cup fifth round tie on 7 February 1970 was sold for £24,000 at a Christie's auction on 13 September 2006. The Northampton goalkeeper in that game, Kim Book, said, "Not even the Berlin Wall could have stopped Best that day." United won the game 8–2 in what was George's first game back for the Reds following a six-week suspension.

## ⚬⚬⚬ FOOTBALLERS' WIVES AND GIRLFRIENDS ⚬⚬⚬

During the 2006 World Cup finals a number of the England players' wives and girlfriends (dubbed "Wags" by the media), including Wayne Rooney's girlfriend Coleen McLoughlin, spent a reported £4,000 in one hour on sunglasses and handbags. In contrast, in 1966 Tina Moore, wife of the legendary England captain, Bobby Moore, took the England players' wives to see "The Black & White Minstrel Show".

## ⚬⚬⚬ BECKHAM PASSES ROBSON ⚬⚬⚬

David Beckham won his 90th cap for England in their 1–0 win over Paraguay at the 2006 World Cup finals. This tied for fifth place on the all-time England international appearances list with his former Manchester United hero, Bryan Robson. Against France in Paris on 26 March 2008, Beckham became the fifth England player to win 100 caps.

## ⚬⚬⚬ REUNION FOR CLASS OF '66 ⚬⚬⚬

The surviving members of England's 1966 World Cup winning team were present at the opening ceremony in the Allianz Arena, Munich for the 2006 World Cup finals.[†] Bobby Charlton, Nobby Stiles et al were among a parade of 158 champions from the seven countries that have won the World Cup to form the largest group of international football stars ever gathered. England had the privilege of leading out the parade on the basis that they had only won the competition once, whilst 55 Brazilian legends came out last. Pele and the model, Claudia Schiffer, carried the World Cup trophy into the stadium.

---

[†]*Although the Allianz Arena looks like a huge Good Year tyre, it is commonly referred to by the nickname Schlauchboot (inflatable boat).*

## ⚉⚉ SPARKY THE KING ⚉⚉

Of all the FA Premier League managers at the start of the 2007–08 season, Mark Hughes – along with Newcastle's Sam Allardyce – spent more years as a professional footballer than any of their peers. Sparky played for 21 years between 1980 and 2001 (Allardyce 1971–92). Sir Alex Ferguson played for 17 years (1957–74), while Chelsea's Jose Mourinho never played a single season of professional football.

## ⚉⚉ POLE BETWEEN POLES ⚉⚉

United signed the West Bromwich Albion and Polish international goalkeeper Tomasz Kuszczak[†] on 10 August 2006 in a deal which included two United players moving in the opposite direction, England Under-18 goalkeeper Luke Steele and defender Paul McShane. The deal for Kuszcak meant that he went to Old Trafford on loan for the 2006–07 season, and then would join the Reds permanently in July 2007.

## ⚉⚉ McCLAREN'S REDS ⚉⚉

When Steve McClaren announced his first squad as England manager he named four United players in it for the game against Greece at Old Trafford on 16 August 2006: Wes Brown, Rio Ferdinand, Gary Neville and Kieran Richardson. Michael Carrick was injured, whilst former Red, Phil Neville, was an unused substitute in England's 4–0 victory.

## ⚉⚉ GIGGS WILL TEAR YOU APART AGAIN ⚉⚉

The inaugural FA Premier League season was in 1992–93, and when Ryan Giggs netted in United's 4–1 win at Aston Villa on 20 October 2007 he joined Bolton Wanderers' Gary Speed as the only players to score in every Premier League campaign.[††] Speed, who scored against Reading on 25 August 2007, left Bolton at the end of 2007 to join Sheffield United, so if the Welsh wizard scores for the Reds in 2008–09, he will stand alone in scoring in every Premier League season.

[†]*On 30 May 2006, during a 2006 World Cup warm-up match between Poland and Colombia, Kuszczak conceded a goal directly from a long punt by the opposing goalkeeper, Luis Enrique Martinez.*

[††]*United fans regularly sing "Giggs Will Tear You Apart Again" to the tune of the Joy Division song "Love Will Tear Us Apart Again".*

## ⟶ ROY KEANE ⟶

Roy Maurice Keane was born in Cork, Republic of Ireland, on 10 August 1971 and began his football career at Rockmount FC in Cork. "Fail to prepare, prepare to fail" is a line from Roy's autobiography simply entitled *Keane,* and this just about summed up his playing career. Roy was a warrior on the pitch as he took the battle to the opposition, leading from the front. He was outspoken, aggressive, often controversially so, powerful and never shirked a tackle, a true midfield general who was the driving force of Manchester United's midfield for 12 years from 1993 to 2005.

Few players can say that they played for two managerial legends, but Keano can. In 1989, Roy signed as a semi-professional with Cobh Ramblers, before joining Brian Clough's Nottingham Forest for £20,000. At the end of the 1992–93 season Forest were relegated and Keano signed for the inaugural FA Premier League winners, Manchester United. Despite overtures from a number of clubs Keano joined Alex Ferguson's emerging force in British football for a record transfer fee of £3.75 million. In his first season at United, Keano won the Double, a feat that the team repeated in season 1995–96. After clinching their fourth Premiership crown in five seasons in 1996–97 Keano was appointed the captain of Manchester United, following the shock retirement of Eric Cantona. However, he missed much of the next season with a cruciate ligament injury, following a poorly timed tackle on Alf Inge Haaland of Leeds United. However, United's inspirational captain returned for the 1998–99 season and helped guide the side to the unprecedented Treble, which included a superhuman performance against Juventus in the UEFA Champions League semi-final. Keano was suspended for United's dramatic 2–1 win over Bayern Munich in the final. In 2000 he was recognised by his fellow professionals, winning the PFA Players' Player of the Year Award.

Keane captained United to nine major honours, making him the club's most successful captain, but also was sent off 11 times in his Old Trafford career. At full international level, Keano played for Ireland 66 times, although his international career may be best remembered for his spat with national coach Mick McCarthy before the 2002 World Cup finals in Japan and South Korea.

In the 2005, Keano set a new record by appearing in his seventh FA Cup final (one with Forest). At United Keano won seven FA Premier League titles, four FA Cups, the European Cup and the Intercontinental Cup. In November 2005 Keano left United and, a month later, fulfilled a boyhood dream by joining Glasgow Celtic, but retired after the 2005–06 season. He was named Sunderland manager in August 2006.

## ENGLAND GAMES AT OLD TRAFFORD

| Date | Result |
|------|--------|
| 17 April 1926 | England 0, Scotland 1 |
| 16 November 1938 | England 7, Northern Ireland 0 |
| 24 May 1997 | England 2, South Africa 1 |
| 6 October 2001 | England 2, Greece 2 |
| 10 October 2001 | England 1, Sweden 1 |
| 10 September 2003 | England 2, Liechtenstein 0 |
| 16 November 2003 | England 2, Denmark 3 |
| 9 October 2004 | England 2, Wales 0 |
| 26 March 2005 | England 4, Northern Ireland 0 |
| 8 October 2005 | England 1, Austria 0 |
| 12 October 2005 | England 2, Poland 1 |
| 30 May 2006 | England 3, Hungary 1 |
| 3 June 2006 | England 6, Jamaica 0 |
| 16 August 2006 | England 4, Greece 0 |
| 2 September 2006 | England 5, Andorra 0 |
| 7 October 2006 | England 0, FYR Macedonia 0 |
| 7 February 2007 | England 0, Spain 1 |

## LOCAL HEROES

United complied with UEFA's rule that all teams in the 2006–07 Champions League had to have at least four "locally trained players" by naming Kieran Richardson, Gary Neville Wes Brown and Ryan Giggs.

## ROCKY IV LOOK-A-LIKE

On 5 January 2006, United signed the Serbia-Montenegro international defender Nemanja Vidic for £7 million from Spartak Moscow. Vidic began his professional career on loan at Spartak Moscow, before returning to Red Star Belgrade, and then signed permanently for Spartak in July 2004, costing the Russian side 6 million euros. Spartak fans compared Vidic to Dolph Lundgren who played the Russian boxer, Ivan Drago, in the movie *Rocky IV*.

## A HISTORIC LION

Former United hero David Beckham's winning strike against Ecuador in Stuttgart on 25 June 2006 put him in the history books by becoming the only England player to have scored in three different World Cup finals (1998, 2002 and 2006).

## ～ THE G-FORCE ～

Football's G-14, comprising European 14 clubs, was founded in 2000 and disbanded on 15 February 2008 with 18 European clubs as members. Many people considered the group's sole aim was to create a European Super League. However, the G-14 always maintained that it was a pressure group acting in the best interests of the clubs. On 29 May 2007, UEFA President Michel Platini called upon G-14 to disband at an extraordinary congress held in Zurich, declaring it was "elitist" and club grievances could be aired through a new UEFA body, the Professional Football Strategy Council (PFSC).

The 14 founder members were:

| | |
|---|---|
| Ajax | Real Madrid |
| Barcelona | Manchester United |
| Borussia Dortmund | Marseille |
| PSV Eindhoven | Milan |
| Internazionale (Milan) | Bayern Munich |
| Juventus | Paris St-Germain |
| Liverpool | Porto |

Four more clubs joined in 2002, making a total of 18, although the group remained the G-14. The four newcomers were Arsenal, Lyon, Bayer Leverkusen and Valencia.

## ～ HARRY'S GAME ～

When Portsmouth beat Manchester United 1-0 at Old Trafford in the FA Cup quarter-final on 8 March 2008, it was the third time United had been knocked out of the competition by a team managed by Harry Redknapp. On 7 January 1984 Harry's AFC Bournemouth, in what was then the Third Division knocked out First Division United – the FA Cup holders – in the third round, 2-0, at Dean Court. On 28 January 2001, then West Ham United's boss, Redknapp beat the Reds 1–0 at Old Trafford in the fourth round.

## ～ TWO FORMER REDS REACH PROMISED LAND ～

When Crystal Palace beat Derby County 2–0 at Selhurst Park on 29 April 2007 it meant that Steve Bruce's Birmingham City and Roy Keane's Sunderland claimed automatic promotion places to the FA Premier League. Bruce and Keane were United team-mates 1993–96.

The 2006–07 Premier League season came down to a two-horse race for the title between Chelsea and Manchester United, with Arsenal and Liverpool fighting it out for third and fourth places. Beneath the top four places there were the usual scraps for UEFA Cup places and to avoid relegation. The latter battle involved two of the three promoted clubs, Sheffield United and Watford, plus West Ham United, Fulham, Wigan Athletic and Charlton Athletic. In the end, Charlton and the two promoted teams were the ones to go down. The surprise package of the season came in the shape of Steve Coppell's Reading, whose first season in the top flight ended with them finishing a highly respectable eighth, one place outside of a European berth. In the end it was United's consistency – they won 4 games more than Chelsea – harnessed to the dazzling displays of Cristiano Ronaldo that won United their first title in four seasons and their ninth FA Premier League crown. Chelsea finished six points behind United to claim the second automatic UEFA Champions League spot. Liverpool pipped Arsenal for third place.

### *Premiership* 2006–2007

| | | P | W | D | L | F | A | W | D | L | F | A | Pts |
|---|---|---|---|---|---|---|---|---|---|---|---|---|---|
| 1. | MANCHESTER UNITED | 38 | 15 | 2 | 2 | 46 | 12 | 13 | 3 | 3 | 37 | 15 | 89 |
| 2. | Chelsea | 38 | 12 | 7 | 0 | 37 | 11 | 12 | 4 | 3 | 27 | 13 | 83 |
| 3. | Liverpool | 38 | 14 | 4 | 1 | 39 | 7 | 6 | 4 | 9 | 18 | 20 | 68 |
| 4. | Arsenal | 38 | 12 | 6 | 1 | 43 | 16 | 7 | 5 | 7 | 20 | 19 | 68 |
| 5. | Tottenham Hotspur | 38 | 12 | 3 | 4 | 34 | 22 | 5 | 6 | 8 | 23 | 32 | 60 |
| 6. | Everton | 38 | 11 | 4 | 4 | 33 | 17 | 4 | 9 | 6 | 19 | 19 | 58 |
| 7. | Bolton Wanderers | 38 | 9 | 5 | 5 | 26 | 20 | 7 | 3 | 9 | 21 | 32 | 56 |
| 8. | Reading | 38 | 11 | 2 | 6 | 29 | 20 | 5 | 5 | 9 | 23 | 27 | 55 |
| 9. | Portsmouth | 38 | 11 | 5 | 3 | 28 | 15 | 3 | 7 | 9 | 17 | 27 | 54 |
| 10. | Blackburn Rovers | 38 | 9 | 3 | 7 | 31 | 25 | 6 | 4 | 9 | 21 | 29 | 52 |
| 11. | Aston Villa | 38 | 7 | 8 | 4 | 20 | 14 | 4 | 9 | 6 | 23 | 27 | 50 |
| 12. | Middlesbrough | 38 | 10 | 3 | 6 | 31 | 24 | 2 | 7 | 10 | 13 | 25 | 46 |
| 13. | Newcastle United | 38 | 7 | 7 | 5 | 23 | 20 | 4 | 3 | 12 | 15 | 27 | 43 |
| 14. | Manchester City | 38 | 5 | 6 | 8 | 10 | 16 | 6 | 3 | 10 | 19 | 28 - | 42 |
| 15. | West Ham United | 38 | 8 | 2 | 9 | 24 | 26 | 4 | 3 | 12 | 11 | 33 | -41 |
| 16. | Fulham | 38 | 7 | 7 | 5 | 18 | 18 | 1 | 8 | 10 | 20 | 42 | 39 |
| 17. | Wigan Athletic | 38 | 5 | 4 | 10 | 18 | 30 | 5 | 4 | 10 | 19 | 29 | 38 |
| 18. | Sheffield United | 38 | 7 | 6 | 6 | 24 | 21 | 3 | 2 | 14 | 8 | 34 | 38 |
| 19. | Charlton Athletic | 38 | 7 | 5 | 7 | 19 | 20 | 1 | 5 | 13 | 15 | 40 | 34 |
| 20. | Watford | 38 | 3 | 9 | 7 | 19 | 25 | 2 | 4 | 13 | 10 | 34 | 28 |

## —— WHEN THE CITY WELL WENT DRY ——

When Manchester United beat Manchester City 1–0 at Eastlands on 5 May 2007, they ensured City had set a new record for the fewest goals scored at home in a season by a club in the England's top division, a mere 10. City had not scored at home since New Year's Day.

## —— UNITED'S TROPHY SWEEP ——

In addition to Manchester United claiming their ninth FA Premier League title in May 2007, The Reds pretty much swept the board when it came to other awards. Cristiano Ronaldo claimed half a dozen awards: PFA Players' Player, PFA Young Player, Fans' Player of the Year, Barclays Premiership Player of the Season, Football Writers' Association Player of the Year and a place in the FA Premier League Team of the Year – United players filled eight of the 11 positions in this fantasy team. Ryan Giggs was presented with the Barclays Premiership Merit Award, in recognition of his record of nine Premier League titles and last, but certainly not least, Sir Alex Ferguson, the man who guided United to all nine of their Premiership crowns since 1993, was presented with the Barclays Manager of the Season award.

### *Did You Know That?*
Cristiano Ronaldo became the first player to win both the PFA Young Player of the Year and Players' Players of the Year awards in 30 years. Andy Gray, then with Aston Villa, collected both awards in 1977.

## —— PULLING IN THE CROWDS ——

A mammoth 1,440,694 fans watched Manchester United's home Premier League matches in 2006–07, the highest ever cumulative total for a single season in the club's 129-year history. The average attendance at the 19 League matches was 75,826 – a British record.

## —— SIR ALEX'S FA CUP CENTURY ——

Manchester United's 4-0 demolition of Arsenal at Old Trafford in the fifth round of the FA Cup on 16 February 2008 was Sir Alex Ferguson's 100th FA Cup game in charge of the club. Goals from Wayne Rooney, Darren Fletcher, 2, and Nani gave Sir Alex his 68th FA Cup victory. The tie was also the 12th meeting between these two rivals in the competition. United have a narrow edge over the Gunners with six wins, five losses and a draw (the memorable 1999 semi-final).

## IRISH REDS PAY TRIBUTE TO A GENIUS

On 22 May 2006, The George Best Carryduff Manchester United Supporters Club held a gala dinner in Belfast City Hall to raise monies in aid of The George Best Foundation. It was the date on which Bestie would have celebrated his 60th birthday, the United legend having passed away on 25 November 2005 after a long battle against liver disease. The dinner was organised by John White and John Dempsey and hosted by the Lord Mayor of Belfast and was attended by Sir Alex Ferguson, David Gill and a former team-mate of the United legend, Paddy Crerand.

## UNITED CATCH AND PASS AN OLD LADY

When Manchester United defeated Olympique Lyonnais 1–0 in the UEFA Champions League at Old Trafford on 4 March 2008, it booked their place in the last 16 of the competition. Cristiano Ronaldo's 30th goal of the season meant that United had equalled Juventus's Champions League record of 10 consecutive home victories set in 1997. By May 2008, United had stretched the record to 12 games, as follows:

| Date | United | Score | Opponents |
| --- | --- | --- | --- |
| 13 September 2006 | United | 3–2 | Glasgow Celtic |
| 17 October 2006 | United | 3–0 | FC Copenhagen |
| 6 December 2006 | United | 3–1 | Benfica |
| 7 March 2007 | United | 1–0 | OSC Lille |
| 10 April 2007 | United | 7–1 | AS Roma |
| 24 April 2007 | United | 3–2 | AC Milan |
| 2 October 2007 | United | 1–0 | AS Roma |
| 7 November 2007 | United | 4–0 | Dynamo Kiev |
| 27 November 2007 | United | 2–1 | Sporting Lisbon |
| 4 March 2008 | United | 1–0 | Olympique Lyonnais |
| 9 April 2008 | United | 1–0 | AS Roma |
| 29 April 2008 | United | 1–0 | Barcelona |

## TALK OF THE DEVILS (11)

"You can't feel the passion and see what you want to see and be involved in what you want to be involved in from afar. Yes, we're from the USA, but we intend to be here very often. We intend to be at the matches. That's why we're involved, to be a part of it, to be associated with it. Just to be part of that, to see it in front of you, to experience it. There's nothing else in the world that can make you feel like that."

*Joel Glazer, after his father Malcolm took overall control of United in 2005*

## THE ELITE FA CUP WINNERS' CLUB

When Manchester United defeated Millwall to lift the FA Cup at Cardiff's Millennium Stadium in 2004, skipper Roy Keane and Ryan Giggs joined an elite group of players to have won four FA Cup-winners' medals. They both won in 1994, 1996, 1999 and 2004. Former United legend Mark Hughes and David Seaman are the only others to have achieved this. Hughes won three at United (1985, 1990 and 1994) and one with Chelsea (in 1997). He is also the only player to have won all of his at Wembley Stadium, while Seaman won his four with Arsenal – in 1993, 1998, 2002 and 2003.

However, for all of their honours, none of them can match the record of the Honourable Arthur Kinnaird, later President of The Football Association. He appeared in nine FA Cup finals in the 1870s and '80s, playing first for Wanderers and then Old Etonians, and he was part of the winning team on a record five occasions. He also scored in both the 1873 and 1878 Finals.

## RED DEVIL TURNED BLACK CAT

Manchester United's on-loan defender, Jonny Evans was named Young Player of the Year when Sunderland held its annual Player of the Year Awards night at the Stadium of Light on 1 May 2007. A Northern Ireland international, Evans played for United in friendlies in 2006, and also in that year's Amsterdam tournament, but he has yet to appear in a competitive match for the Reds.

## HAPPY HALF CENTURY

When Manchester United travelled to play Newcastle United at St James's Park on 1 January 2007, it was their 50th match played on New Year's Day. The game ended in a 2–2, Paul Scholes scoring both of United's goals.

## SUPER SWEDE QUICK OFF THE MARK

Swedish legend Henrik Larsson came to Old Trafford on a three-month loan spell from his home club Helsingborg and made a scoring debut for United in a 2–1 FA Cup third round win over Aston Villa at Old Trafford on 7 January 2007. At Scottish giants Celtic, he had won just about every domestic medal and with Barcelona he won a UEFA Champions League winner's medal. Helsingborg offered to extend his loan deal at United until the end of the season, but Larsson declined it.

## ⸺ RYAN GIGGS, OBE ⸺

Ryan Joseph Wilson was born on 29 November 1973 in Cardiff, Wales. To say that he has had a magnificent career with Manchester United is a gross understatement; not only has he won more medals with Manchester United than any other in the club's history but also his medal haul – comprising ten Premier League winners' medals, four FA Cup winners' medals, two UEFA Champions League winners' medal, a World Club Championship winners' medal, a European Super Cup winners' medal and two League Cup winners' medals – makes him the most deorated British footballer ever. When he played in the 2008 UEFA Champions League Final, he passed Sir Bobby Charlton's United appearance record with 759.

Ryan joined United in 1990, signing professional forms later that year. In 1991 he adopted his mother's maiden name and became Ryan Giggs. He made his League debut in March 1991 against Everton at Old Trafford and two months later scored the only goal in a derby win over Manchester City. In October 1991, aged 17 years and 321 days, Ryan played for Wales against Germany, becoming Wales's youngest-ever full international. A month later he won his first medal as United beat Red Star Belgrade to take the European Super Cup. His first domestic medal arrived in March 1992, after United beat Nottingham Forest in the League Cup final, and he finished the season earning the PFA Young Player of the Year Award.

In 1992–93 Ryan won his first Premier League winners' medal and he became the first player to be named PFA Young Player of the Year twice. In 1993–94 and 1995–96 Ryan was part of United's Double-winning squads. A fourth Premiership medal in 1997 was the prelude to the unforgettable 1998–99 campaign. Ryan played a significant part in United's unprecedented, and unequalled, Treble of Premiership, FA Cup and UEFA Champions League. On the way, Ryan scored what has since been voted the greatest ever goal in the history of the FA Cup in United's 2–1 FA Cup semi-final replay win over Arsenal. In November 1999 he won the World Club Championship against Palmeiras of Brazil in Tokyo. Two more Premiership titles followed in 2000 and 2001.

On 23 August 2002 he scored his 100th goal for United in a 2–2 draw at Chelsea. The following May, Ryan his eighth Championship winners' medal. A year later, he won his fourth FA Cup winners' meal in his native Cardiff after Millwall had been beaten. On 2 June 2007, shortly after collecting his ninth Premiership winners' medal Ryan won his 64th and final cap for Wales. Just like George Best, he did not play on the world stage as Wales never qualified for a major championship.

### Did You Know That?
In season 2006–07 Ryan made his 700th appearance for United.

*Substitutes*
Edwin *VAN DER SAR*, Steve *BRUCE*, David *BECKHAM*,
Cristiano *RONALDO*, Ruud *VAN NISTELROOY*
*Manager*
Sir Alex *FERGUSON, CBE*

### *Did You Know That?*
When France failed to qualify for the 1994 World Cup finals, Cantona and David Ginola were made the scapegoats by the French FA, and neither were ever picked again. At both Euro 2004 and the 2006 World Cup, Eric supported England and not France.

—— LEADING THE LEAGUES ——

During his career, Dutch international striker Ruud van Nistelrooy has been the leading goal scorer in three different European leagues. He also collected League championship winners' medals with these three clubs, but Ruud has not won a medal in European competition, either at club or international level.

| Country | Club | League | Season/s |
|---|---|---|---|
| **Holland:** | PSV Eindhoven | Eredivisie | 1998–99/1999–2000 |
| **England:** | Manchester United | Premiership | 2002–03 |
| **Spain:** | Real Madrid | La Liga | 2006–07/2007–08 |

## BLUES' SPOT OF BOTHER IN COMMUITY SHIELD

The 99th FA Community Shield (previously the FA Charity Shield), played at Wembley on 5 August 2007, was won by Manchester United thanks to a marvellous hat-trick of saves in the penalty shootout by Edwin van der Sar after the match had finished 1–1. Ryan Giggs, making his tenth appearance in the prestige season's curtain-raiser, opened the scoring in the 35th minute but Chelsea's new French striker Florent Malouda levelled matters on the stroke of half-time. Van der Sar took over in the penalty shoot-out, which went as follows:

| Chelsea Player | Result | United player | Result | Score |
|---|---|---|---|---|
| Claudio Pizarro | Save | Rio Ferdinand | Goal | 0–1 |
| Frank Lampard | Save | Michael Carrick | Goal | 0–2 |
| Shaun Wright-Phillips | Save | Wayne Rooney | Goal | 0–3 |

## MUNICH ANNIVERSARY PERFECTLY OBSERVED

Manchester United played Manchester City on 10 February 2008, just four days after the 50th anniversary of the Munich Air Disaster. There had been a variety of events commemorating that fateful day in 1958, but fears of City fans disrespecting the minute's silence before the kick-off proved to be totally unfounded as the tribute was marked with complete silence around Old Trafford. The FA Premier League gave both teams permission to wear a special kit for this fixture, without any sponsors' logo or markings and the players' shirts were numbered 1 to 11. Only the the match itself didn't go as United had planned: City ran out 2–1 winners.

## A KNIGHT FOR ALL SEASONS

Sir Alex Ferguson, CBE collected the 2006–07 PFA Merit Award. He took charge of Manchester United in November 1986 and won his ninth championship in 2007. It was the 19th major trophy Sir Alex – who was also named the Barclays Manager of the Season for 2006–07 – had won in his 20 full seasons in England.

## UNITED'S LAME DEFENCE OF THEIR TROPHY

On 7 November 2006 Southend United caused one of the biggest upsets in the history of the League Cup when the Championship strugglers knocked out Manchester United, the Carling Cup holders, in the fourth round with a shock 1–0 win at Roots Hall.

Including the 2007 edition, Manchester United have played in 24 of the 99 FA Charity/Community Shields, winning 16, sharing four and losing only four. Ryan Giggs, meanwhile, won his sixth winners' medal in 2007 to equal Ray Clemence's record (five with Liverpool and one with Tottenham Hotspur).

***Did You Know That?***
United drew 1–1 with Chelsea in the 1997 Charity Shield at the "old" Wembley Stadium, but won 4–2 in the penalty shootout.

~~~ THE UNITED–LIVERPOOL RIVALRY ~~~

Manchester City are, of course, Manchester United's biggest rivals, attracting fans from the same city. However, in terms of competitive rivalry, there is nothing to match the one between United and Liverpool. No player has moved directly from United to Liverpool since Phil Chisnall left Old Trafford for Anfield in 1964. Indeed, in 2007 United refused Gabriel Heinze permission to join Liverpool, the defender moving to Real Madrid instead. The last player to play for both clubs was Paul Ince, who spent two years in Italy between his departure from Manchester in 1995 and his arrival on Merseyside in 2007. On the field, the clubs have met 175 times in all competitions – up to the end of 2007–08 – with United holding a narrow advantage in the results column. This is United's record:

| Competition | Played | Wins | Draws | Defeats |
|---|---|---|---|---|
| League | 150 | 58 | 43 | 49 |
| FA Cup | 15 | 8 | 4 | 3 |
| League Cup | 4 | 1 | 0 | 3 |
| Other | 6 | 1 | 3 | 2 |
| Total | 175 | 68 | 50 | 57 |

~~~ BLUES STOPPED IN THEIR TRACKS ~~~

Manchester United, the only team ever to win the Premier League title three seasons in a row – and the first to win the top division title three consecutive years since Liverpool in the 1980s – ended Chelsea's dreams of emulating Sir Alex Ferguson's squads of 1999–2001. Chelsea went into the 2006–07 season as the reigning Premier League Champions, but it was United who claimed their ninth title, six points clear of the Blues.

## —ᴠᴠ— BELFAST BOY ON THE MONEY —ᴠᴠ—

On 27 November 2006, the Ulster Bank immortalized former Manchester United and Northern Ireland soccer legend George Best with a commemorative £5 banknote. The bank issued the limited edition – there were one million of them – run of notes to commemorate the first anniversary of the death of the man voted the greatest ever Manchester United player by United fans. It depicts the Belfast Boy in both his Manchester United and Northern Ireland colours. George's father, Dickie Best, was presented with banknote number 1,000,000.

## —ᴠᴠ— UNITED MAUL ITALIAN WOLVES —ᴠᴠ—

When AS Roma entered Old Trafford on 10 April 2007 holding a 2–1 lead after the first leg of their UEFA Champions League quarter-final tie, they had a confidence based on history. United had not overturned a first-leg deficit since a 1983–84 Cup-Winners Cup victory over Barcelona. the 23-year drought was ended in spectacular fashion as United produced an awesome display of breathtaking attacking football to run out 7–1 winners on the night (8–3 on aggregate). Cristiano Ronaldo., making his 27th appearance for United in Europe, scored his first two goals, and he was joined on the scoresheet by Michael Carrick (two), Alan Smith, Wayne Rooney and Patrice Evra.

## —ᴠᴠ— UNITED'S VILLA PARK FORTRESS —ᴠᴠ—

Manchester United beat Watford 4–1 in the 2007 FA Cup semi-final at Villa Park, with goals from Wayne Rooney, two, Kieran Richardson and Cristiano Ronaldo. Villa Park is a favourite venue for United: since losing on the opening day of the 1995–96 season they have recorded 15 wins and three draws in 18 visits. In FA Cup semi-finals the Reds' record is almost as good with seven wins and four draws from 11 matches. It was, of course, the venue for Ryan Giggs' wonder-goal in the 1999 FA Cup semi-final against Arsenal.

## —ᴠᴠ— TALK OF THE DEVILS (12) —ᴠᴠ—

"I will never be surprised what Sir Alex Ferguson can do because I know what he is like as a person and as a manager. Whoever writes him off he always proves them wrong – and he has done it again."

*David Beckham, reflecting on United 2007 Premier League championship*

## SIR ALEX GIVES SPARKY A EUROPEAN GIFT

Former Old Trafford favourite Mark Hughes received a gift from Manchester United at the end of the 2005–06 season. United had qualified for the UEFA Cup, courtesy of winning the Carling Cup. But because they finished in the top two of the FA Premier League, United went into the UEFA Champions League, which opened up an extra spot for an English club in Europe's second competition. The beneficiaries of this were manager Mark Hughes and his Blackburn Rovers team.

## GIGGS NEARLY CAUSES WALK-OFF

When Ryan Giggs scored with a quickly-taken free kick late in the first leg of United's UEFA Champions League last 16 tie away to Lille in Lens on 20 February 2007 it gave the Reds a priceless away goal. Lille's players were furious, especially goalkeeper Tony Sylva who protested that he was still lining-up his wall when the Welsh wizard curled the ball into the net. Sylva was booked for his outburst and several Lille players looked set to walk off the pitch in protest. Play was held up for some time until they were persuaded to resume the game, which United won 1-0.

## A RUUD £1M

In June 2007, 11 months after leaving Manchester United, Ruud van Nistelrooy earned the club a £1m windfall. When United allowed the Dutch international striker to leave Old Trafford in July 2006, to join Real Madrid for £10.2m, Sir Alex Ferguson insisted on a series of clauses being put into the deal. These included a pair of £500,000 bonuses for United, one if Real Madrid won La Liga and the other if van Nistelrooy finished the season as Spain's top scorer. Madrid won the title on the final day of the season and Ruud finished the campaign with 25 goals to his name, best in La Liga.

## £5M BOOK WORM

When Wayne Rooney signed the largest sports book deal in British publishing history with HarperCollins in March 2006, the young star agreed to a £5m deal, plus royalties, in return for a minimum five books to be published over a 12-year period. His first book under the deal, *Wayne Rooney, My Story So Far*, was published shortly after the 2006 World Cup Finals.

## ᨑᨑ CRISTIANO RONALDO ᨑᨑ

Cristiano Ronaldo dos Santos Aveiro was born on 5 February 1985 in Funchal, on the Portuguese island of Madeira. In 1993, Ronaldo played for his first team, Andorinha – where his father was the kit manager. At the age of 10 he signed for CD National. In season 1999–2000, still only 15, he helped CD Nacional to the Portuguese Second Division Championship and then went on a three-day trial with Sporting Clube of Lisbon, who wasted little time in signing him. He scored twice on his debut for Sporting against Moreirense and, in 2003, when Manchester United travelled to Portugal to play the Lisbon club in a match to commemorate the official opening of their new Jose Alvalade XXI Stadium, the United players were so impressed with his display on both wings in Sporting's 3-1 win that they urged Sir Alex to buy him. Having having just lost David Beckham to Real Madrid, United paid Sporting £12.24m to take over on the right hand side of their midfield.

On arriving at Old Trafford he asked for the No.28 shirt, his number at Sporting, but Sir Alex handed him the No.7, the shirt made famous by George Best and Beckham. Ronaldo made his Manchester United debut on the opening day of the 2003–04 Premier League season, coming on as a substitute against Bolton Wanderers at Old Trafford. United were leading 1–0 at the time and within minutes the new No.7 had won a penalty and helped United to win 4–0. In his first season at United he played 39 times and scored six goals. A year later he appeared 50 times and scored nine goals. In 2005–06 he played 47 games and scored 12 goals. He was named FIFPro Special Young Player of the Year in 2005 and 2006.

In the summer of 2006, United fans feared Ronaldo might leave after he was accused of persuading the referee to send off Wayne Rooney when Portugal knocked England out of the World Cup. Instead, he extended his contract until 2010. Ronaldo improved on his previous figures in 2006–07, scoring 23 goals from 52 matches en route to helping the Reds clinch their ninth Premiership crown. In addition, he won Barclays Player of the Month Awards for November and December, the PFA Young Player of the Year, PFA Players' Player of the Year, Football Writers' Association Player of the Year, Portuguese Sports Personality of the Year (2006) and Portuguese Player of the Year (2007) awards. However good that was, Ronaldo exceeded these feats in 2007–08, scoring 42 goals in all competitions as United swept to a third consecutive Premier League title and won a third UEFA Champions League. He also retained his individual Barclays, FWA, Manchester United and PFA Player of the Year awards.

### *Did You Know That?*
His parents named him after the former US President, Ronald Reagan.

## ⟶ EXIT THE DRAGON ⟵

On 2 June 2007, Ryan Giggs played his 64th and final international for Wales. He captained his country in a 0–0 draw against the Czech Republic in a Euro 2008 qualifier at the Millennium Stadium, Cardiff. In the final minute of the game, John Toshack, the Welsh manager, sent on Robert Earnshaw for Ryan, thereby permitting the Welsh legend to walk off the pitch to receive a standing ovation from the 30,714 fans in attendance – including some from the Czech Republic who unveiled their own banners. Giggs scored 12 goals in his 15-year career for Wales.

### Did You Know That?
No player in English football history can match Ryan Giggs' collection of 18 major winners' medals. He has won the Premier League nine times, four FA Cup finals, the Uefa Champions League, World Club Championship, European Super Cup and two Football League Cups.

## ⟶ A TEAM FULL OF DEVILS ⟵

Every year at their annual awards presentation, the Professional Footballers' Association selects a team of the season for each of the top four divisions of English football. In 2006–07, the Premier League XI contained eight Manchester United players. This was the team selected by PFA members (Manchester United unless stated):

Edwin van der Sar
Gary Neville
Rio Ferdinand
Patrice Evra
Nemanja Vidic
Ryan Giggs

Paul Scholes
Cristiano Ronaldo
Steven Gerrard (Liverpool)
Dimitar Berbatov (Spurs)
Didier Drogba (Chelsea)

## ⟶ SIR ALEX'S MANAGEMENT CLASS ⟵

Four managers in the Premier League in 2007–08 had played under Sir Alex Ferguson either at Manchester United or Aberdeen.

**Steve Bruce:** Birmingham City and Wigan Athletic
**Mark Hughes:** Blackburn Rovers
**Roy Keane:** Sunderland
**Alex McLeish:** Birmingham City

The 2007–08 Premier League title went to Manchester United thanks to the division's most potent attack and stingiest defence. United scored 80 goals and conced only 22 in 38 matches. Their home record, which saw them drop just four points was also a factor as the Reds finished two clear of Chelsea and four ahead of Arsenal. Liverpool were fourth, 11 points clear of Everton, who won a UEFA Cup spot. At the bottom Derby County set new records for both fewest wins, one, and points, 11. They finished 24 points behind 19th-placed Birmingham City. Also relegated were Reading as Fulham survived on goal difference.

### Premiership
### 2007–2008

| | | P | W | D | L | F | A | W | D | L | F | A | Pts |
|---|---|---|---|---|---|---|---|---|---|---|---|---|---|
| 1. | MANCHESTER UNITED | 38 | 17 | 1 | 1 | 47 | 7 | 10 | 5 | 4 | 33 | 15 | 87 |
| 2. | Chelsea | 38 | 12 | 7 | 0 | 36 | 13 | 13 | 3 | 3 | 29 | 13 | 85 |
| 3. | Arsenal | 38 | 14 | 5 | 0 | 37 | 11 | 10 | 6 | 3 | 37 | 20 | 83 |
| 4. | Liverpool | 38 | 12 | 6 | 1 | 43 | 13 | 9 | 7 | 3 | 24 | 15 | 76 |
| 5. | Everton | 38 | 11 | 4 | 4 | 34 | 17 | 8 | 4 | 7 | 21 | 16 | 65 |
| 6. | Aston Villa | 38 | 10 | 3 | 6 | 34 | 22 | 6 | 9 | 4 | 37 | 29 | 60 |
| 7. | Blackburn Rovers | 38 | 8 | 7 | 4 | 26 | 19 | 7 | 6 | 6 | 24 | 29 | 58 |
| 8. | Posrtsmouth | 38 | 7 | 8 | 4 | 24 | 14 | 9 | 1 | 9 | 24 | 26 | 57 |
| 9. | Manchester City | 38 | 11 | 4 | 4 | 28 | 20 | 4 | 6 | 9 | 17 | 33 | 55 |
| 10. | West Ham United | 38 | 7 | 7 | 5 | 24 | 24 | 6 | 3 | 10 | 18 | 26 | 49 |
| 11. | Tottenham Hotspur | 38 | 8 | 5 | 6 | 46 | 34 | 3 | 8 | 8 | 20 | 27 | 46 |
| 12. | Newcastle United | 38 | 8 | 5 | 6 | 25 | 26 | 3 | 5 | 11 | 20 | 39 | 43 |
| 13. | Middlesbrough | 38 | 7 | 5 | 7 | 27 | 23 | 3 | 7 | 9 | 16 | 30 | 42 |
| 14. | Wigan Athletic | 38 | 8 | 5 | 6 | 21 | 17 | 2 | 5 | 12 | 13 | 34 | 40 |
| 15. | Sunderland | 38 | 9 | 3 | 7 | 23 | 21 | 2 | 3 | 14 | 13 | 38 | 39 |
| 16. | Bolton | 38 | 7 | 5 | 7 | 23 | 18 | 2 | 5 | 12 | 13 | 36 | 37 |
| 17. | Fulham | 38 | 5 | 5 | 9 | 22 | 31 | 3 | 7 | 9 | 16 | 29 | 36 |
| 18. | Reading | 38 | 8 | 2 | 9 | 19 | 25 | 2 | 4 | 13 | 22 | 41 | 36 |
| 19. | Birmingham City | 38 | 6 | 8 | 5 | 30 | 23 | 2 | 3 | 14 | 16 | 39 | 35 |
| 20. | Derby County | 38 | 1 | 5 | 13 | 12 | 43 | 0 | 3 | 16 | 8 | 46 | 11 |

—— TALK OF THE DEVILS (13) ——

"The closest I got to him was when we shook hands at the end of the game."

*Northampton Town defender Roy Fairfax, who had tried to mark George Best in a 1970 FA Cup tie (Best scored six times in United's 8–2 win)*

## GIGGS BREAKS SIR BOBBY'S RECORD

When Ryan Giggs came on for Paul Scholes in the 87th minute of the 2008 UEFA Champions League Final against Chelsea in Moscow's Luzhniki Stadium, he became Manchester United's all-time leading appearance-maker with 759 games. With United's penalty shoot-out victory Giggs also collected his 18th senior medal, a British record and, to cap it all, the Welsh wizard converted his spot-kick, the winning one that put United 6–5 ahead.

## MUNICH MEMORIALS

On 6 February 2008, in the Manchester Suite, at Old Trafford, a memorial service was led by United's Chaplain, the Reverend John Boyers. It included by two of the survivors of the crash, Sir Bobby Charlton and Harry Gregg, as well as a message from Prince Charles. Also in attendance were three other survivors: Albert Scanlon, Bill Foulkes and Kenny Morgans, as well as the three sons of owner Malcolm Glazer. More than 1,000 people attended the service, in the suite and outside, where the service was relayed by loudspeakers.

On the same day, just outside of Munich Airport, a plaque was unveiled commemorating the crash. The plaque – on a piece of granite – contains the outline of a football pitch. Along the two touchlines, there is a message written in both English and German, the English version reading,:"In memory of all those who lost their lives here in the Munich Air Disaster on the 6th February 1958." Between the messages, in two blocks of names, is a list of the 23 who died, the upper one being the 11 Manchester United staff and players: Walter Crickmer, Tom Curry, Bert Whalley, Roger Byrne, Geoff Bent, Eddie Colman, Duncan Edwards, Mark Jones, David Pegg, Tommy Taylor and Liam (Billy) Whelan.

At Trudering, the actual site of the crash, an English-speaking Catholic priest led a service attended by Bayern Munich President Karl-Heinz Rummenigge and around 400 mourners, many of whom left flags and scarves as a tribute to the dead. Rummenigge said, "February 6, 1958 was a black day in the history of Manchester United, but also for football in general."

## AS IT WAS IN THE BEGINNING

United's 2007–08 season began with a 3–0 penalty shoot-out victory over Chelsea in the FA Community Shield, and ended with a 6–5 win in a shoot-out against the Blues in the UEFA Champions League Final.

## UNITED TOP FORBES RICH LIST

On 1 May 2008 *Forbes Magazine* issued its Football Rich List. Manchester United were quoted as the most valuable football club in the world, ahead of Real Madrid, who topped the February 2008 list published by Deloitte (this list being based on turnover as opposed to value). The top ten clubs in Forbes's list are below, but proof of the success of the Premier League can be gauged by the fact that six more English clubs made the overall top 24:

| Rank | Club | Value £ | Value US$ |
| --- | --- | --- | --- |
| 1. | Manchester United | 900m | 1.8b |
| 2. | Real Madrid | 643m | 1.285b |
| 3. | Arsenal | 600m | 1.2b |
| 4. | Liverpool | 525m | 1.05b |
| 5. | Bayern Munich | 458m | 917m |
| 6. | AC Milan | 399m | 798m |
| 7. | Barcelona | 392m | 784m |
| 8. | Chelsea | 382m | 764m |
| 9. | Juventus | 255m | 510m |
| 10. | Schalke 04 | 235m | 470m |

## ENLISTING GOD'S HELP

On the morning of the 1966 World Cup final, 30 July, Manchester United midfielder Nobby Stiles walked from the England hotel to a church in Golders Green where he attended mass.

## UNITED'S TRANSFER TREBLE

On 31 May 2007, Manchester United signed the 19-year old Brazilian international Anderson from FC Porto and the 20-year old Portuguese winger Nani from Sporting Lisbon. Meanwhile, United also confirmed that England midfielder Owen Hargreaves would be signing for the club on 1 July 2007 from Bayern Munich.

## BORN ON THE SAME DAY (2)

The following Manchester United people were born on the same day:

5 Feb ..... David Sadler, Lee Martin, Cristiano Ronaldo and Carlos Tevez
9 Aug ................. Albert Quixall, Gary Bailey and Mikael Silvestre
21 Oct .......................................... Paul Ince and Nemanja Vidic

## ⟿ SELECT BIBLIOGRAPHY ⟿

*A–Z of Manchester United, 100 Years of Rivalry 1878–1978*
Derek Brandon, Boondoggle Limited (1978).
*The Complete Manchester United Trivia Fact Book*
Michael Crick, Signet Books, Penguin Publishing Group (1996).
*Denis Law – An Autobiography*
Futura Publications Limited (1979).
*England – The Football Facts*
Nick Gibbs, Facer Publishing Limited (1988).
*Facts and Figures on the Football League Clubs (1888–1978)*
*No.2 Manchester United,*
Norman Lovett, British Programme Club (1980).
*Football Wizard, The Billy Meredith Story*
John Harding, Robson Books (1998)
*The Gibson Guarantee – The Saving of Manchester United 1931–1951*
Peter Harrington, Imago Publishing (1994).
*The Good, the Bad and the Bubbly*
George Best with Ross Benson, Pan Books (1990).
*The History of Manchester United Football Club*
Tony Pullein, Direct Printing Limited (1974).
*Manchester United 1997*
Ian Morrison & Alan Shury, A Zone Production, (1997).
*Manchester United 1998*
Week per Page Diary, A Zone Production,
A Zone Production (1998).
*Manchester United – A Complete Record 1878 – 1892*
Alan Shury & Ian Morrison, The Breedon Books Publishing
Company Limited (1992).
*Manchester United – Official Members' Yearbook 2003/04*
Manchester United Books (2004).
*Manchester United Pictorial History and Club Record*
Charles Zahra, Joseph Muscat, Iain McCartney & Keith Mellor,
Temple Nostalgia (1986).
*Manchester United Pocket Annual 1994–95*
Edited by Phil Bradley, Words On Sport Limited (1995).
*Manchester United Pocket Annual 1995–96*
Edited by Andy & Phil Bradley, Words On Sport Limited (1996).
*Manchester United – The Mirror Pocket Annual 1997–98*
Bookman Projects (1998).
*The Official Manchester United Illustrated Encyclopedia*
Manchester United Books (2001).
*The Rough Guide to Manchester United – 2002–03 Season*
Jim White & Andy Mitten, Rough Guides Limited (2002).

*They Died Too Young – The Busby Babes*
David Sandison, Parragon (1996).
*The United Alphabet – A Complete Who's Who of Manchester United FC*
Garth Dykes, ACL & Polar Publishing (UK) Limited (1994).
*United Yearbook 1997–98*
Parragon (1998).
*Keane: The Autobiography*
Roy Keane & Eamonn Dunphy, Penguin Books Ltd (2003).

## RECOMMENDED WEBSITES

www.manutd.com
www.prideofmanchester.com/index.htm
www.unitedonline.co.uk
www.stallions.com.au
www.duncan-edwards.co.uk
www.manutdzone.com
www.scottishleague.net
www.manchesteronline.co.uk
www.redcafe.net
www.femalefirst.co.uk
www.footballrefugees.com
www.christies.com
www.rednews.co.uk
www.ave-it.net
www.biogs.com
www.wikipedia.org
www.pmsa.org.uk
www.manunited.net
www.manutd.soccer24-7.com
www.englandfootballonline.com
www.thefa.com
www.royoftherovers.com
www.brainyquote.com
www.footymad.net
www.redissue.co.uk
www.manchester2002-uk.com/ten-towns
www.stretfordend.co.uk
http://en.wikipedia.org/wiki/Roy_Keane
www.soccerfiesta.net

# INDEX